Library Outreach, Partnerships, and Distance Education: Reference Librarians at the Gateway

Library Outreach, Partnerships, and Distance Education: Reference Librarians at the Gateway has been co-published simultaneously as *The Reference Librarian*, Numbers 67/68 1999.

The *Reference Librarian* Monographic "Separates"

Below is a list of "separates," which in serials librarianship means a special issue simultaneously published as a special journal issue or double-issue *and* as a "separate" hardbound monograph. (This is a format which we also call a "DocuSerial.")

"Separates" are published because specialized libraries or professionals may wish to purchase a specific thematic issue by itself in a format which can be separately cataloged and shelved, as opposed to purchasing the journal on an on-going basis. Faculty members may also more easily consider a "separate" for classroom adoption.

"Separates" are carefully classified separately with the major book jobbers so that the journal tie-in can be noted on new book order slips to avoid duplicate purchasing.

You may wish to visit Haworth's website at . . .

http://www.haworthpressinc.com

. . . to search our online catalog for complete tables of contents of these separates and related publications.

You may also call 1-800-HAWORTH (outside US/Canada: 607-722-5857), or Fax 1-800-895-0582 (outside US/Canada: 607-771-0012), or e-mail at:

getinfo@haworthpressinc.com

Library Outreach, Partnerships, and Distance Education: Reference Librarians at the Gateway, edited by Wendi Arant and Pixey Anne Mosley (No. 67/68, 1999). *Focuses on community outreach in libraries toward a broader public by extending services based on recent developments in information technology.*

From Past-Present to Future-Perfect: A Tribute to Charles A. Bunge and the Challenges of Contemporary Reference Service, edited by Chris D. Ferguson, PhD (No. 66, 1999). *Explore reprints of selected articles by Charles Bunge, Bibliographies of his published work, and original articles that draw on Bunge's values and ideas in assessing the present and shaping the future of reference service.*

Reference Services and Media, edited by Martha Merrill, PhD (No. 65, 1999). *Gives you valuable information about various aspects of reference services and media, including changes, planning issues, and the use and impact of new technologies.*

Coming of Age in Reference Services: A Case History of the Washington State University Libraries, edited by Christy Zlatos, MSLS (No. 64, 1999). *A celebration of the perserverance, ingenuity, and talent of the librarians who have served, past and present, at the Holland Library reference desk.*

Document Delivery Services: Contrasting Views, edited by Robin Kinder, MLS (No. 63, 1999). *Reviews the planning and process of implementing document delivery in four university libraries–Miami University, University of Colorado at Denver, University of Montana at Missoula, and Purdue University Libraries.*

The Holocaust: Memories, Research, Reference, edited by Robert Hauptman, PhD, and Susan Hubbs Motin (No. 61/62, 1998). *"A wonderful resource for reference librarians, students, and teachers . . . on how to present this painful, historical event." (Ephraim Kaye, PhD, The International School for Holocaust Studies, Yad Vashem, Jerusalem)*

Electronic Resources: Use and User Behavior, edited by Hemalata Iyer, PhD (No. 60, 1998). *Covers electronic resources and their use in libraries, with emphasis on the Internet and the Geographic Information Systems (GIS).*

Philosophies of Reference Service, edited by Celia Hales Mabry (No. 59, 1997). *"Recommended reading for any manager responsible for managing reference services and hiring reference librarians in any type of library." (Charles R. Anderson, MLS, Associate Director for Public Services, King County Library System, Bellevue, Washington)*

Business Reference Services and Sources: How End Users and Librarians Work Together, edited by Katherine M. Shelfer (No. 58, 1997). *"This is an important collection of papers suitable for all business librarians. . . . Highly recommended!" (Lucy Heckman, MLS, MBA, Business and Economics Reference Librarian, St. John's University, Jamaica, New York)*

Reference Sources on the Internet: Off the Shelf and onto the Web, edited by Karen R. Diaz (No. 57, 1997). *Surf off the library shelves and onto the Internet and cut your research time in half!*

Reference Services for Archives and Manuscripts, edited by Laura B. Cohen (No. 56, 1997). *"Features stimulating and interesting essays on security in archives, ethics in the archival profession, and electronic records." ("The Year's Best Professional Reading" (1998), Library Journal)*

Career Planning and Job Searching in the Information Age, edited by Elizabeth A. Lorenzen, MLS (No. 55, 1996). *"Offers stimulating background for dealing with the issues of technology and service. . . . A reference tool to be looked at often." (The One-Person Library)*

The Roles of Reference Librarians: Today and Tomorrow, edited by Kathleen Low, MLS (No. 54, 1996). *"A great asset to all reference collections. . . . Presents important, valuable information for reference librarians as well as other library users." (Library Times International)*

Reference Services for the Unserved, edited by Fay Zipkowitz, MSLS, DA (No. 53, 1996). *"A useful tool in developing strategies to provide services to all patrons." (Science Books & Films)*

Library Instruction Revisited: Bibliographic Instruction Comes of Age, edited by Lyn Elizabeth M. Martin, MLS (No. 51/52, 1995). *"A powerful collection authored by respected practitioners who have stormed the bibliographic instruction (BI) trenches and, luckily for us, have recounted their successes and shortcomings." (The Journal of Academic Librarianship)*

Library Users and Reference Services, edited by Jo Bell Whitlatch, PhD (No. 49/50, 1995). *"Well-planned, balanced, and informative. . . . Both new and seasoned professionals will find material for service attitude formation and practical advice for the front lines of service." (Anna M. Donnelly, MS, MA, Associate Professor and Reference Librarian, St. John's University Library)*

Social Science Reference Services, edited by Pam Baxter, MLS (No. 48, 1995). *"Offers practical guidance to the reference librarian. . . . a valuable source of information about specific literatures within the social sciences and the skills and techniques needed to provide access to those literatures." (Nancy P. O'Brien, MLS, Head, Education and Social Science Library, and Professor of Library Administration, University of Illinois at Urbana-Champaign)*

Reference Services in the Humanities, edited by Judy Reynolds, MLS (No. 47, 1994). *"A well-chosen collection of situations and challenges encountered by reference librarians in the humanities." (College Research Library News)*

Racial and Ethnic Diversity in Academic Libraries: Multicultural Issues, edited by Deborah A. Curry, MLS, MA, Susan Griswold Blandy, MEd, and Lyn Elizabeth M. Martin, MLS (No. 45/46, 1994). *"The useful techniques and attractive strategies presented here will provide the incentive for fellow professionals in academic libraries around the country to go and do likewise in their own institutions." (David Cohen, Adjunct Professor of Library Science, School of Library and Information Science, Queens College; Director, EMIE (Ethnic Materials Information Exchange); Editor, EMIE Bulletin)*

School Library Reference Services in the 90s: Where We Are, Where We're Heading, edited by Carol Truett, PhD (No. 44, 1994). *"Unique and valuable to the the teacher-librarian as well as students of librarianship. . . . The overall work successfully interweaves the concept of the continuously changing role of the teacher-librarian." (Emergency Librarian)*

Reference Services Planning in the 90s, edited by Gail Z. Eckwright, MLS, and Lori M. Keenan, MLS (No. 43, 1994.) *"This monograph is well-researched and definitive, encompassing* *reference service as practices by library and information scientists. . . . it should be required reading for all professional librarian trainees."* (Feliciter)

Librarians on the Internet: Impact on Reference Services, edited by Robin Kinder, MLS (No. 41/42, 1994). *"Succeeds in demonstrating that the Internet is becoming increasingly a challenging but practical and manageable tool in the reference librarian's ever-expanding armory."* (Reference Reviews)

Reference Service Expertise, edited by Bill Katz (No. 40, 1993). *This important volume presents a wealth of practical ideas for improving the art of reference librarianship.*

Modern Library Technology and Reference Services, edited by Samuel T. Huang, MLS, MS (No. 39, 1993). *"This book packs a surprising amount of information into a relatively few number of pages. . . . This book will answer many questions."* (Science Books and Films)

Assessment and Accountability in Reference Work, edited by Susan Griswold Blandy, Lyn M. Martin, and Mary L. Strife (No. 38, 1992). *"An important collection of well-written, real-world chapters addressing the central questions that surround performance and services in all libraries."* (Library Times International)

The Reference Librarian and Implications of Mediation, edited by M. Keith Ewing, MLS, and Robert Hauptman, MLS (No. 37, 1992). *"An excellent and thorough analysis of reference mediation. . . . well worth reading by anyone involved in the delivery of reference services."* (Fred Batt, MLS, Associate University Librarian for Public Services, California State University, Sacramento)

Library Services for Career Planning, Job Searching and Employment Opportunities, edited by Byron Anderson, MA, MLS (No. 36, 1992). *"An interesting book which tells professional libraries how to set up career information centers. . . . Clearly valuable reading for anyone establishing a career library."* (Career Opportunities News)

In the Spirit of 1992: Access to Western European Libraries and Literature, edited by Mary M. Huston, PhD, and Maureen Pastine, MLS (No. 35, 1992). *"A valuable and practical [collection] which every subject specialist in the field would do well to consult."* (Western European Specialists Section Newsletter)

Access Services: The Convergence of Reference and Technical Services, edited by Gillian M. McCombs, ALA (No. 34, 1992). *"Deserves a wide readership among both technical and public services librarians. . . . highly recommended for any librarian interested in how reference and technical services roles may be combined."* (Library Resources & Technical Services)

Opportunities for Reference Services: The Bright Side of Reference Services in the 1990s, edited by Bill Katz (No. 33, 1991). *"A well-deserved look at the brighter side of reference services. . . . Should be read by reference librarians and their administrators in all types of libraries."* (Library Times International)

Government Documents and Reference Services, edited by Robin Kinder, MLS (No. 32, 1991). *Discusses access possibilities and policies with regard to government information, covering such important topics as new and impending legislation, information on most frequently used and requested sources, and grant writing.*

The Reference Library User: Problems and Solutions, edited by Bill Katz (No. 31, 1991). *"Valuable information and tangible suggestions that will help us as a profession look critically at our users and decide how they are best served."* (Information Technology and Libraries)

Continuing Education of Reference Librarians, edited by Bill Katz (No. 30/31, 1990). *"Has something for everyone interested in this field. . . . Library trainers and library school teachers may well find stimulus in some of the programs outlined here."* (Library Association Record)

Weeding and Maintenance of Reference Collections, edited by Sydney J. Pierce, PhD, MLS (No. 29, 1990). *"This volume may spur you on to planned activity before lack of space dictates 'ad hoc' solutions."* (New Library World)

Serials and Reference Services, edited by Robin Kinder, MLS, and Bill Katz (No. 27/28, 1990). *"The concerns and problems discussed are those of serials and reference librarians everywhere. . . . The writing is of a high standard and the book is useful and entertaining. . . . This book can be recommended." (Library Association Record)*

Rothstein on Reference: . . . with some help from friends, edited by Bill Katz and Charles Bunge, PhD, MLS (No. 25/26, 1990). *"An important and stimulating collection of essays on reference librarianship. . . . Highly recommended!" (Richard W. Grefrath, MA, MLS, Reference Librarian, University of Nevada Library)* Dedicated to the work of Sam Rothstein, one of the world's most respected teachers of reference librarians, this special volume features his writings as well as articles written about him and his teachings by other professionals in the field.

Integrating Library Use Skills Into the General Education Curriculum, edited by Maureen Pastine, MLS, and Bill Katz (No. 24, 1989). *"All contributions are written and presented to a high standard with excellent references at the end of each. . . . One of the best summaries I have seen on this topic." (Australian Library Review)*

Expert Systems in Reference Services, edited by Christine Roysdon, MLS, and Howard D. White, PhD, MLS (No. 23, 1989). *"The single most comprehensive work on the subject of expert systems in reference service." (Information Processing and Management)*

Information Brokers and Reference Services, edited by Bill Katz, and Robin Kinder, MLS (No. 22, 1989). *"An excellent tool for reference librarians and indispensable for anyone seriously considering their own information-brokering service." (Booklist)*

Information and Referral in Reference Services, edited by Marcia Stucklen Middleton, MLS and Bill Katz (No. 21, 1988). *Investigates a wide variety of situations and models which fall under the umbrella of information and referral.*

Reference Services and Public Policy, edited by Richard Irving, MLS, and Bill Katz (No. 20, 1988). *Looks at the relationship between public policy and information and reports ways in which libraries respond to the need for public policy information.*

Finance, Budget, and Management for Reference Services, edited by Ruth A. Fraley, MLS, MBA, and Bill Katz (No. 19, 1989). *"Interesting and relevant to the current state of financial needs in reference service. . . . A must for anyone new to or already working in the reference service area." (Riverina Library Review)*

Current Trends in Information: Research and Theory, edited by Bill Katz, and Robin Kinder, MLS (No. 18, 1984.) *"Practical direction to improve reference services and does so in a variety of ways ranging from humorous and clever metaphoric comparisons to systematic and practical methodological descriptions." (American Reference Books Annual)*

International Aspects of Reference and Information Services, edited by Bill Katz, and Ruth A. Fraley, MLS, MBA (No. 17, 1987). *"An informative collection of essays written by eminent librarians, library school staff, and others concerned with the international aspects of information work." (Library Association Record)*

Reference Services Today: From Interview to Burnout, edited by Bill Katz, and Ruth A. Fraley, MLS, MBA (No. 16, 1987). *Authorities present important advice to all reference librarians on the improvement of service and the enhancement of the public image of reference services.*

The Publishing and Review of Reference Sources, edited by Bill Katz, and Robin Kinder, MLS (No. 15, 1987). *"A good review of current reference reviewing and publishing trends in the United States . . . will be of interest to intending reviewers, reference librarians, and students." (Australasian College Libraries)*

Personnel Issues in Reference Services, edited by Bill Katz, and Ruth Fraley, MLS, MBA (No. 14, 1986). *"Chock-full of information that can be applied to most reference settings. Recommended for libraries with active reference departments." (RQ)*

Reference Services in Archives, edited by Lucille Whalen (No. 13, 1986). *"Valuable for the insights it provides on the reference process in archives and as a source of information on the different ways of carrying out that process." (Library and Information Science Annual)*

Conflicts in Reference Services, edited by Bill Katz, and Ruth A. Fraley, MLS, MBA (No. 12, 1985). *This collection examines issues pertinent to the reference department.*

Evaluation of Reference Services, edited by Bill Katz, and Ruth A. Fraley, MLS, MBA (No. 11, 1985). *"A much-needed overview of the present state of the art vis-à-vis reference service evaluation. . . . excellent. . . . Will appeal to reference professionals and aspiring students." (RQ)*

Library Instruction and Reference Services, edited by Bill Katz, and Ruth A. Fraley, MLS, MBA (No. 10, 1984). *"Well written, clear, and exciting to read. This is an important work recommended for all librarians, particularly those involved in, interested in, or considering bibliographic instruction. . . . A milestone in library literature." (RQ)*

Reference Services and Technical Services: Interactions in Library Practice, edited by Gordon Stevenson and Sally Stevenson (No. 9, 1984). *"New ideas and longstanding problems are handled with humor and sensitivity as practical suggestions and new perspectives are suggested by the authors." (Information Retrieval & Library Automation)*

Reference Services for Children and Young Adults, edited by Bill Katz, and Ruth A. Fraley, MLS, MBA (No. 7/8, 1983). *"Offers a well-balanced approach to reference service for children and young adults. " (RQ)*

Video to Online: Reference Services in the New Technology, edited by Bill Katz, and Ruth A. Fraley, MLS, MBA (No. 5/6, 1983). *"A good reference manual to have on hand. . . . well-written, concise, provide[s] a wealth of information." (Online)*

Ethics and Reference Services, edited by Bill Katz, and Ruth A. Fraley, MLS, MBA (No. 4, 1982). *Library experts discuss the major ethical and legal implications that reference librarians must take into consideration when handling sensitive inquiries about confidential material.*

Reference Services Administration and Management, edited by Bill Katz and Ruth A. Fraley, MLS, MBA (No. 3, 1982). *Librarianship experts discuss the management of the reference function in libraries and information centers, outlining the responsibilities and qualifications of reference heads.*

Reference Services in the 1980s, edited by Bill Katz (No. 1/2, 1982). *Here is a thought-provoking volume on the future of reference services in libraries, with an emphasis on the challenges and needs that have come about as a result of automation.*

Library Outreach, Partnerships, and Distance Education: Reference Librarians at the Gateway

Wendi Arant
Pixey Anne Mosley
Editors

Library Outreach, Partnerships, and Distance Education: Reference Librarians at the Gateway has been co-published simultaneously as *The Reference Librarian*, Numbers 67/68 1999.

The Haworth Information Press
An Imprint of
The Haworth Press, Inc.
New York • London • Oxford

Published by

The Haworth Press Information Press, 10 Alice Street, Binghamton, NY 13904-1580, USA

The Haworth Information Press, is an imprint of The Haworth Press, Inc., 10 Alice Street, Binghamton, NY 13904-1580 USA.

Library Outreach, Partnerships, and Distance Education: Reference Librarians at the Gateway has been co-published simultaneously as *The Reference Librarian*, Numbers 67/68 1999.

The development, preparation, and publication of this work has been undertaken with great care. However, the publisher, employees, editors, and agents of The Haworth Press and all imprints of The Haworth Press, Inc., including The Haworth Medical Press® and Pharmaceutical Products Press®, are not responsible for any errors contained herein or for consequences that may ensue from use of materials or information contained in this work. Opinions expressed by the author(s) are not necessarily those of The Haworth Press, Inc.

Cover design by Thomas J. Mayshock Jr.

Library of Congress Cataloging-in-Publication Data

Library outreach, partnerships, and distance education: reference librarians at the gateway/Wendi Arant [and] Pixey Anne Mosley, editors.
     p. cm.
    "Co-published simultaneously as The reference librarian, numbers 67/68, 1999."
    Includes bibliographical references and index.
    ISBN 0-7890-0842-4 (alk. paper–ISBN 0-7890-0953-6 (alk. paper)
    1. Library outreach programs–United States. 2. Academic libraries–United States. 3. Electronic reference services (Libraries)–United States. 4. Libraries–United States–Special collections–Electronic information resources. I. Arant, Wendi. II. Mosley, Pixey Anne.
Z711.7.L54 2000
025.5'2777–dc21
                                    00-021759

INDEXING & ABSTRACTING

Contributions to this publication are selectively indexed or abstracted in print, electronic, online, or CD-ROM version(s) of the reference tools and information services listed below. This list is current as of the copyright date of this publication. See the end of this section for additional notes.

- *Academic Abstracts/CD-ROM*
- *Academic Search: data base of 2,000 selected academic serials, updated monthly*
- *BUBL Information Service: An Internet-Based Information Service for the UK Higher Education Community <URL:http//bubl.ac.uk/>*
- *CNPIEC Reference Guide: Chinese National Directory of Foreign Periodicals*
- *Current Awareness Abstracts of Library & Information Literature, ASLIB (UK)*
- *Current Index to Journals in Education*
- *Educational Administration Abstracts (EAA)*
- *FINDEX www.publist.com*
- *Handbook of Latin American Studies*
- *IBZ International Bibliography of Periodical Literature*
- *Index to Periodical Articles Related to Law*
- *Information Science Abstracts*
- *Informed Librarian, The www.infosourcespub.com*
- *INSPEC*
- *Journal of Academic Librarianship: Guide to Professional Literature, The*
- *Konyvtari Figyelo-Library Review*
- *Library & Information Science Abstracts (LISA)*

(continued)

- *Library and Information Science Annual (LISCA)*
  www.lu.com/arba

- *Library Literature*

- *MasterFILE: updated database from EBSCO Publishing*

- *Newsletter of Library and Information Services*

- *OT BibSys*

- *PASCAL*
  www.inist.fr

- *Referativnyi Zhurnal (Abstracts Journal of the All-Russian Institute of Scientific and Technical Information)*

- *Sage Public Administration Abstracts (SPAA)*

Special bibliographic notes related to special journal issues (separates) and indexing/abstracting:

- indexing/abstracting services in this list will also cover material in any "separate" that is co-published simultaneously with Haworth's special thematic journal issue or DocuSerial. Indexing/abstracting usually covers material at the article/chapter level.
- monographic co-editions are intended for either non-subscribers or libraries which intend to purchase a second copy for their circulating collections.
- monographic co-editions are reported to all jobbers/wholesalers/approval plans. The source journal is listed as the "series" to assist the prevention of duplicate purchasing in the same manner utilized for books-in-series.
- to facilitate user/access services all indexing/abstracting services are encouraged to utilize the co-indexing entry note indicated at the bottom of the first page of each article/chapter/contribution.
- this is intended to assist a library user of any reference tool (whether print, electronic, online, or CD-ROM) to locate the monographic version if the library has purchased this version but not a subscription to the source journal.
- individual articles/chapters in any Haworth publication are also available through the Haworth Document Delivery Service (HDDS).

Library Outreach, Partnerships, and Distance Education: Reference Librarians at the Gateway

CONTENTS

ABOUT THE EDITORS

Wendi Arant is Coordinator of Electronic Reference Services for the Texas A&M University General Libraries. She also functions as Humanities Reference Librarian, dedicated to faculty and students in the English Department, developing the collection, providing reference and in-depth research service, and doing specialized bibliographic instruction. She has a B.A. in Humanities and Romance Languages, followed by an M.L.S. in Librarianship from the University of Washington and is currently pursuing an M.S. in Information and Operations Management from Texas A&M University.

Pixey Anne Mosley is Coordinator of Instructional Services for the Texas A&M University General Libraries. She also serves as a Science and Engineering Reference Librarian, with liaison and collection development responsibilities for the Aerospace Engineering Department. Her education background includes a B.S. in Aerospace Engineering from Texas A&M University, an M.S. in Aeronautical Engineering from The Wichita State University (Wichita, Kansas), and an M.L.S. from Louisiana State University. She was recently granted tenure and promoted to Associate Professor rank at Texas A&M University.

Introduction

Wendi Arant
Pixey Anne Mosley

Outreach is a concept that is gaining more and more significance for libraries, particularly with the recent developments in information technology. Dictionaries define it as "the act of extending services, benefits, etc., to a wider section of the population." This definition also implies a mission to communicate a particular message to an audience in order to gain their support. Its meaning for libraries is profound, having consequences for fundraising, public service and public relations.

In a world where information and scholarly communication is now transmitted virtually and physically, librarians must be less desk-bound and building-centered. Technology has freed them up to seek out patrons rather than having patrons come to them. They are able to bring knowledge out of the library and bring it to a selected audience in their own environment, as well as adapt the ambience of the library to be more welcoming and user-friendly, whether this means changes to the physical location or a presence electronically. This is a more personalized approach to information service, but it goes beyond this primary mission to offer other benefits.

There are many issues currently affecting libraries, including the growth of technology, emerging literacy issues, at-risk populations, diversity and multiculturalism, and distance education. For libraries to move past the image of musty old book warehouses, they must be

[Haworth co-indexing entry note]: "Introduction." Arant, Wendi, and Pixey Anne Mosley. Co-published simultaneously in *The Reference Librarian* (The Haworth Information Press, an imprint of The Haworth Press, Inc.) No. 67/68, 1999, pp. 1-4; and: *Library Outreach, Partnerships, and Distance Education: Reference Librarians at the Gateway* (ed: Wendi Arant, and Pixey Anne Mosley) The Haworth Press, Inc., 2000, pp. 1-4. Single or multiple copies of this article are available for a fee from The Haworth Document Delivery Service [1-800-342-9678, 9:00 a.m. - 5:00 p.m. (EST). E-mail address: getinfo@haworthpressinc.com].

proactive in developing new services and making patrons aware of already existing services and the value of collections. Librarians need to meet patrons in their own context and build mutually beneficial relationships. More and more, this requires non-traditional library skills, such as marketing, initiating non-library partnerships, implementing business plans, and utilizing technological tools. Divided into four sections, this volume will present ideas and strategies implemented around the country to reach out to traditional and new user communities.

TECHNOLOGY AND OUTREACH

The presence of technology in libraries, and in turn the prevalence of information systems in society, is an undeniable fact. The technological tools have changed both the nature of information and the manner in which it is provided. For some patrons (and for some librarians), technology is eagerly embraced. Others find it to be a challenge or hurdle that must be overcome. The five featured manuscripts present a variety of proposals and cautions on incorporating electronic resources into reference services. The opening article by Lilly and Van Fleet takes a look at some leading academic library home pages for ADA compliance issues and offers valuable tips on making web-based services inclusive to disabled users. Meola and Stormont discuss the implementation of a real-time reference service with the use of Internet technology, providing a just-in-time view of information service that is becoming more critical in this technology-dependent world. Continuing in this manner, Hart, Coleman and Yu examine the knowledge and use of such technology by academic faculty. Several articles offer ideas for expanding traditional reference and instructional services utilizing a variety of electronic mediums. The last two manuscripts in the section, by Morales and Rosen, and Tickle, look at using technology to increase awareness and use of reference services with relation to specialized collections.

TARGETING SPECIAL CONNECTIONS: SPECIFIC USER GROUPS AND LIAISON PARTNERS

Librarians are fully aware that libraries do not exist in a vacuum. However, traditionally, library service has centered around the library as a physical structure and on aiding to those who come to the building. Thus, librarians have been hesitant to initiate relationships outside of the profession. These six manuscripts give insights into developing successful working relationships in the great wide world. One consistent theme that runs throughout the articles is the need to first establish an environment of mutual respect and appreciation of the library's role as well as an understanding of roles and expectations. Opening with issues of early education and emergent literacy, Kars and Doud relate an ambitious collaboration with a variety of partners not generally associated with a public library. This section provides a variety of different concepts concerning library partnerships; Kahn presents ideas on a workshop that educates high school English teachers on how their students use the public library; Puffer-Rothenberg and Thomas relate a program expanding services for at-risk populations such as student athletes; and Kudlay, Norlin and Morris, and Gresham and Van Tassel look at gaining a better understanding of minority and diversity outreach opportunities for libraries.

A DIFFERENT APPROACH: NEW USER PROGRAMS, OUTREACH SERVICES, AND PUBLIC RELATIONS

"Marketing" used to be anathema and unnecessary when discussing "public good" services. However, economic and political issues have forced many libraries into budget battles, where effective resource utilization and service justifications are familiar concepts to administrators and managers. This, in turn, requires libraries to be more aware of their image and their impact on their clientele and community, surveying and counting their customers. In many cases, libraries are trying new techniques more commonly seen in the commercial or non-profit organizational arena than in higher education or public service. This evolution may require a significant restructuring of reference services and the roles of reference librarians. Similarly, services may be expanded to focus toward a particular segment of the user population. The initial article in this section by Odom and Strout-Dapaz introduces the idea of holding an Open House extravaganza to introduce users to library facilities and services; Zwemer and Mitchell elaborate on this concept of community involvement in the library. In a different tone, Hendrix discusses how a commitment to outreach has led to major reorganizations in the roles and responsibilities of reference librarians. Mazak and Manista focus on partnering with teaching faculty to familiarize freshmen with library and archival research. Finally, Ury, Meldrem and Johnson take this course-based collaboration to the electronic environment with web-based research aids and intensive consultation.

OUTREACH IN AN ACADEMIC LIBRARY: OVERVIEW, ISSUES, AND BACKGROUND

Last but certainly not least is a section providing a constructive overview of more traditional library outreach proposals, for those librarians seeking to get general programs off the ground. The first article by McCasland and Golden give some concrete directions for making services more accessible to persons with disabilities, discussing everything from audio enhancement packages to braille peripherals. The next two articles provide an overview of successful outreach programs at different sized academic libraries. These articles by Neely et al. and Landry-Hyde discuss programs at Colorado State University and Texas A&M University, Corpus Christi, covering a range of topics including community users, distance education, and document delivery. The concluding article by Caspers focuses on the growing number of distance education students, what services they need and how their information needs can be met by the library. With an extensive list of references, this article will be most appropriate for those libraries being introduced to the demands of distance learners.

The included authors, and indeed, the editors, find outreach to be a critical issue for libraries in this and in the next millennium. It has a measurable impact on service, funding and community relations–one that may work to the library's advantage. With the evolution of technology, there are opportunities for libraries to recreate their services to support new and existing clientele. In closing, we hope you find this volume to be informative and provide you with real-world ideas for increasing the public service and outreach activities in your library setting.

I. TECHNOLOGY AND OUTREACH

Wired But Not Connected: Accessibility of Academic Library Home Pages

Erica B. Lilly
Connie Van Fleet

SUMMARY. The main library Web pages representing *Yahoo!*'s list of the "100 Most Wired Colleges" were analyzed for accessibility to people with disabilities. Forty of the pages were judged accessible using Bobby, the online automated service developed by the Center for Applied Special Technology. Frequencies of accessibility errors, recommendations, questions, tips, and browser compatibility errors are provided. The study found no relationship between accessibility of the library

Erica B. Lilly is Coordinator, Electronic Information Services, Library and Media Services, Kent State University, Kent, OH 44242 (E-mail: elilly@kent.edu). Connie Van Fleet is Associate Professor, School of Library and Information Science, Kent State University, Kent, OH 44242 (E-mail: vanfleet@slis.kent.edu).

The authors wish to acknowledge Sarah Cofer, graduate assistant in the Kent State University School of Library and Information Science, for her assistance with data collection.

[Haworth co-indexing entry note]: "Wired But Not Connected: Accessibility of Academic Library Home Pages." Lilly, Erica B., and Connie Van Fleet. Co-published simultaneously in *The Reference Librarian* (The Haworth Information Press, an imprint of The Haworth Press, Inc.) No. 67/68, 1999, pp. 5-28; and: *Library Outreach, Partnerships, and Distance Education: Reference Librarians at the Gateway* (ed: Wendi Arant, and Pixey Anne Mosley) The Haworth Press, Inc., 2000, pp. 5-28. Single or multiple copies of this article are available for a fee from The Haworth Document Delivery Service [1-800-342-9678, 9:00 a.m. - 5:00 p.m. (EST). E-mail address: getinfo@haworthpressinc.com].

home pages and indicators of institutional resources, as represented by *Yahoo!* ranking (computer resources), Association of Research Libraries composite ranking (extent of library resources), and Carnegie Classification (range and extent of academic and research resources). Guidelines for accessible Web pages and an Adaptive PC Computer Workstation are included. *[Article copies available for a fee from The Haworth Document Delivery Service: 1-800-342-9678. E-mail address: getinfo@haworthpressinc. com <Website: http://www.haworthpressinc.com>]*

KEYWORDS. Internet, university libraries, handicap accessibility, web pages, ADA, adaptive technology

INTRODUCTION

According to recent statistics, there are approximately 48 million people in the U.S. who have a physical or learning disability (Cunningham and Coombs 1997, 2). The Americans with Disabilities Act of 1990 (ADA) ". . . prohibits discrimination on the basis of disability in employment, programs and services provided by state and local governments, goods and services provided by private companies, and in commercial facilities" (U.S. Department of Justice 1998). It is ironic that one of the most free and equitable environments, the Internet, and specifically the World Wide Web, may present one of the most obvious barriers to equitable information access. With the advent of graphical Web browsers, beginning with Mosaic and evolving through the most current versions of Netscape Navigator, Microsoft Internet Explorer, and others, Web page designers have exploited the various visual and aural features of this highly interactive environment. Unfortunately for those with visual impairments, hearing impairments, learning and perceptual disabilities, or motor limitations, navigating within this information venue may provide a less than satisfying or successful experience.

Imperatives for Equal Access

The ADA requires that programs and facilities be made accessible to people with disabilities (Crispen 1993, 9). Taking this requirement one step further, a recent United States Department of Justice Policy ruling affirmed that ADA Titles II and III require that state and local governments and the business sector provide effective communication whenever they communicate through the Internet (Waddell 1998).

"This effective communication rule applies to covered entities using the Internet for communications regarding their programs, goods, or services since they must be prepared to offer those communications via an accessible medium (Waddell 1998). Moreover, the *Library Bill of Rights* states that "Electronic information, services, and networks provided directly or indirectly by the library should be equally, readily and equitably accessible to all library users" (American Library Association 1998).

Electronic Outreach

It appears that most colleges and universities have focused on providing on-campus accommodations for people with disabilities, and that academic librarians have supported institutional priorities. On-site accessible work stations are essential, but they may be insufficient to ensure equitable access to information services and resources to all users. (See Appendix A, Suggested Adaptive PC Computer Workstation Configuration.) Academic libraries increasingly use the Web as a platform from which they can provide one-stop access for their users to numerous electronic resources and tools (Fraser, Comden, and Burgstahler 1998). As the Web becomes a more prominent service point for library users, it is imperative that any library's Web site be viewed as an important outreach tool and designed in a manner that allows maximum accessibility for all users.

Barriers to Web Access

The Web has become an increasingly multimedia environment, integrating sight, sound, and motion. Just as computer technology for people with disabilities is usually categorized by the area of disability being accommodated (Jones 1993), so may the issues of access to the Web. It is estimated that up to 90 percent of all Web pages have some barriers to users with physical or cognitive disabilities (Moeller 1998).

Vision Impairments. Individuals who are blind, have low vision, have functional vision, or are color blind are included in this category (Cunningham & Coombs 1997, 4; Paciello 1996b; Trace Research and Development Center 1998). They may often encounter difficulties seeing computer screens and keyboards and using a mouse to interact with electronic information (Cunningham and Coombs 1997; Paciello 1996b). Web pages with large amounts of graphics or a cluttered design may not be easily interpreted by adaptive equipment used by persons with visual impairments. Screen readers, for example, respond to text, not graphics (Cunningham & Coombs, 1997, 121). For some users, graphics may appear as the word [*image*] or as a non-downloadable file (Beck 1995). Navigation of Web pages with multicolumn formats may also be difficult, as screen readers read one line of text at a time and jump across rather than down each column (Paciello 1996b).

Hearing Impairments. People who are hard-of-hearing or deaf belong in this category (Cunningham and Coombs 1997, 5). As the Web incorporates the use of sounds for both site enhancement and conveying content, these individuals may experience difficulty in accessing important information, unless alternate forms of presenting the same information are made available (Paciello 1996a; Trace Research and Development Center 1998).

Mobility Impairments. This category includes people who use wheelchairs as well as those with limited or no hand usage. Both groups may include persons with paralysis, missing limbs, and limited body control or movement (Cunningham and Coombs 1997, 4). These individuals will vary in their use of computer input devices (e.g., standard keyboard, mouse, mouth stick, headpointer, eyegaze-operated keyboard, or infrared device) (Pacillo 1996a, Trace Research and Development Center 1998). Web pages with small navigation buttons or closely spaced links may be difficult for these users to navigate easily.

Learning Disabilities. Individuals may experience a range of disabilities, from visual perception problems to aural processing difficulties (Cunningham and Coombs 1997, 5). Certain learning disabilities may make it difficult for an individual to find his or her place on a computer screen (Cunningham and Coombs 1997, 98). Overly colorful or cluttered Web pages may be difficult for these users to access. A person with a learning disability may benefit from the use of simple displays, use of patterns, and simple sequences (Trace Research and Development Center 1998).

Universal Design Principles and Library Web Pages

Why is it important to provide Web pages that are accessible to all users? According to the *GVU's 9th User Survey,* conducted by the Graphic, Visualization, and Usability Center at the Georgia Institute of Technology (1998), approximately 8 percent of users reported having a disability (e.g., vision, hearing, motor, cognitive). Of this number, half reported having a visual impairment. The benefits of adaptive computing technology and support services for students with disabilities may often be realized by some very tangible benefits. These include higher grade point averages, students being able to take more classes per semester, lower probation and drop-out rates, and a greater likelihood that students will pass all of their classes (Cunningham and Coombs 1997, 6). The library should be an integral part of this success.

A selected overview of the literature of home page development reveals that librarians and other educators are becoming increasingly interested in designing home pages with maximum accessibility for all users (Descy 1997; Gregory and Brown 1997; Matsco and Campbell 1996; Peters-Walters 1998; Schnell 1997; Schuyler 1997). Major companies such as Apple Computer, IBM, Microsoft, and Sun Microsystems are developing products and suggesting guidelines to developers to encourage greater Web accessibility for users with disabilities (Apple Computer, Inc. 1998; IBM Corporation 1998; Microsoft Corporation 1998; Sun Microsystems 1998).

Universal design (UD) may be defined as "the design of products and environments to be usable by all people, to the greatest extent possible, without the need for adaptation or specialized design" (Connell et al. 1995). Universal design ensures that services are designed for persons with a wide range of abilities and that care is taken to prepare in advance for the range of users who will access them (Fraser, Comden, and Burstahler 1998). In terms of Web design, such an inclusive approach tries to accommodate all readers, regardless of disability (Sullivan and Manning 1997). Vanderheiden (1996) contends that, "In general, when products, environments, or systems are made more accessible to persons with limitations, they are usually easier for more able-bodied persons to see. Some of the potential benefits include lower fatigue, increased speed, and lower error rates." Universal design may result in more elegantly designed and easily accessible Web pages for everyone.

The WAI Accessibility Guidelines: Page Authoring describes a number of prioritized guidelines, rationales and techniques for making Web site navigation, context, and orientation more accessible (Vanderheiden, Chisolm, and Jacobs 1998). A survey of the literature concerned with creating accessible Web sites reveals that there are consistently recommended features of HTML that could easily be incorporated into the design of Web pages (DO-IT 1997; Fontaine 1995; Fraser, Comden, and Burgstahler 1998; Laux 1998; National Federation of the Blind 1998; Starling Access Services 1997; Vanderheiden 1995; Waters 1997). The resulting Web pages would be accessible to all users. Selected guidelines are summarized in Table 1.

Applying these and additional principles of accessible Web design delineated in the *WAI Accessibility Guidelines* will ensure that any Web pages "transform" or "degrade" gracefully, remaining usable independent of user, available technology, or situation (Vanderheiden, Chisholm, and Jacobs 1998; Burstein 1998).

HOW ACCESSIBLE ARE LIBRARY HOME PAGES?

Established, suggested guidelines exist which facilitate accessible Web page design. Librarians are concerned with providing information to their users. Does there exist a synthesis of these two schools of thought? This study was designed to explore the following questions:

- How accessible are college and university library home pages?
- What are the most common accessibility problems encountered in using them?
- Do institutional characteristics and resources as represented by *Yahoo!* ranking, Association of Research Libraries ranking, and Carnegie Classification influence accessibility?

METHODOLOGY

A sample of 100 college and university library home pages was selected. The pages were analyzed for accessibility using the Bobby 3.0 online service. Institutional characteristics as reflected by Association of Research Libraries ranking, Carnegie Classification, and *Yahoo!* ranking were recorded.

Sample Selection:
"America's 100 Most Wired Colleges"

This study examines the library home pages of the colleges and universities found on *Yahoo!*'s 1998 list of "America's 100 Most Wired Colleges" (Greenman, Bernstein, and Gan 1998). Inclusion on the list is based on self-reported data regarding use of computer technology and electronic resources. Being listed in *Yahoo!* has become a source of pride for colleges and universities. The list provides an intentional sample of institutions that are conscious of the possibilities afforded by electronic access and have the resources to take advantage of those opportunities.

TABLE 1. Selected Guidelines for Accessible Web Pages

Page Design and Layout	Benefits
Develop a consistent and simple page layout for your site.	A consistent "look and feel" coupled with obvious navigation between pages will assist all visitors to your Web site, especially those with learning or cognitive disabilities.
Keep backgrounds simple and be sure there is sufficient contrast with page text. Test your site on many different types of monitors, color and monochrome, if you can.	Web pages with clean backgrounds and high contrast with page text will be easier to read by those with low vision or learning disabilities. Busy or textured backgrounds or color combinations with low contrast are difficult for most users to really see easily.
Use standard HTML. Provide alternative pages if you must use non-HTML (e.g. PDF, Shockwave) technologies or proprietary browser features.	All browsers should be able to access your Web pages if you use the HTML specifications defined by the World Wide Web Consortium (Vanderheiden, Chisolm, and Jacobs 1998). By providing HTML or plain text formats of PDF or Shockwave information, you increase the accessibility of the information on our Web site.
Design and use large buttons.	Larger sized buttons are easier for users with mobility impairments to select when navigating our Web site.
Include a note or statement concerning accessibility.	Visitors to your site will see that access is an important issue to your library. By defining your position on accessibility, you may encourage dialogue with users about this topic.
Use the "ALT" attribute to include short, descriptive alternative text for all images, applets, and image maps.	The text in the "ALT" attribute will display for visually impaired visitors using a voice output program with a text-based browser or for those users of a graphical browser who choose to load Web pages with the images turned off.

TABLE 1 (continued)

Page Design and Layout	Benefits
Provide descriptions for any pictures, scripts, or applets not fully described in the alternative text or document content. This includes any images of scanned manuscripts.	An alternative text description will allow important information presented via graphs, charts, diagrams, etc., to be accessible to persons with visual impairments. It may also assist users with learning disabilities and those for whom English is a second language.
Provide text captions, transcriptions or descriptions for audio clips.	Alternative text presentation of audio information (speeches, singing, etc.) allows users with hearing impairments or those connecting through systems without audio support to access the same information.
Provide captioned video and verbal descriptions of moving information, in both auditory and text formats.	This allows actions, body language and other visual clues to be accessible to persons with visual and hearing impairments.
Provide text alternatives for tabular information.	Visitors with visual impairments using screen readers and magnifiers will be better able to access your Web site. Most screen readers interpret information in tables from left to right rather than in up and down. Magnifiers may render large tables unreadable.
Use frames only when necessary. Provide alternate means of accessing the same information by giving users options on an introductory page that allows them to choose between a frame and non-frame option or by creating individual pages for each frame on a page and placing links on the page that links between frames.	Visitors with visual impairments using screen readers and magnifiers will be better able to access your Web site. Most screen readers interpret information in tables from left to right rather than in up and down. Magnifiers may render large tables unreadable.
Provide alternative methods for gathering form-based information.	Allowing users to e-mail or fax you information increases the input options for users with visual impairments.
Test all Web pages across various versions of different Web browsers, computer platforms, and types of monitors.	Multiple testing of Web pages in different environments ensures maximum accessibility to the most users.

Accessibility Analysis:
Bobby 3.0

The Bobby Web site, developed by the Center for Applied Special Technology (CAST), was selected as the instrument to evaluate library home pages. "Bobby is a Web-based public service offered by CAST that analyzes Web pages for their accessibility to people with disabilities as well as their compatibility with various browsers" (Center for Applied Special Technology 1998). It incorporates the guidelines recommended by the *WAI Accessibility Guidelines: Page Authoring* (Vanderheiden, Chisolm, and Jacobs 1998).

Institutional Computer Resources:
"America's 100 Most Wired Colleges"

Using *Yahoo!*'s "100 Most Wired" list ensured that the college and university Web pages were supported by a superior computer infrastructure. Inclusion on the list also implied a degree of sophistication and available expertise. In addition to providing an appropriate sample, the ranked order of the list reflected the technological resource base of the institutions.

Institutional Academic and Research Resources:
Carnegie Classification

"The 1994 Carnegie Classification includes all colleges and universities in the United States that are degree-granting and accredited by an agency recognized by the U.S. Secretary of Education" (The Carnegie Foundation for the Advancement of Teaching 1998). Carnegie classification reflects the institution's range of degrees and level of research activity. The status of each institution in the *Yahoo!* list was determined by examining the classified list as published in the annual almanac issue of *The Chronicle of Higher Education* (*Chronicle* 1997b).

Library Resources:
Association of Research Libraries

The Association of Research Libraries (ARL) is a not-for-profit organization comprised of libraries of North American research institutions (Association of Research Libraries 1998a). Its programs and services "promote equitable access to and effective use of recorded knowledge in support of teaching, research, scholarship, and community services" (Association of Research Libraries 1998b). Membership in ARL is by invitation only, and its 121 members share a commitment to providing materials needed for study and research (Association of Research Libraries 1998b). ARL assigns a composite ranking based on an index designed to measure the relative size of university libraries. The index reflects such factors as collection size and growth, operating expenditures, and number of personnel. This study uses the 1995-96 ranking as reported in the 1997 *Chronicle of Higher Education (Chronicle* 1997a).

Procedure

The address for the main library home page for each college or university in the sample was identified. Each address was then submitted to Bobby 3.0 online, which analyzed the Web page. In each case, the HTML 3.2 version of the page was specified, as this was the most commonly used version at the time of the study. In cases where both graphical and text versions of the page were available, both versions were analyzed for accessibility. These cases are noted, but for the sake of consistency, only the graphical version was included in the general data analysis.

A report of the category and number of accessibility errors, recommendations, questions (about elements which require human judgment and observation), tips, and the category and number of browser compatibility errors was generated for each page. Frequencies were calculated for the number of pages with accessibility errors, the categories of accessibility errors, recommendations, questions, tips, and the categories of browser compatibility errors.

The nature of the accessibility variable (bi-variate) and the institutional resource variables (rankings) dictated use of a nonparametric test of association. Relationships between accessibility and each of institutional resource variables were tested using Kolmogorov-Smirnov routine in SPSS-PC.

FINDINGS

Accessibility of Library Web Pages

Appendix B provides a summary of data, including accessibility findings. Forty of the 100 library home pages were rated accessible.

That is, no accessibility errors were recorded by Bobby. Fifteen sites were available in graphical and text versions. While only the graphical versions were included in the general data analysis, both versions were analyzed for accessibility. Of the dual version sites, both versions were approved at 5 of the 15 sites; the text version only was approved at another 5; the graphical version only at 3; and neither version of the page was approved at 2 sites. Table 2 lists the colleges or universities with both text and graphical versions of the main library home page.

TABLE 2. Approval Patterns for Sites with Both Text and Graphical Versions n = 15

College	Text	Graphic	Both	Neither
University of Arizona			x	
Baylor University				x
University of California-Davis			x	
University of California-Los Angeles	x			
Claremont McKenna College*		x		
Duke University			x	
Harvey Mudd College*		x		
Haverford College	x			
Johns Hopkins University	x			
University of Missouri-Rolla				x
Occidental College			x	
Pomona College*		x		
Rice University	x			
Temple University	x			
Worcester Polytechnic			x	
Totals	5	3	5	2

*Share "The Libraries of Claremont Colleges" page.

Accessibility Errors

Accessibility errors and frequency are presented in Table 3. Accessibility errors are those that could seriously affect the use of the page by a person with a disability. The most commonly occurring category of error was the failure to provide alternative text for all images. This error appeared in 53 of the 100 pages. Other accessibility errors, in order of descending frequency were failure to provide alternative text for all image map hot-spots (17); use of server-side image maps when functions were not available through other mechanisms (9); failure to provide text for all image submit buttons (3); and including blinking or scrolling text (2).

Recommendations

In some cases, there are elements of a page that could be improved, but the flaw is not so serious as to make the page inaccessible. Bobby provides recommendations to improve accessibility and universal design. These are listed by frequency in Table 4. The most common recommendation "If possible, avoid using tables to format text documents in columns" appeared in response to 97 pages, while the three other recommendations were recorded for 25 pages ("Client side image map contains a link not presented elsewhere on the page"), 6 pages ("Provide alternative content for each SCRIPT that conveys important information of function"), and 1 page ("Create link phrases that make sense when read out of context").

TABLE 3. Frequency of Accessibility Errors by Category (The number of pages which prompted this error message.) n = 100

Error message	# pages
Provide alternative text for all images.	53
Provide alternative text for all image map hot-spots.	17
Do not use server-side image maps unless the same functions are available through other mechanisms.	9
Provide alternative text for all image submit buttons.	3
Avoid blinking or scrolling text.	2

TABLE 4. Frequency of Recommendations (The number of pages which prompted this recommendation.) n = 100

Recommendation	# pages
If possible, avoid using tables to format text documents in columns.	97
Client-side image map contains a link not presented elsewhere on the page.	25
Provide alternative content for each SCRIPT that conveys important information or function.	6
Create link phrases that make sense when read out of context.	1

Questions

Accessibility questions are those that cannot be answered by Bobby's automated service. They require human judgment and assessment by the page's creator. As the Bobby FAQ page (Center for Applied Special Technology 1998) defines them, "The accessibility questions are all those places where Bobby thinks there might be an access error, but has no way of telling." One question, "Does this image convey important information beyond what is in its ALT text description?" appeared in response to virtually every page (97), while two other questions were asked infrequently. "Is this image button being used as a server-side image map?" was prompted by 3 pages. "Is there an alternative page where "auto-refreshing" is only done on the user's request?" was prompted by 1 (Table 5).

Tips

The Bobby report also includes a section of tips for improving overall accessibility of the page. There is a great deal of variance in the frequency with which these tips appear (Table 6). While the caveat "Avoid ASCII art" was prompted by all of the pages in the sample, "Make sure that style sheets fail gracefully" appeared only 6 times. Supporting document structure by use of proper elements (98), using color effectively (94), and using an alternative version of a page to ensure accessibility (60) were tips that appeared in response to more than half of the pages. Three more tips: nesting headings properly (30), separating adjacent links (30), and encoding list structures properly (27) were prompted by more than a quarter of the pages.

TABLE 5. Frequency of Questions (The number of pages which prompted this question.) n = 100

Question	# pages
Does this image convey important information beyond what is in its ALT text description?	97
Is this image button being used as a server-side image map?	3
Is there an alternative page where "auto-refreshing" is only done on the user's request (manual refreshing only)?	1

TABLE 6. Frequency of Tips (The number of pages which prompted this tip.) n = 100

Tip	# pages
Avoid ASCII art. Replace it with an image and alternative text.	100
Make sure that document structure is supported by the proper use of structural elements.	98
Make sure that text, image, and background colors contrast well and that color is not used as the sole means of conveying important information.	94
If you can't figure out any other way to make a page accessible, construct an alternate version of the page which is accessible.	60
Make sure that headings are nested properly.	30
Adjacent links should be separated.	30
Encode list structures and list items properly.	27
Make sure that style sheets fail gracefully.	6

Browser Compatibility Errors

The browser compatibility section of the Bobby report is useful in identifying HTML elements and element attributes that are not compatible with particular browsers. A Web page may contain browser compatibility errors and still be approved as accessible by the Bobby program. The most common browser compatibility error was "unknown attribute in element," which was noted in 74 pages (Table 7).

TABLE 7. Frequency of Browser Compatibility Errors by Category (The number of pages which prompted this error message.) n = 100

Error	# pages
Unknown attribute in element.	74
Attribute in element must be assigned an integer.	21
Unknown element name.	20
Required attribute is missing from tag.	18
Attribute in element must be assigned a color.	9
Attribute in element is assigned an incorrect value.	5
The closing tag of the element cannot contain attributes.	3

Fewer than 25 of the pages prompted the remaining error messages: "attribute in element not assigned a required integer" (21), "unknown element name" (20), "required element missing from tag" (18), "attribute in element not assigned required color" (9), "attribute in element assigned an incorrect value" (5), and "closing tag of the element cannot contain attributes" (3). A more complete explanation of these messages is available at the Bobby site (Center for Applied Special Technology, 1998).

Accessibility and Institutional Characteristics

Relationships among variables were analyzed using the Kolmogorov-Smirnov test. The test revealed no significant relationship between library Web page accessibility and *Yahoo!* ranking ($z = .939$, $p = .3412$), accessibility and Association of Research Libraries composite rank ($z = .3674$, $p = .9993$), nor accessibility and Carnegie classification ($z = .6124$, $p = .8475$).

IMPLICATIONS

The results of this study indicate that equal access to library services is a matter of institutional and individual philosophy and commitment, rather than a reflection of the university's status or available resources. Libraries in small liberal arts colleges, where one might assume greater attention to the individual, are no more or less likely to provide accessible pages than large universities, where one might assume a larger resource base.

While strides have been made in recognizing the need for accessible on-campus services and facilities for students with disabilities, awareness of the need for access to the library's electronic resources may be another matter. While the Web is being used more frequently as a means for providing convenient access to information resources, its obvious role as an outreach mechanism for students with disabilities has not been exploited. It is discouraging that fewer than half of the sample academic library Web pages are offering equitable access to Web sites, particularly given the high level of support for computer technology and services implied by their parent institutions' inclusion in the *Yahoo!* "100 Most Wired Colleges" list. This is consistent, however, with the lack of correlation with Carnegie Classification, which implies greater academic and research resources, and Association of Research Library ranking, which reflects extent of library resources.

The Bobby site offers an invaluable service. Automatic testing for compliance with the World Wide Web Consortium *Web Accessibility Initiative Page Authoring Guidelines* is quick and convenient. For librarians and others who wish to revise their pages to conform to the principles of universal design, the detailed error messages listed in the report are specific and can save page designers a great deal of time. This is a valuable service that is freely available and is an important first step. While not a guarantee of accessibility, working with recommendations provided by the Bobby analysis ensures that the site is as accessible as possible.

Ultimately, however, "accessibility is a human endeavor" (Center for Applied Special Technology 1998). Bobby asks questions that can be answered only through human observation and analysis; revising pages is the work of individuals. This study indicates that accessibility is not just a "human endeavor," but the result of personal and individual commitment to equitable access. Librarians who are truly committed to the concept of electronic information, services, and networks that are "equally, readily, and equitably accessible to all library users" (American Library Association 1998) will make that concept a reality. Until then, "For students with disabilities, the Web [will continue to] be like a classroom without a ramp" (*Chronicle* 1998).

REFERENCES

American Library Association. 1998. "The Library Bill of Rights." Available from http://www.ala.org/oif/electacc.html

Apple Computer, Inc. 1998. "Disability Resources." Available from http://www.apple.com/education/k12/disability/

Association of Research Libraries. 1998a. "ARL Fact Sheet." Available from http://www.arl.org/arl/arlfacts.html

Association of Research Libraries. 1998b. "Statement on Qualifications for Membership in the Association of Research Libraries." Available from http://www.arl.org/arl/arlfacts.html

Banks, Richard and Norman Coombs. 1998. "Adapting On-site Facilities for Patrons with Disabilities." Available from http://www.ohiolink.edu/ostaff/ada_report/

Beck, Susan Gilbert. 1995. A galaxy of rustling stars: places on the web and other library and information paths for the Deaf. *Library Hi Tech* 13(4): 93-100.

Burstein, Cari D. 1998. "Viewable with Any Browser: Accessible Site Design." Available from http://www.anybrowser.org/campaign/abdesign.sHTML#degradability

Center for Applied Special Technology. 1998. "Bobby 3.0." Available from http://www.cast.org/bobby/

The Chronicle of Higher Education. 1997a. "Facts & Figures: Holdings of Research Libraries in U.S. and Canada, 1995-96." Available from http://chronicle.com/che-data/info . . . brary.dir/97resour.dir/library.htm

The Chronicle of Higher Education. 1997b. The Nation: Institutions. *The Chronicle of Higher Education Almanac* 44(1): 37.

Connell, Bettye Rose, Mike Jones, Ron Mace, Jim Mueller, Abir Mullick, Elaine Ostroff, Joe Sanford, Ed Steinfeld, Molly Story, and Gregg Vanderheiden. 1995. "The Principles of Universal Design (version 1.1)." Available from http://trace.wisc.edu/docs/ud_princ/ud_princ.htm

Crispen, Joanne L., ed. 1993. *The Americans with Disabilities Act: Its Impact on Libraries The Library's Responses in "Doable" Steps.* Chicago: American Library Association.

Cunningham, Carmela and Norman Coombs. 1997. *Information Access and Adaptive Technology.* Phoenix: Oryx Press.

Descy, Don E. 1997. All aboard the internet: accessible web page design. TechTrends 42(6): 3-6.

DO-IT (Disabilities, Opportunities, Internetworking, and Technology). 1997. "World Wide Access: Accessible Web Design." Available from http://Weber.u.washington.edu/~doit/Brochures/Technology/universal.design.html

Fraser, Beth, Dan Comden and Sheryl Burgstahler. 1998. Including Users with Disabilities: Designing Library Web Sites for Accessibility. *Choice* 35 (Supplement): 35-37.

Fontaine, Paul. 1995. "Writing Accessible HTML Documents." Available from http://www.yuri.org/Webable/htmlcode.html

Graphic, Visualization, and Usability Center. Georgia Institute of Technology. 1998. "GVU's 9th User Survey." Available from http://www.gvu.gatech.edu/user_surveys/survey-1998-04/

Greenman, Ben, Rob Bernstein, and Dina Gan. 1998. "America's Most Wired Colleges." Available from http://www.zdnet.com/yil/content/college/index.html

Gregory, Gwen and M. Marlo Brown. 1997. World Wide Web page design: A structured approach. *Journal of Interlibrary Loan, Document Delivery & Information Supply* 7(3): 45-59.

IBM Corporation. 1998. *Web Accessibility.* Available from http://www.austin.ibm.com/sns/accessWeb.html

Jones, Richard R. 1993. Adaptive computer technology: an overview. *Library Hi Tech* 11(1): 30-3.

Kautzman, Amy M. 1998. Virtuous, virtual access: Make Web pages accessible to people with disabilities. *Searcher: The Magazine for Database Professionals* 6(6): 42-49.

Laux, Lila. 1998. Designing Web pages and applications for people with disabilities. p. 87-95 in *Human Factors and Web Development*, edited by Chris Forsythe, Eric Grose, and Julie Ratner. Mahwah, NJ: Lawrence Erlbaum Associates.

Matsco, Sandra and Sharon Campbell. 1996. Writing a library home page. *Public Libraries* 35: 284-6.

Microsoft Corporation. 1998. "Accessibility Page." Available from http://www.microsoft.com/enable/

Moeller, Michael. 1998. Disabling Web barriers. *PC Week* 15(19): 27.

National Federation for the Blind. 1998. *Guidelines for Web Accessibility.* Available from http://www.nfb.org/Webacc.htm

Paciello, Mike. 1996a. Making the Web accessible for the deaf, hearing, and mobility impaired. *Florida Libraries* 39(5): 83, 91.

Paciello, Mike. 1996b. Making the World Wide Web accessible for the blind and visually impaired. *Florida Libraries* 39(1): 5, 15.

Peters-Walters, Stacy. 1998. Accessible Web site design. *Teaching Exceptional Children* 30(5): 42-47.

Schnell, Eric H. 1997. Principles of Web document structure and design. *Medical Reference Services Quarterly* 16(1): 47-51.

Schuyler, Michael. 1997. Web (Dis)Content. *Computers in Libraries* 17(3): 38-39, 42.

Starling Access Services. 1997. "Accessible Web Page Design: General Design Tips." Available from http://www.igs.net/~starling/acc/acgen.htm

Sullivan, Terry and Krystyn Manning. 1997. "Could Helen Keller Read Your Page?" Available from http://www.pantos.org/atw/35412.html

Sun Microsystems. 1998. "New Technologies Open the Web to Everyone." Available from http://www.sun.com/980629/enable/

Trace Research and Development Center. (1998). "A Brief Introduction to Disabilities." Available from http://trace.wisc.edu/text/univdesn/populat/populat.HTML

U.S. Department of Justice. 1998. "Americans with Disabilities Act: ADA Home Page." Available from http://www.usdoj.gov/crt/ada/adahom1.htm

Vanderheiden, Gregg C. 1995. "Design of HTML Pages to Increase Their Accessibility to Users with Disabilities: Strategies for Today and Tomorrow (version 6.0)." Available from http://www.yuri.org/Webable/htmlglds.html

Vanderheiden, Gregg C. 1996. "Thirty Something (Million): Should They Be the Exceptions?" Available from http://trace.wisc.edu/docs/30_some/30_some.htm
Vanderheiden, Gregg, Wendy Chisolm, and Ian Jacobs (eds). 1998. "WAI Accessibility Guidelines: Page Authoring." Available from http://www.w3.org/TR/WD-WAI-PAGEAUTH/
Waddell, Cynthia D. 1998. "Applying the ADA to the Internet: A Web Accessibility Standard." Available from http://www.rit.edu/~easi/law/Weblaw1.htm
Waters, Crystal. 1998. *Universal Web Design*. Indianapolis, IN: New Riders.
World Wide Web Consortium. 1998. "HyperText Markup Language." Available from http://www.w3.org/MarkUp/

APPENDIX A

Suggested Adaptive PC Computer Workstation Configuration

Coombs and Cunningham (1997) suggest that when planning an adaptive workstation, it is best to begin with the easiest and least expensive approaches. "Move to the more expensive, more complicated approaches only when the simpler ones won't work (Cunningham and Coombs 1997, 60). The Office of Civil Rights has specified a scanner and relevant software as an important tool for a library to meet the obligation of providing equal access (Banks and Coombs 1998). Adequate training in adaptive technology for disabled students must also be a major consideration of any library, whether it takes place within the library or within a campus computing facility (Banks and Coombs 1998). Specific recommendations for equipment and software become outdated quickly in this rapidly developing field. The following selective list is derived from two sources, Banks and Coombs (1998) and Cunningham and Coombs (1997). It should be used as a starting point; every library must examine its own environment to implement an appropriately configured adaptive workstation.

1. Work Space

    A.   Adjustable-height table

    B.   Extra lighting

2. Hardware and Accessories

    A.   PC with a Pentium processor, 166 MHz or higher

    B.   Windows 95

    C.   32 MB RAM

    D.   1 GB Hard Drive

    E.   Sound card

    F.   Braille keyboard overlay

    G.   Glare screen or some way of allowing the monitor to be tilted

APPENDIX A (continued)

3. Software

A. Screen Magnification software (benefits users with visual and learning disabilities)
Example: *Zoom Text Xtra* Level 2 (demo version available at http://www.aisquared.com/contents.htm)

B. Screen Reader software (benefits users with visual disabilities)
Example: *Jaws for Windows* 3.2 (includes a software synthesizer)

C. On-Screen Keyboard and Switch-Adapted Mouse (SAM) Trackball (benefits users with permanent or temporary hand mobility impairments)
Example: *Cooper's On-Screen Keyboard with WordComplete* (demo version available at http://www.rjcooper.com/page7.htm#onscreen)

D. Browser software (benefits users with visual disabilities)
Example: *Microsoft Internet Explorer*
(Accommodates users with both cognitive and visual disabilities in terms of selecting screen options that eliminate distractions, expanding alternate text for images, and more.)
Example: *PwWebSpeak/pwWebSpeak Plus* (ver. 1.4.3)
(This browser interacts with the HTML coding on a Web page, allowing it to support forms processing, use of Internet search engines, and client-side image maps. Release version 1.4.3 supports frames. Future versions are expected to support Javascripts and Java Applets. Demo version available at http://www.prodworks.com)

4. More Extensive (and Expensive!) Equipment

A. Scanner and Optical Scanning Software, packaged with software to facilitate its use (benefits users with visual or learning disabilities and those who cannot manipulate books easily to read independently)
Example: *Arkenstone's An Open Book*

B. Braille Embosser and software to prepare electronic text for brailling
Example: *Enabling Technology's Juliet Pro Braille Embosser*

APPENDIX B

Data Summary

Name	Yahoo! Rank	ARL Rank*	Carnegie Class**	Bobby Approved
Dartmouth College	1	79	Doctoral II	No
New Jersey Institute of Technology	2	NR	Doctoral II	Yes
Massachusetts Institute of Technology	3	73	Research I	Yes
Rensselaer Polytechnic Institute	4	NR	Research II	Yes
University of Illinois at Urbana-Champaign	5	6	Research I	Yes
Carnegie Mellon University	6	NR	Research I	No
California Institute of Technology	7	NR	Research I	No
Indiana University at Bloomington	8	13	Research I	Yes
University of Oregon	9	80	Research II	Yes
Worcester Polytechnic Institute	10	NR	Doctoral II	Yes
University of Delaware	11	89	Research II	No
Dakota State University	12	NR	Not Ranked	Yes
Emerson College	13	NR	Not Ranked	Yes
Rhodes College	14	NR	Liberal Arts	Yes
Virginia Polytechnic Institute	15	85	Research I	No
University of Virginia	16	20	Research I	No
Northwestern University	17	32	Research I	No
Drexel University	18	NR	Doctoral I	No
College of Saint Benedict	19	NR	Liberal Arts	Yes
New York University	20	24	Research I	No
Sweet Briar College	21	NR	Liberal Arts	Yes
Baylor University	22	NR	Doctoral II	No
University of California at Los Angeles	23	3	Research I	No
University of California at Santa Cruz	24	NR	Research II	No

APPENDIX B (continued)

Name	*Yahoo!* Rank	ARL Rank*	Carnegie Class**	Bobby Approved
East Carolina University	25	NR	Not Ranked	No
University of Central Florida	26	NR	Doctoral II	Yes
Stanford University	27	5	Research I	No
Middlebury College	28	NR	Liberal Arts	No
Ohio State University	29	22	Research I	No
Yale University	30	2	Research I	No
University of Notre Dame	31	53	Research II	Yes
University of Vermont	32	NR	Research II	No
Florida State University	33	83	Research I	Yes
Rochester Institute of Technology	34	NR	Not Ranked	Yes
Saint Johns University	35	NR	Liberal Arts	No
University of Mississippi	36	NR	Research II	No
Michigan State University	37	37	Research I	No
Texas A&M University	38	42	Research I	No
University of Maryland, College Park	39	43	Research I	No
University of Missouri at Rolla	40	NR	Doctoral I	No
Saint Louis University	41	NR	Research II	No
University of California at Berkeley	42	4	Research I	No
University of Southern California	43	38	Research I	No
Washington State University	44	96	Research II	No
Hamilton College	45	NR	Liberal Arts	No
Loyola College	46	NR	Not Ranked	No
Santa Clara University	47	NR	Not Ranked	No
Iowa State University	48	66	Research I	Yes
Skidmore College	49	NR	Liberal Arts	No
Kenyon College	50	NR	Liberal Arts	No

Name	*Yahoo!* Rank	ARL Rank*	Carnegie Class**	Bobby Approved
University of Toledo	51	NR	Doctoral I	No
Vanderbilt University	52	58	Research I	No
Auburn University	53	72	Research II	No
College of the Holy Cross	54	NR	Liberal Arts	No
Cornell University	55	11	Research I	Yes
Marquette University	56	NR	Doctoral I	Yes
Duke University	57	23	Research I	Yes
Bucknell University	58	NR	Liberal Arts	Yes
Vassar College	59	NR	Liberal Arts	No
Duquesne College	60	NR	Doctoral II	Yes
Oberlin College	61	NR	Liberal Arts	No
University of Connecticut	62	50	Research I	Yes
Case Western Reserve University	63	102	Research I	No
Franklin & Marshall College	64	NR	Liberal Arts	No
Colby College	65	NR	Liberal Arts	Yes
Princeton University	66	16	Research I	No
Swarthmore College	67	NR	Liberal Arts	No
University of Arizona	68	27	Research I	Yes
University of California at Davis	69	35	Research I	Yes
Pomona College	70	NR	Liberal Arts	Yes
Columbia University	71	9	Research I	Yes
Kent State University	72	87	Research II	Yes
Harvard University	73	1	Research I	No
Rice University	74	108	Research II	No
University of Michigan	75	7	Research I	No
University of Richmond	76	NR	Not Ranked	No

APPENDIX B (continued)

Name	*Yahoo!* Rank	ARL Rank*	Carnegie Class**	Bobby Approved
Wake Forest University	77	NR	Doctoral II	No
Williams College	78	NR	Liberal Arts	Yes
Claremont McKenna College	79	NR	Liberal Arts	Yes
Harvey Mudd College	80	NR	Not Ranked	Yes
Occidental College	81	NR	Liberal Arts	Yes
Pennsylvania State University	82	19	Research I	Yes
Southern Methodist University	83	NR	Doctoral I	Yes
University of Chicago	84	18	Research I	Yes
University of Washington	85	12	Research I	No
University of Wisconsin at Madison	86	14	Research I	Yes
Wellesley College	87	NR	Liberal Arts	No
Whitman College	88	NR	Liberal Arts	No
Bates College	89	NR	Liberal Arts	Yes
State University of New York at Geneseo	90	NR	Not Ranked	Yes
Syracuse University	91	81	Research II	No
University of Northern Texas	92	NR	Doctoral I	No
Carleton College	93	NR	Liberal Arts	No
Haverford College	94	NR	Liberal Arts	No
Johns Hopkins University	95	39	Research I	No
Temple University	96	84	Research I	No
Birmingham–Southern College	97	NR	Not Ranked	No
Cedarville College	98	NR	Not Ranked	No
Drake University	99	NR	Not Ranked	Yes
Grinnell College	100	NR	Liberal Arts	No

*NR = Not Ranked
**Liberal Arts = Selective Liberal Arts; Not Ranked = Not Ranked in *The Chronicle of Higher Education* (1997b)

Real-Time Reference Service
for the Remote User:
From the Telephone and Electronic Mail
to Internet Chat, Instant Messaging,
and Collaborative Software

Marc Meola
Sam Stormont

SUMMARY. Academic libraries now provide reference service for the remote user in at least two ways: by the telephone and by electronic mail. The remote user at a computer workstation, however, may not have access to a telephone and may be poorly served by the asynchronous nature of electronic mail. New technologies and collaborative software for serving remote users in real-time such as Internet chat, paging and instant messaging, whiteboard, application sharing, and audio and video conferencing offer new possibilities for remote access to reference services. In this article we review these technologies and report the results of a trial project at Temple University. The results are promising for

Marc Meola is Reference Librarian at Temple University, Paley Library (017-00), 1210 W. Berks Street, Philadelphia, PA 19122-6088 (E-mail: mmeola@astro.ocis. temple.edu); Sam Stormont is Electronic Reference Services Coordinator at Temple University, Paley Library (017-00), 1210 W. Berks Street, Philadelphia, PA 19122-6088 (E-mail: stormont@astro.ocis.temple.edu). The networking of computer workstations through the Internet has increased the number of users who can access library collections remotely. Remote users now include users in computer centers, homes, and offices, from locations a few miles to hundreds of miles away.

[Haworth co-indexing entry note]: "Real-Time Reference Service for the Remote User: From the Telephone and Electronic Mail to Internet Chat, Instant Messaging, and Collaborative Software." Meola, Marc, and Sam Stormont. Co-published simultaneously in *The Reference Librarian* (The Haworth Information Press, an imprint of The Haworth Press, Inc.) No. 67/68, 1999, pp. 29-40; and: *Library Outreach, Partnerships, and Distance Education: Reference Librarians at the Gateway* (ed: Wendi Arant, and Pixey Anne Mosley) The Haworth Press, Inc., 2000, pp. 29-40. Single or multiple copies of this article are available for a fee from The Haworth Document Delivery Service [1-800-342-9678, 9:00 a.m. - 5:00 p.m. (EST). E-mail address: getinfo@haworthpressinc.com].

real-time reference services. *[Article copies available for a fee from The Haworth Document Delivery Service: 1-800-342-9678. E-mail address: getinfo@haworthpressinc.com <Website: http://www.haworthpressinc.com>]*

KEYWORDS. Reference, remote users, electronic mail, internet chat, instant messaging, paging, audio and video conferencing, collaborative software, TalkBack, NetMeeting

INTRODUCTION

Emerging digital libraries are often conceived of solely as collections of electronic materials that may be accessed from a remote location.[1] New software designed for collaboration between computer users, however, points to a larger conception of the digital library that includes not only electronic access to sources, but electronic access to services as well. In this vision, it is assumed that electronic access to sources by itself does not obviate the need for librarian-patron interaction. In fact, access to an array of sources that differ in terms of accessibility, interface, organization, and content increases the need for interaction, especially when patrons are not physically in the library. Reference librarians have long used the telephone for remote interaction, and more recently electronic mail. New collaborative software such as internet chat, instant messaging and paging, whiteboard, application sharing, and audio and video conferencing offer more possibilities for remote access to services, and libraries are beginning to take advantage of these possibilities.[2] This article compares more established technologies for reaching remote users such as the telephone and electronic mail with emerging technologies such as Internet chat, instant messaging, and collaborative software. It discusses efforts at Temple University to reach remote users in real-time with an interactive pager program called TalkBack.

WHO IS THE REMOTE USER?

The remote user is defined as any user not physically in front of a reference desk. This definition includes users in computer centers in the library itself; users at computer centers in buildings on campus but not in the library; users in dorm rooms, homes, and offices who are affiliated with the university, as well as users not affiliated with the university who seek to use the Libraries' collections. The definition also includes users with a disability that in some way prevents them from receiving traditional reference service but whose problem is ameliorated by certain technologies. The number of remote library users has been increasing as catalogs, citation and full text databases, and world wide web sites have become accessible from locations outside the library. It is a mistake to assume that remote users do not have questions about information finding strategies that require mediation by professional librarians. Remote users have reference questions just as in-library patrons have reference questions. In-library patrons can ask their questions in person; remote users should be able to ask their questions remotely.

HOW TO PROVIDE REFERENCE SERVICE
TO THE REMOTE USER?

Telephone

The telephone is the most traditional way of providing reference service to remote users. In today's jargon, the telephone is a real-time interactive audio application. Some librarians may object to newer interactive services (such as Internet chat, for example) on the grounds that such services do not offer anything beyond service by telephone, which most libraries already provide. A glance at the types of remote users who are now able to access library collections refutes this argument. A student in a computer lab usually does not have access to a telephone. Persons in dorm rooms, at home, or in offices who are dialed into the library network do not have access to a telephone unless they have two telephone lines. Users at greater distances will have to pay long distance charges to use the telephone. In addition, some users may have a disability that prevents them from using the telephone, but it may be possible for them to type and receive a message by a computer keyboard. Telephone reference is tried and true, tested and proven. It is an example of librarians adopting technology to serve users. The success of telephone reference is not an argument against new forms of interactive reference, but proof that interacting through technology with users at a distance is necessary, desirable, and doable. Telephone reference will continue to play a role in serving remote users, but its use will be limited, as all interactive programs are, to persons who have access to the technology. In the networked workstation environment, there are increasing numbers of users who will find it easier and more convenient to contact the reference desk through an interactive web-based program (such as paging software or a variation of internet chat for example) than by the telephone.

Electronic Mail

Libraries began using electronic mail in reference service in the late 1980s and the service is now fairly commonplace and uncontroversial.[3] A link with an e-mail address and a form can be placed on a library's homepage and questions can be integrated into the reference department's workflow. Temple University Libraries began offering e-mail reference service in 1995. Questions are distributed to all members of the reference department through a listserv and responses are sent within twenty-four hours. Responsibility for answering questions is rotated weekly. Service is provided to Temple University students, faculty, and staff, or users with a question relating to an aspect of the collections of the Temple University Libraries. Postings are monitored by the Head of Reference and the Electronic Reference Services Coordinator for accuracy, thoroughness, and timely completion.

E-mail reference differs from telephone and traditional desk reference in at least three ways: answers to questions are in written form, answers may be distributed by listerv allowing all reference staff to view, and communication is asynchronous instead of in real time. Since e-mail reference answers are written instead of spoken, reference staff may have to spend more time formulating answers so they are accurate and able to be understood, especially since their answers are being reviewed by their colleagues. Written answers may benefit users who can save the answer for review at a later time or print the answer out if it contains instructions or a referral. Since questions are not answered in real time, reference staff can, if necessary, take the time to provide a detailed answer to a question, but this also can be a disadvantage for some who may spend too much time on a question.

The number and types of questions received through e-mail have changed since 1995. When our e-mail service was first proposed, some librarians feared that reference staff would be overwhelmed with questions, but this did not occur.[4] Initially, the number of questions fluctuated but stabilized at four to five questions a week when a direct link to their homepage was established in 1997. Early questions tended to be of two types: questions about the mechanics of access (how do I connect to this database from home?), and questions about specific materials (do you have the *Evening Bulletin* from 1932?). With the Fall 1998 semester, questions doubled to eight to ten a week, and staff began to wonder if remote users might benefit from the more immediate attention that could be provided with Internet chat or instant messaging.

Internet Chat and Instant Messaging

Internet chat is text-based real-time communication. Users on one end of a networked computer type messages through a computer keyboard and message recipients at the end of another networked computer see the message on their monitors and respond in kind. Chat does not require users in a computer lab or users at home to use a telephone, and answers to questions can be communicated immediately, unlike e-mail. Text-based Internet chat is a blending of telephonic and e-mail communication, which would seem to be particularly useful for a library service such as reference which is often defined as "the process of answering questions."[5] Yet, although Internet chat has been in existence roughly as long as e-mail, the use of chat as a means of providing reference service in libraries has been limited.

One possible reason is that chat has a shady reputation and is often viewed negatively by some librarians. Librarians may be wary of students occupying computer terminals designated for research use by chatting with their fellow students, often sitting a few terminals away. This is a common problem at many schools, but it cannot be the only reason chat is not used in reference service since libraries have a similar problem with students using electronic mail, but many offer electronic mail reference.[6]

Another possible reason is that chat has been technically complicated to configure for the reference environment and less widespread than electronic mail. With the advent of the World Wide Web and Java-enabled browsers that permit chat programs to be integrated into web pages, however, this situation is changing. Chat is now one of the most popular features of the Internet: of the 107 million people who use the Internet, 40 to 50 million use chat.[7] America Online reports that its users spend more time in chat rooms than they do surfing websites.[8] Chat is currently being used by businesses to provide customer service, by the entertainment industry to promote film personalities and authors, and by educational institutions in distance learning.[9]

The reference staff believe chat is valuable because it connects remote users with reference librarians in real-time. Although currently underutilized in academic libraries, it has potential as an intermediate step between electronic mail reference and real time audio and video conferencing. In the summer of 1998, staff began conceptualizing a chat reference service for Temple University Libraries. They formulated a list of desiderata for the program and service:

- the program should be simple to use with a minimum of instructions for users and librarians,
- the program should be directly accessible from the library web page; users should not have to download any software,
- the program should allow library staff to limit interactions to one-to-one discussions between user and librarian rather than group discussions in rooms to avoid security problems and use of the service for non-research related conversations,
- the program should require little or no programming or scripting on our part,
- the program should not require us to show advertising,
- the program should be free or of relatively low cost.

The user would be able to click on a link on our web page, type a message in an interactive form, and be able to establish a real-time connection with a member of our reference staff. For simplicity, it was decided not to create chat rooms where multiple users could talk to each other. Initially, interaction would occur while reference staff were on the reference desk, but if this proved too hectic or confusing, staff would be assigned chat hours, either at the desk or at another location in the library.

Although a large number of chat programs are available for downloading on the World Wide Web, most did not fit the parameters in that they either required advertising, required programming or scripting, or were beyond the budget. We discovered that the State University of New York at Morrisville was using a program called TalkBack to offer real-time reference service. The program coordinators were immediately interested in TalkBack because it met all our criteria: it is simple to use, web-based, it does not require the user to download any software, it does not have advertising, and it is free.

TalkBack is a paging program that works in conjunction with server software. A link on a web page connects the user to a TalkBack form. The remote user types a message into the form and then clicks on a button to send the message. When the message is sent, a window pops up on the machine where the software is installed allowing the message to be read. A reply can be sent back to the remote user. The process can then be repeated if necessary. Talkback is not exactly an internet chat application; its author describes it as a "world wide web interactive pager." Paging and instant messaging programs are becoming increasingly popular on the Internet as alternatives to chat rooms.[10]

Temple University Libraries began testing TalkBack for reference service in the fall of 1998. A link to the Talkback service was placed on the Libraries home page, but no publicity was used to announce or promote the service. The service was described as being for Temple University students, faculty, and staff. TalkBack was installed on a computer at Temple University's Paley Library reference desk and questions were answered by reference staff who were on the desk during regular reference hours (Monday through Friday 9:00 a.m. to 9:00 p.m., Saturday 10:00 a.m.-6:00 p.m., Sunday 12:00 noon to 8 p.m.). All members of the reference staff were trained in how to use the software and were required to answer TalkBack questions in addition to in-person and telephone reference questions. If reference staff are working with an in-person patron at the time of an incoming TalkBack question, Talkback software sends a message to the user that the reference staff is busy and invites them to send an email question instead. The TalkBack program includes a log that records all exchanges and enables program coordinators to track and analyze the program's use.

For the initial six week period beginning November 12 and ending December 24, 1998, the following can be reported from the Temple University experience:

- Reference staff received 86 questions through TalkBack compared with 54 questions through the traditional electronic mail reference service for the same time period.
- Of the 86 questions, 61 were answered in real-time, the remaining 25 were referred to an electronic mail form. Of the 25 referred to the email form, 22 users submitted questions by email and received answers.

- The most frequently asked questions were requests for a specific journal, book or document; and requests for help searching or accessing a specific database.
- Patron reaction was positive including several comments on the usefulness of the quick response. There were no complaints about the software and no frivolous or obscene messages.
- Staff reaction was mixed, especially regarding the short amount of time in which to respond to a question.

The program coordinators were surprised and encouraged by the high number of questions we received through TalkBack. Since they received more questions through TalkBack than through established email reference service for the same six week period, they believe this indicates a clear willingness of patrons to use software to ask questions in real-time. Since reference staff were able to answer 71% of those questions in real-time (the remaining were referred to email), they believe those prospects for real-time reference services are promising.

There are two drawbacks to the TalkBack program. One is that staff must respond to the pop-up window within sixty seconds or the program will timeout and default to the e-mail reference form. The other is that the program does not display a running text of the dialogue, making it difficult to keep track of a conversation, particularly if reference staff is interrupted by an in-person patron. The staff realized this would be a problem and anticipated that TalkBack would work best for relatively simple questions and uninterrupted exchanges. They believe these problems are problems related to the software but not to the idea of real-time reference service. One program which may have the potential for overcoming these drawbacks is Microsoft's NetMeeting.

Audio and Video Conferencing and Collaborative Software

There have been a number of experiments with video conferencing in reference service in the past few years.[11] Most have focused primarily on video and have been limited to a group of specific users during certain hours of the day. These early experiments revealed some of the limitations of using video conferencing in reference: users need access to video technology, and the technology itself is limited by available bandwidth. At the time that trailblazing librarians tested video conferencing, the technology was so new that not enough remote users could use it consistently from locations where they most often worked, and the technology itself either did not work consistently or users were uncomfortable and unsure how to use it. With new collaborative software programs, however, video is one option out of many for real time collaboration, thereby increasing the possibility that the interaction will be successful. For example, if a user does not have a video camera or does not want to be seen, the user may still communicate in real time using chat. A librarian may also communicate with chat and demonstrate concepts with whiteboard and application sharing (these terms will be explained below).

The authors learned of collaborative software programs being considered for use in Temple classes by attending workshops run by the Temple University Attention to Teaching and Teaching Improvement Center. The software demonstrated included Daedalus, GroupWise Web Publisher, Norton Connect Net, Microsoft NetShow, Microsoft NetMeeting, and Reilly WebBoard. These programs fall into two groups: software designed for writing classes so that students can share files and comment on each other's work, and software designed for businesses and other groups to hold conferences at a distance. They saw the possibility of applying this software to reference by attempting to simulate traditional reference exchanges for remote users with a combination of chat software and audio and video applications. It was encouraging that classes at the University were considering using the software, since this meant students would be more likely to be familiar with the software before using it to connect to our reference desk.

Microsoft's NetMeeting was the most appealing program to us because its features are most adaptable to a reference transaction, the program (at this writing) is free, and Academic Computing Services at Temple University supports the program by maintaining a server that affiliated users may use to connect with each other. One drawback is that users will have to download the program instead of simply being able to access the service from our web page. The program does come bundled with new computers that have Windows 95 and 98, however.

Microsoft NetMeeting runs on Windows 95, Windows 98, and Windows NT 4.0. Features include chat, whiteboard, application sharing, file sharing, and audio and video sharing. The chat feature allows real time communication to take place in a window. Whiteboard is a window in which a librarian and remote user may write text, draw lines, highlight text, circle text, or point to images. For example, the image of a library's home page may be pasted into the whiteboard and a librarian can then point to or highlight a link for the user. Application sharing allows a librarian and remote user to view the same application. For example, if a remote user has a question about searching an online catalog or database, a librarian may demonstrate the search and the remote user may view the search as it is taking place. Similarly, the librarian may observe a remote user executing a search and advise if necessary. File sharing allows two users to share files and is probably more useful for two librarians collaborating on a paper than for a librarian and remote user involved in a reference transaction. Audio sharing allows remote users to communicate with each other in real time using audio. A sound card, speakers, and a microphone are required. Video sharing occurs in a small window in NetMeeting; participants need either a video-capture card and camera or a video camera that connects through the computer's parallel (printer) port.

The program coordinators are currently configuring NetMeeting for use at Temple University. The initial trial will focus on the remote users in Temple University computing centers since the program may be installed on those workstations. Reference staff will use the program at the reference desk at first and move to a less hectic location later if necessary. Initially, the chat feature will be utilized as the primary way of communicating with the remote user, but staff will move toward audio and video sharing. NetMeeting permits flexibility in that a service does not need to start out as two-way video conferencing: conferees can begin with real time chat and progress as equipment permits. For many reference transactions, chat and application sharing may be sufficient to help the user, even though full simulation of traditional reference transactions is the ultimate goal.

CONCLUSION

Just as there are different databases, different vendors, and different formats in our libraries, there are now a number of different technologies that may be used to serve remote users. The plain old telephone is no longer sufficient to meet the needs of all remote users, any more than the printed book on paper is. As is always the case, each library must find its own mix of technologies that best serves its users, which may include differing combinations of the telephone, electronic mail, chat, and collaborative software, or aspects of all of them at once. Paging programs such as TalkBack and collaborative software programs such as Microsoft's NetMeeting offer real possibilities for libraries to simulate traditional reference service for remote users. Doing so will ensure that digital libraries will include remote access to services as well as remote access to sources.

NOTES

1. Michael Lesk defines digital libraries as " . . . organized collections of digital information." Michael Lesk, *Practical Digital Libraries: Books, Bytes, and Bucks* (San Francisco: Morgan Kaufmann Publishers, 1997) ix. Carol Tenopir and Lisa Ennis, "The Digital Reference World of Academic Libraries," *Online*, July 1998 is source centered. Ronald J. Heckart speculates that the disappearance of human help may be inherent in the logic of the digital library in "Machine Help and Human Help in the Emerging Digital Library," *College and Research Libraries* 59, no. 3 (May 1998): 250-259.

2. Michigan State University uses chat and the State University of New York at Morrisville uses paging software to deliver real time reference service. Nova Southeastern University uses NetMeeting to provide library instruction to distance students, see Paul R. Pival and Johanna Tunon, "NetMeeting: A New and Inexpensive Alternative For Delivering Library Instruction to Distance Students" *College and Research Libraries News* 59, no. 10 (November 1998): 758-760.

3. Christine M. Roysdon and Laura Lee Elliott, "Electronic Integration of Library Services Through a Campuswide Network," *RQ* no. 28 (Fall 1988): 82-93.

4. This does not seem to have happened at other universities either, see: Lara Bushallow-Wilbur, Gemma DeVinney, and Fritz Whitcomb, "Electronic Mail Reference Service: A Study," *RQ* 35, no. 3 (1996): 359-371.

5. William A. Katz, *Introduction to Reference Work*, 6th ed., vol. 1, *Basic Information Sources* (New York: McGraw-Hill Inc., 1992) 3.

6. Lisa Guernsey, "Off-Campus Users Swamp College Libraries, Seeking Access to Web and E-Mail," *Chronicle of Higher Education* 94, no. 47 (July 31, 1998): A17.

7. Michel Marriott, "The Blossoming of Internet Chat: Moving from Gossip, Flirting and Worse to Education, Consumer Service and Even More Gossip." *New York Times*, 2 July 1998, Web edition.

8. Ibid.

9. Ibid.

10. Lisa Napoli, "Instant Messages: the New Pace of Business." *New York Times*, 14 November 1998, Web edition.

11. Ruth Pagell, "The Virtual Reference Librarian: Using Desktop Videoconferencing for Distance Reference," *The Electronic Library*, 14, no. 1 (February, 1996): 21-26; Kathleen M. Folger, "The Virtual Librarian: Using Desktop Videoconferenc-

ing to Provide Interactive Reference Assistance,'' (paper presented at the 1997 Association of College and Research Libraries national conference), accessible at www. ala.org/acrl/papers.html; Susan Lessick, Kathyrn Kjaer, and Steve Clancy, "Interactive Reference Service (IRS) at UC Irvine: Expanding Reference Service Beyond the Reference Desk," (paper presented at the 1997 Association of College and Research Libraries national conference), accessible at www.ala.org/acrl/papers. html.

Marketing Electronic Resources and Services: Surveying Faculty Use as a First Step

Judith L. Hart
Vicki Coleman
Hong Yu

SUMMARY. In an effort to provide desktop access to information at Texas A&M University, an increasingly greater portion of the University Libraries' budget is being spent on electronic resources and services. This study, a survey of a random sample of the faculty and teaching staff, was designed to determine if these resources and services are being used by the targeted population and, if not, why. The results of the study indicate that a lack of information is the greatest obstacle to the use of electronic resources/services, and they suggest that the Libraries should place greater emphasis on outreach to the faculty and improved marketing strategies. *[Article copies available for a fee from The Haworth Document Delivery Service: 1-800-342-9678. E-mail address: getinfo@haworthpressinc. com <Website: http://www.haworthpressinc.com>]*

KEYWORDS. University faculty, usage of electronic resources, marketing library services, outreach, faculty survey

---

Judith L. Hart is Senior Science Reference Librarian, Sterling C. Evans Library, Texas A&M University, College Station, TX 77843-5000 (E-mail: jlhart@tamu.edu). Vicki Coleman is Head, Spahr Engineering Library, Lawrence, KS 66045-2800 (E-mail: vcoleman@ukans.edu). Hong Yu is Assistant Research Librarian, Information and Technology Exchange Center, Texas Transportation Institute, P.O. Box 3135, College Station, TX 77843 (E-mail: hong-yu@tamu.edu).

[Haworth co-indexing entry note]: "Marketing Electronic Resources and Services: Surveying Faculty Use as a First Step." Hart, Judith L., Vicki Coleman, and Hong Yu. Co-published simultaneously in *The Reference Librarian* (The Haworth Information Press, an imprint of The Haworth Press, Inc.) No. 67/68, 1999, pp. 41-55; and: *Library Outreach, Partnerships, and Distance Education: Reference Librarians at the Gateway* (ed: Wendi Arant, and Pixey Anne Mosley) The Haworth Press, Inc., 2000, pp. 41-55. Single or multiple copies of this article are available for a fee from The Haworth Document Delivery Service [1-800-342-9678, 9:00 a.m. - 5:00 p.m. (EST). E-mail address: getinfo@haworthpressinc.com].

INTRODUCTION

Two years ago, Dr. Leonard Berry, Director of the Center of Retailing Studies at Texas A&M University (TAMU), spoke at the American Library Association (ALA) Annual Conference regarding the future of libraries and the need for them to market their services. He told of how a family-owned boutique in a small Texas city draws customers from throughout the state. The owners make their largest profit from their basic clothing sales, but market their beautiful scarves to attract and pull customers into the shop. At the close of his presentation, he posed the following questions to librarians: (1) What is your "scarf?" (2) If your library was to disappear tomorrow, would your customers miss it (Berry et al., 1996)?

To survive and prosper in today's technological information age, libraries must offer their users resources and services that they cannot readily find anywhere else, whether it be access to electronic information resources or services provided by a knowledgeable library staff. The concept of marketing library services puts emphasis on satisfying customers and meeting their expectations. For this to happen, customers must know the resources and services the library provides and the benefits they gain by using the services. This requires marketing and outreach on the part of the library.

One component of a successful marketing strategy is determining the needs of a targeted customer base. Other components include clearly defining the resources and services offered so that they are instantly recognized by name (e.g., PEAK as a package of Elsevier full-text journals, OVID as a company name for many databases, etc.); informing customers of the price/value of the resources/services used (e.g., how many people realize the full cost of ordering a journal article through Interlibrary Loan Services?); promotion and public relations. Quality service should pervade every step of the process.

This study is the beginning of a marketing strategy for the electronic resources and services offered at the Texas A&M University (TAMU) Libraries. TAMU is a land grant university with over 43,000 students, 2,300 faculty, and a library collection of approximately 2.5 million volumes held in one main library and two branch libraries. The 1997 American Research Libraries (ARL) annual statistics show that Texas A&M has the fifth largest collection of computer files among ARL institutions. The same statistics show that the ratio of computer files to volumes held at TAMU ranks fourth (Association of Research Libraries, 1998). Due to the large number of electronic resources pro-vided by the libraries, it is crucial to know if these resources are being used and, if not, why.

LITERATURE REVIEW

A 1988 survey of Texas A&M University "revealed that 21 percent of the faculty surveyed were searching databases from their offices and labs without centralized funding or assistance from the Library" (Clark and Gomez, 1990). The researchers who performed the survey concluded that convenience was a major factor in determining where faculty did their electronic searching. In fact, many faculty were pay-ing for the use of databases when the same databases were available at the Library. In the past five years, the TAMU library system has expanded to include branch libraries and an emphasis has been placed on providing remote access to electronic resources. The convenience of the faculty and students has been taken into consideration. At the time of the survey, the University Libraries provided remote access to over one hundred databases and approximately 1,500 full-text elec-tronic journals and access to additional databases in the libraries. Presently, the Libraries provide remote access to over 3,500 electronic resources. Due to the greatly expanded number of electronic resources available, 1998 was an appropriate time to conduct another survey to assess faculty needs for and uses of the electronic resources and ser-vices currently available at their desktops.

Several universities and institutions have conducted studies to as-sess faculty use of electronic information technologies and resources (Abels et al., 1996; Adams et al., 1995; Borgman et al., 1985; Clark and Gomez, 1990; Fiscella and Proctor, 1995; Vander Meer et al., 1997; Wilkins and Nantz, 1995). The present study will most closely resemble the research conducted by Adams et al. (1993), who sent surveys to faculty in all academic disciplines at the State University of New York's four graduate University Centers (Albany, Binghamton, Buffalo, and Stony Brook). The results of the study showed inequities in access to electronic technologies among the disciplines and lack of knowledge of library resources. A more recent survey conducted at Western Michigan University focused on the "relationship between faculty use of university libraries and faculty use of computers" (Vander Meer et al., 1997). Their findings indicated that faculty who are frequent library users are more likely than non-users to use computer applications. Implications for library services included the need for: standardization among electronic interfaces to ease the steep learning curve for efficient use of electronic resources, user assistance and instruction, collaboration with University Computing Services, marketing electronic services and communicating with faculty.

OBJECTIVES

The objectives of this research were to (1) assess the awareness and usage of current electronic resources and services by a segment of the Libraries' customer base, the faculty and teaching staff, (2) assess the obstacles to use of electronic information, and (3) determine how to increase the use of the available technologies and services. The information gained will allow the Libraries to provide electronic services and resources to meet the specific needs and preferences of the faculty, thereby serving the faculty community more effectively.

METHODOLOGY

The survey used was a modification of a survey originally designed to determine the needs, preferences, and usage of electronic resources by faculty (Adams et al., 1993). The survey was updated to reflect modern information technologies (see Appendix). A random sample of 400 faculty (including teaching assistants) was generated by computer from a population of over 2,300. Surveys were sent to 400 faculty with a self-addressed return envelope in the Spring semester of 1998. For anonymity, surveys and return envelopes were not numbered. To encourage participation, respondents had the opportunity to win either two tickets to a local theatrical performance or a dinner for two at a local restaurant. Also, the first fifty respondents had the opportunity to participate in a free unmediated document-delivery project. Faculty were given three weeks to respond.

FINDINGS

Thirty-nine percent of the recipients of the survey responded. Demographics of the respondents (professorial rank, number of years of post-secondary teaching experience, and academic college) are given in Charts 1-3. Nearly 98% of the respondents have access to a computer either at home or in the office; however, the type of computer and peripheral equipment varies considerably. Over 75% have connections to the campus network via either their office or/and home computer. With the exception of the TAMU Online Public Access Catalog (OPAC), contracts license required connections through the campus network to obtain remote access to the library's electronic journals and databases. One set of questions in the survey instrument pertained to the level of usage of networked resources by faculty. The majority of the faculty at TAMU who answered the survey do use the library's OPAC and the journal indexes available through the OPAC's operating system. Most of the respondents also use the electronic journal indexes, electronic journals, and listservs either at the office or at home as opposed to in the library. The Lexis-Nexis database and CD-ROM databases show higher usage in the library because at the time of the survey, special permission was required to obtain remote access to them (see Chart 4).

The faculty indicated that the top three obstacles to using electronic information technology are lack of information about available databases (68% of the respondents), lack of time (42.7%), and lack of necessary

CHART 1. Faculty Rank

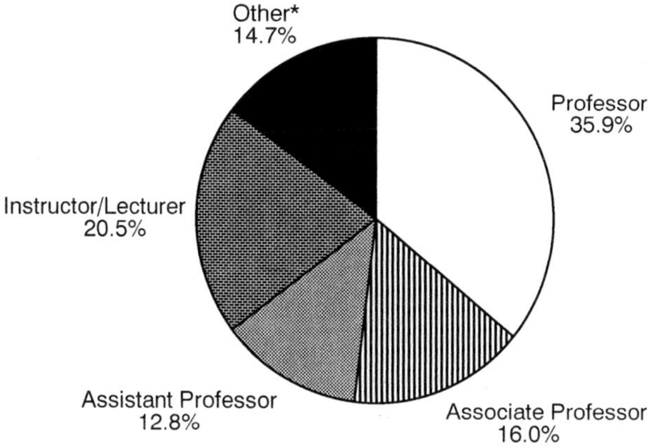

Other*
14.7%

Professor
35.9%

Instructor/Lecturer
20.5%

Assistant Professor
12.8%

Associate Professor
16.0%

*Denotes teaching graduate students and teacher assistants.

CHART 2. Number of Years Post-Secondary Teaching Experience

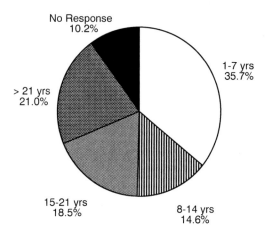

CHART 3. Academic College

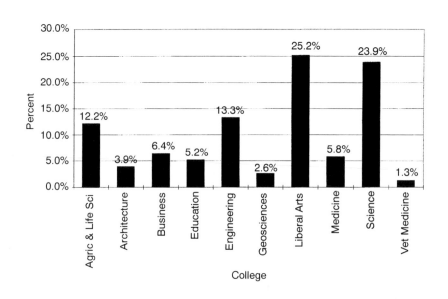

CHART 4. Faculty Use of Networked Resources

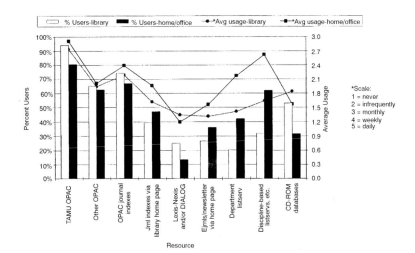

training (40.8%) (see Chart 5). When asked what might increase their use of electronic technologies and services, 70.7% of the faculty responded that provision of more information about the resources available to them would increase their usage, approximately 38% cited instruction in the use of computer software, and approximately 33% cited instruction in the use of electronic resources (see Chart 6). Only 44.6% were aware of the full-text electronic journals available to them through the Libraries' online subscriptions, 36.9% of the Interlibrary loan request form on the Libraries' Web page, and 10.8% of the "Ask a Reference Question," which is also on the Libraries' Web page. Eighty-seven percent of the faculty reported that their department has access to a microcomputer specialist or Local Area Network (LAN) administrator to assist with computing problems. Of those desiring training related to electronic technologies, most preferred small group sessions, the availability of printed help-manuals, and online tutorials.

FACULTY COMMENTS

The last part of the survey consisted of a section for open-ended comments. Over one-third of the participants took advantage of this

CHART 5. Obstacles to Using Information Technology

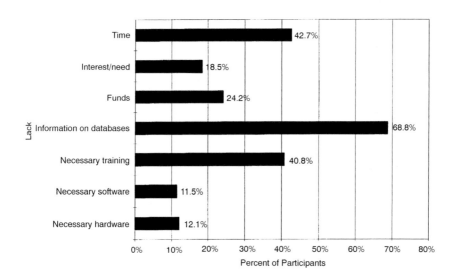

CHART 6. Ways to Increase Use of Electronic Resources

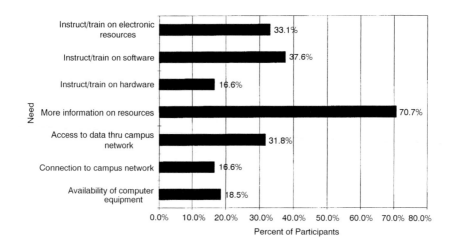

opportunity to express their opinions. The fact that the faculty's response to being asked to participate in the survey was very positive cannot be over-emphasized. The comment, "Thanks for asking," epitomizes this point.

Lack of information on resources and services was mentioned numerous times. "Your questionnaire revealed how much I don't know about what is happening." "Admittedly, I was not even aware that the library had a home page until reading this questionnaire." Several of the comments mentioned adding a service which the libraries already offered.

Training was another area repeatedly mentioned. There were a variety of suggestions, from online help and clearly written manuals to one-on-one instruction and frequent short courses. One response was that there is "No substitute for human help." A major problem can be transferring skills learned on computers in labs or in the libraries to office computers. "Classes are helpful, but so often when I go back to my computer, it does not work and I become frustrated." Time also was mentioned as a obstacle to learning new formats. "I have the technical skill and the appropriate equipment to take advantage of the library's electronic resources, but I have not taken the time to learn about these resources."

General comments on electronic resources and services of interest were: "I have to be dragged kicking and screaming (to the computer) but then I'm usually glad" and "If 'direct requests for articles' (that is unmediated document delivery) is a euphemism for 'downsizing the library staff,' I want no part of it."

IMPLICATIONS OF THE FINDINGS AND CONCLUSIONS

Currently at TAMU, various methods are used to market library services and resources to faculty. Flyers advertizing major databases are occasionally placed in the campus mail to faculty; each semester a Sci/Tech newsletter promoting new services and electronic resources is distributed (via campus mail and Web page) to faculty; quarterly meetings are held with faculty representatives from each academic college; annual meetings are held with faculty library representatives from each department; and the Coordinator of Instructional Services maintains contact with faculty from all disciplines and is present with a poster display at new faculty orientations. Help guides for using the

Libraries' remotely accessible databases can be downloaded from a Web page. The same Web site also provides forms for users to ask reference questions, request materials through interlibrary loan, suggest books for the collection, and schedule library tours with a librarian. With all this said, the most common cited obstacle to using information technology is lack of information; to increase use of electronic resources the Libraries need to provide more information and instruction on available resources. Obviously, current promotional efforts have not been sufficient. Referring back to the Leonard Berry parable at the beginning of this article, clearly, TAMU needs to find it's "scarf," that marketable element that draws users to the services and resources provided by the Libraries.

Sterling C. Evans Library, the main TAMU library, is in the process of decentralizing its reference desk into three reference service units–Education and Media Services, Science and Engineering Services, and Humanities and Social Sciences Services. A consequence of this is that each unit has a smaller audience to target. As a part of this re-organization, reference librarians have the added responsibility of being bibliographers; they develop and maintain collections in their subject specialities and serve as liaison librarians to the related academic departments. Presently, individual liaison librarians are attending departmental meetings, arranging for training sessions by vendors for faculty/graduate students on new databases (e.g., Beilstein and SciFinder Scholar), giving demonstrations of databases to classes/seminars, and corresponding via e-mail to departmental library representatives and broadcasting informational messages to the entire department.

Perhaps the liaison librarians will be our "scarf." They will know the needs of their targeted customer base, be able to clearly define the resources and services offered, and inform, instruct, promote, and build a two-way communication between academic departments and the Libraries. They will need to be innovative in finding ways to effectively communicate with the faculty. It will take time to develop the trust needed for a sound relationship. Every personal contact a librarian makes with a faculty member or student is an opportunity to market the Libraries electronic resources and services. This survey, itself a marketing tool, is the beginning. The challenge is before us.

REFERENCES

Abels, Eileen G., Peter Liebscher, and Daniel W. Denman. "Factors That Influence the Use of Electronic Networks by Science and Engineering Faculty at Small Institutions. Part I. Queries." *Journal of the American Society for Information Science* 47 (February 1996): 146-158.

Adams, Judith A., and Sharon C. Bonk. "Electronic Information Technologies and Resources: Use by University Faculty and Faculty Preferences for Related Library Services." *College & Research Libraries* 56 (March 1995): 119-131.

Adams, Judith A., Deborah Lines Andersen, Sharon C. Bonk, Sue R. Faerman, and Thomas J. Galvin. "Electronic Information Access Technologies: A Faculty Needs Assessment." (1993). ERIC Document Reproduction Service No. ED 381 160.

Association of Research Libraries. *Association of Research Libraries Statistics Ranked Lists for Academic Institutions.* Online. Available: http://fisher.lib.Virginia.EDU/newarl/list.html. 25 March 1998.

Berry, Leonard, Vicki Coleman, Daniel Xiao and Ellen Metter. "Great Service Now: Framework for Action." Slide presentation for the American Libraries Association–Reference and Adult Services Division President's Program. ALA Annual Conference, New York. 8 June 1996.

Borgman, Christine L., Donald O. Case, and Dorothy Ingebretsen. "University Faculty Use of Computerized Databases: An Assessment of Needs and Resources." *Online Review* 9.4 (1985): 307-332.

Clark, Katharine E., and Joni Gomez. "Faculty Use of Databases at Texas A&M University." *RQ* 30 (Winter 1990): 241-248.

Fiscella, Joan B., and Edward Proctor. "An Approach to Assessing Faculty Use of Local Loaded Databases." *College & Research Libraries* 56 (September 1995): 446-458.

Vander Meer, Patricia Fravel, Howard Poole, and Thomas Van Valey. "Are Library Users Also Computer Users? A Survey of Faculty and Implications for Services." *The Public-Access Computer Systems Review* 8.1 (1997):6-31. Online. Available: http://info.lib .uh.edu/pr/v8/n1/van8n.1.html. 25 March 1998.

Wilkins, Marilyn L., and Karen S. Nantz. "Faculty Use of Electronic Communications Before and After a LAN Installation: A Three-Year Analysis." *Journal of End User Computing* (Winter 1995): 4-11.

Survey of Faculty Access to Electronic Technologies and Information Resources

The purpose of this survey is to help the Sterling C. Evans Libraries determine how we may better provide access to electronic databases, electronic journals and online resources. You have been randomly selected to participate in this survey because we need to know your needs in order to provide the best service. Your prompt response is crucial to us.

I. Which of the following equipment is now readily available to you in your office or home? *Check all that apply.*

	OFFICE	HOME
1. PC Windows '95/NT	_____	_____
2. PC Windows (all other versions)	_____	_____
3. PC DOS	_____	_____
4. Macintosh	_____	_____
5. Workstation (such as Sun)	_____	_____
6. Laser Jet Printer (HP4Si or higher)	_____	_____
7. Ink Jet Printer	_____	_____
8. Dot Matrix Printer	_____	_____
9. Connection to campus network (TAMUNET)	_____	_____
10. Fax (telefascimile)	_____	_____
11. Have no computer equipment	_____	_____
12. Other (please specify):	_____	_____
_____	_____	_____
_____	_____	_____

II. The following is a list of information resources available through networks. Please indicate the frequency of use in each location by writing the appropriate **number** on the corresponding line.

	Frequency Used in LIBRARY	Frequency Used in OFFICE/HOME
1. TAMU campus library online catalog (NOTIS) *1) never 2) infrequently 3) monthly 4) weekly 5) daily*	_____	_____
2. Other libraries' online catalogs *1) never 2) infrequently 3) monthly 4) weekly 5) daily*	_____	_____
3 Journal index databases on NOTIS (e.g., Wils, AGRICOLA) *1) never 2) infrequently 3) monthly 4) weekly 5) daily*	_____	_____
4. Journal index databases via the Library Home Page *1) never 2) infrequently 3) monthly 4) weekly 5) daily*	_____	_____
5. Journal index databases via commercial vendor on a personal or department account (e.g., DIALOG, Compuserve) *1) never 2) infrequently 3) monthly 4) weekly 5) daily*	_____	_____
6. Lexis-Nexis and/or DIALOG electronic databases in the libraries *1) never 2) infrequently 3) monthly 4) weekly 5) daily*	_____	_____
7. Electronic journals and newsletters via the Library Home Page *1) never 2) infrequently 3) monthly 4) weekly 5) daily*	_____	_____
8. Department listserv *1) never 2) infrequently 3) monthly 4) weekly 5) daily*	_____	_____
9. Discipline-based electronic bulletin boards, listservs, etc. *1) never 2) infrequently 3) monthly 4) weekly 5) daily*	_____	_____
10. CD-ROM index databases available in the libraries (e.g., ERIC, AGRICOLA, GeoRef, PsycINFO, Compendex, etc.) *1) never 2) infrequently 3) monthly 4) weekly 5) daily*	_____	_____

III 1. List (if any) the electronic databases, CD-ROM databases, or electronic journals that you currently use for your teaching and research. (e.g., Sociofile, INSPEC, GeoRef, ABI/INFORM, Lexis-Nexis, Project Muse, MLA, etc.)

_____   _____

_____   _____

   2. Does a student do 1) all 2) some or 3) none of your electronic database searching. *Circle one.*

SURVEY (continued)

IV.   Currently, which of the following represent obstacles to your use of electronic information technology? *Circle all that apply.*

    1. lack necessary hardware (computer, modem, etc.)
    2. lack necessary sottware (e.g., TAMUNET sottware package)
    3. lack necessary training
    4. lack information about available databases
    5. lack operating funds to pay costs of searching and/or document delivery
    6. lack of interest or need
    7. lack of time
    8. other, please specify_____

V.   Which of the following might increase your use of the technologies and services. *Circle all that apply.*

    1. availability of computer equipment in my office or home
    2. connection to campus network
    3. access to data and text files through campus computer network
    4. more information about resources available through networks
    5. instruction/training in the use of computer hardware
    6. instruction/training in the use of computer sottware (e.g., Adobe Acrobat)
    7. instruction/training in the use of e-mail, network sources, online databases
    8. funding
    9. other, please specify_____

VI.   If you were to participate in training related to electronics technologies which type(s) of training would you prefer? *Circle all that apply.*

    1. small group classes/workshops
    2. printed manuals
    3. formal classes
    4. one-on-one tutorials
    5. telephone assistance
    6. on-line tutorials (computer-assisted instruction)
    7. assistance via e-mail

VII.   Does your department/building have a Microcomputer Specialist, LAN Administrator or other technical person who can assist you with computing problems? *Circle one.*

    1. Yes
    2. No
    3. Don't Know

VIII .   Do your regular classrooms have Ethernet connections? *Circle one.*   1. Yes   2. No   3. Don't know

IX.   List any electronic databases, CD-ROMs, or electronic journals/newsletters that you want to use to which you do not currently have adequate access or funding to support access.

    _____   _____

    _____   _____

X.   Would you be interested in document delivery to your office via fax or email? *Circle one.* 1. Yes 2. No

XI.   Are you aware of the following electronic services and resources? *Circle all that apply.*

    1. Interlibrary loan requests via Internet
    2. Ask a Reference Question via Internet
    3. Electronic journals/newsletters via the Internet

Information About You

XII. Your department _____

XIII. Your building _____

XIII. Your Faculty Rank/Professional Title. *Please circle one.*

    1. Professor
    2. Associate Professor
    3. Assistant Professor
    4. Instructor/Lecturer
    5. Other, please specify _____

    6. Number of years of post-secondary teaching experience _____

XIV. Please offer any comments you might have regarding libraries, electronic information resources, or resource sharing.

_____

_____

_____

_____

_____

_____

Thank you for taking the time to complete this survey. Please return the survey to:

Judy Hart
Reference Dept.
Sterling C. Evans Library
MS-5000

Accessing the Old and the New: Outreach via Web Exhibits and Archive Collections at the University of Arizona Library

Micaela Morales
Jeff Rosen

SUMMARY. The University of Arizona Library's tradition of outreach to the surrounding community is reflected in two examples of projects detailed here. The first project is a series of Web exhibits created by librarians and individuals from the community that explore the history of Tucson and southern Arizona. Some of the Web exhibits detail the experiences of immigrant and Native American cultures in the area while other Web exhibits deal more generally with the history of the area. The second project involves a Federal grant that will make certain parts of library's Special Collections more accessible to the community by building new facilities that are open longer hours, digitizing some of the materials and adding computer workstations for users. *[Article copies available for a fee from The Haworth Document Delivery Service: 1-800-342-9678. E-mail address: getinfo@haworthpressinc.com <Website: http://www. haworthpressinc.com>]*

KEYWORDS. Library archives, digital collections, library exhibits, marketing, community outreach, World Wide Web, southwestern history

---

Micaela Morales is Electronic Information Teaching Support Specialist, Harvard Business School. Baker Library 100E, Harvard Business School, Boston, MA 02163. Jeff Rosen is Assistant Librarian, Social Sciences Team, Main Library, University of Arizona, P.O. 210055, University of Arizona Library, Tucson, AZ 85721.

[Haworth co-indexing entry note]: "Accessing the Old and the New: Outreach via Web Exhibits and Archive Collections at the University of Arizona Library." Morales, Micaela, and Jeff Rosen. Co-published simultaneously in *The Reference Librarian* (The Haworth Information Press, an imprint of The Haworth Press, Inc.) No. 67/68, 1999, pp. 57-67; and: *Library Outreach, Partnerships, and Distance Education: Reference Librarians at the Gateway* (ed: Wendi Arant, and Pixey Anne Mosley) The Haworth Press, Inc., 2000, pp. 57-67. Single or multiple copies of this article are available for a fee from The Haworth Document Delivery Service [1-800-342-9678, 9:00 a.m. - 5:00 p.m. (EST). E-mail address: getinfo@haworthpressinc.com].

INTRODUCTION

The University of Arizona (UA) began classes in 1891 as a state supported land grant institution. Today, the University serves approximately thirty-four thousand students.[1] In keeping with its status as a land grant institution, the University Library has had a commitment to serving the surrounding community that is reflected in a long history of outreach projects. For the last two years the library has designated outreach to the surrounding community as a major strategic goal and an annual plan project. The University Library undertook a total of forty-five separate outreach projects during the 1997/98 academic year. These have been widely ranging projects such as the *Teacher as Docent* program offered to local school teachers by the Center for Creative Photography (a campus unit that is part of the University Library). Additionally, the library worked with the Arizona AgNIC Project (Agricultural Networked Information Consortium)–a project that is part of a national initiative and which includes a campus team comprised of librarians, information professionals, and rangeland experts from the University's College of Agriculture. Among other tasks this project has undertaken digitizing the backfiles of the *Journal of Range Management.*[2] Other outreach projects in the last year have included training counselors and staff of the Southern Arizona Aids Foundation to use the Web effectively and projects that involved bringing in public school students and teachers for training in using digital resources.

This paper will focus on two very different outreach projects, one that was started several years ago and which promises to continue to grow and evolve and one that is planned to begin in the next year and which may have far-reaching ramifications. The first outreach project is the series of exhibits presented by the University of Arizona Library that take some of the unique resources of the library and of the Tucson and Southern Arizona community and make them available in one of the newest formats–the World Wide Web. The second outreach project will focus on making the library's Special Collections–some of the oldest and traditionally least accessible items held by the UA Library–more accessible and available to those who come to the library to use these materials.

WORLD WIDE WEB EXHIBITS:
ORIGINAL IMPETUS FOR THE EXHIBITS

In early 1995, the Web was still a relatively new medium. The full potential of the Web to highlight and showcase library collections was just beginning to be explored. UA Librarians realized that the wealth of information in our own Special Collections and Archives as well as the rich cultural resources in the community, could be placed on the Web and thereby gain greater exposure than was possible previously.

Two types of Web exhibits, both dealing with local history and culture began to take shape: The *Through Our Parents' Eyes* pages (see appendix for URL's) are the portion of the exhibit that looks at Tucson's rich history of "pioneer" and native American cultures, from the firsthand viewpoint of a variety of ethnic groups that helped to settle Tucson and other southern Arizona areas. The remaining Web exhibits deal with the general history of southern Arizona and with the history of the Southwest not related to the pioneer experience including such varied topics as Japanese internment camps in Arizona, the sinking of the U.S.S. Arizona at Pearl Harbor, natural hazards due to comets and asteroids and Tucson's turn of the century street railway.

Another reason for deciding to put up the Web exhibits was that the library wanted to alert the public in the local area to the rich bounty that the library has to offer and to solidify the library's role as part of the local community. The library was also interested in partnering with educational/cultural organizations in the area to strengthen the connection between the University of Arizona Library and the Pima Community College Library (Tucson) and the public schools in Tucson.

WHY THIS PARTICULAR OUTREACH PROJECT?

This type of project and the nature of the exhibits were such that Web exhibits would take relatively little effort compared to the amount of positive impact they would generate. There was also the recognition that Web culture is heavily oriented to young people and that perhaps the exhibits would reach new audiences who might not traditionally come to the University Library, as well as reaching those who are unable to physically visit the library.

Another consideration was that the Tucson area has a great deal of local history resources that are unknown or deteriorating and that this would provide an opportunity to demonstrate how digitization can play an important role in the preservation and dissemination of these materials. For example, an elderly gentleman in Tucson has an extensive collection of photographs that document the changing nature of Chinese markets and merchants in the area, spanning many decades. The Library now has efforts underway to secure and digitize this collection.

WHICH POTENTIAL EXHIBITS TO CHOOSE?

Early in 1995, the Web was still relatively new and not yet appreciated. Many archivists, who are usually accustomed to dealing with print materials, had not explored the possibility of using the Web for exhibiting materials.

Soon however, several projects began to take shape simultaneously. Dr. James Griffith, Coordinator (ret.) of the Southwest Folklore Center at the University of Arizona had begun to work with Stuart Glogoff, Assistant Dean for Library and Information Systems. The two began to explore the possibility of an online exhibit dealing with mission churches established by Father Eusebio Kino in the Sonoran desert regions of The United States and Mexico. For this exhibit, Dr. Griffith drew from his extensive collection of slides of the area taken over the last three decades. This exhibit is titled *Mission Churches of the Sonoran Desert.*[3]

At the same time Roger Myers, of the UA Library Special Collections, began work on a fascinating Web exhibit, *War Relocation Authority Camps in Arizona 1942-1946,* about the internment camps set up by the U.S. government in Arizona, interring Japanese-Americans during World War II. In this way, the first two exhibits concerned with the general history of Tucson and southern Arizona came about.

Meanwhile, Stuart Glogoff began collaborating with the Judaic Studies program at the University of Arizona to secure the Bloom Archives for the UA Library. This is a large collection of materials related to the pioneer Jewish settlements in the Southwestern United States. The Bloom Archives provided the materials for the first ethnic group related exhibit that served as a model and opened a lot of doors to other potential groups that might help create exhibits.

Stuart and Louise Glogoff, Bibliographic Database Manager at Pima Community College, then began working with a Chinese American who had many photographs and much information about the early Chinese immigrants to Tucson. This material became an important element of the exhibit *The Promise of Gold Mountain: Tucson's Chinese Heritage*. With the connection to the Jewish archives exhibit and possibility of many other exhibits based on the experiences of ethnic immigrant groups to the area, the group of Web exhibits known as *Through Our Parents' Eyes* was born. Thus, the two major tracks of the Library's Web exhibits, immigrant history of southern Arizona and general history of southern Arizona and the Southwestern U.S., were well underway.

The next exhibit added to the site was initiated by Dr. Michael Engs of Pima Community College who was working with the Arizona Historical Society on oral history projects related to the African American experience. The result of this collaboration was the exhibit *In the Steps of Esteban: Tucson's African American Heritage*. Shortly after this exhibit, Gene Spesard of the library's systems team created *USS Arizona–"that terrible day"*–an exhibit about the sinking of the USS Arizona during the attack on Pearl Harbor. This exhibit is the most popular of all the Web exhibits and has hosted over eighty-one thousand visitors since being published on the Web.

FORMALIZING THE WEB EXHIBITS PROCESS

The Web exhibits at the University of Arizona Library were started when HTML and Web page design was in its infancy. As time went on the people working on the project looked at what worked and what didn't and how people responded to. Reassessing exhibits in view of new innovations and now some reformatting efforts are underway. For example: the Bloom Southwest Jewish Archives exhibit was recently redone because "it looked like it was designed in 1995," that is to say, Web design has come a long way in the last few years.

On the strength of the exhibits that were already on the Web, the library received a fifteen thousand-dollar grant in early 1997 from the Fear Not Foundation to develop Web exhibits. At this time a process was started to cross train library staff in planning a Web exhibit, how to do HTML markup and digital image scanning–that is to say, a process for developing Web exhibits was formalized. Developing this process for creating the Web exhibits was important because library staff did not have any special background in Web design or exhibits. Many things had to be learned along the way: page layout, what constitutes good design, working with graphics to maximize presentation impact. Among other work, the exhibit *Tucson's Ronstadt Family* emerged during this period.

SHOWING SUCCESS: WEB PROJECTS AS SUCCESSFUL OUTREACH

Demonstrating that people are visiting and using a Web based exhibit can be tricky. We have the technology to measure the amount of "hits" on a given Web site but that doesn't really tell us how many people gained information or had an enriching experience. "Guest books" try to gather information in the same way that paper equivalents in real life museum exhibits do by recording who visits and any comments they may have.

A number of other indicators have been helpful in measuring the outreach success of the UA Library Web exhibits: the page counters on the exhibits indicate high usage, and letters and E-mail messages from a variety of users including alumni have been very positive. Media support has included an article that ran in the local newspaper about the Web exhibits and a short piece on the exhibits on the local public radio news show. Community feedback has included E-mail from the mother of a fifth grade student who had successfully used an exhibit for her school project, and use of the Web exhibits by some Tucson area schools to study the African American migrant experience in the area.

WHAT WAS LEARNED BY DOING THE EXHIBITS?

Library staff that have worked on the Web exhibits report that a great deal of learning took place. First, the library has learned that the Web is a great vehicle for outreach. The ability to display older or deteriorating materials along with text and the fact that these resources are universally available to anyone with access to a Web browser makes the Web an ideal medium for these type of exhibits. E-mail messages from local residents as well as from people all over the country and around the world that found and used the library's exhibits have confirmed this. As the librarians involved in the project began to collaborate with other historical and archival collections in the area, they realized how comparatively technologically rich the university library is. That is to say, most of the local museums and historical societies are technologically poor or under-funded and so another aspect of the outreach was to open up these organizations and their resources to the community. Moreover, these Web exhibits are not simply more Web pages created by librarians about the library. What defines the exhibits as "outreach" is that local people who wanted to share their story helped create the exhibits and that these exhibits have actively been used in a variety of ways by the local community.

PLANS FOR CONTINUATION OF THE WEB EXHIBITS

Several plans are currently in development to continue expanding the Web exhibits coordinated by the University of Arizona Library. The library is reaching out to the Native American community in the Tucson area, specifically the Tohono Odam and Yaqui tribes. Three grant projects are just commencing that involve the University of Arizona, Pima Community College and the Tucson Unified School District. These efforts will hopefully lead to Web exhibits that deal with community history and we hope that the relationships and the process that has been established, will allow the Web exhibits to continue to grow and expand.

RENOVATION OF SPECIAL COLLECTIONS

Another project at the University of Arizona Library that aims to improve outreach efforts is the renovation of the areas that house Special Collections. Special Collections at the University of Arizona Library was established in 1958 to accommodate resource materials on Arizona, the Southwest and the U.S./Mexico Borderlands. It houses an extensive collection consisting of many formats–books, pamphlets, ephemera, broadsides, photographs, and significant primary resources in the manuscript and archival collections. Recently, the Congressional Archives were established by the University of Arizona to serve scholars and the general public, as well as students of all ages (K-12, undergraduates, and graduates). These Archives, including the personal and professional papers of former Arizona Congressman Morris K. Udall, and the Senatorial papers of former Arizona Senator Dennis DeConcini, are a leading repository of information in the country for those interested in the people, ecology, economics, and politics of Arizona and the Southwest.

This next section will describe how a $2 million federal appropriation grant awarded to the University of Arizona Library will enhance outreach efforts by improving accessibility (electronic and otherwise) of Special Collection materials and by creating new collection and user space.

IMPROVING ACCESS

Although the Library has directed significant resources in the past in terms of personnel, equipment, space, and archival supplies towards processing these unique collections, the renovation will address issues that continue to impede access to the collections. The most obvious limitation to access is the hours of operation. Currently, regular weekday hours are 10 a.m. to 5 p.m., with limited hours on weekends. Another limitation is that not everything in Special Collections is included in the library's online catalog and this impedes users from knowing what is in the collections. Additionally, finding aids are seldom cataloged. Finding aids are typically lengthy inventories prepared in linear fashion using word processing software, and may provide item-level information or a summary description of the contents of a manuscript of archival collection.[4] Also, many items in Special Collections are very old and fragile; therefore, access to these collections is limited due to preservation issues.

The above mentioned limitations can be addressed by utilizing emerging technologies to improve access to the collections. For example, the Library has created a World Wide Web page highlighting what is contained in the Congressional Archives for the Congressman Morris K. Udall papers (http://www.library.arizona.edu/moudall). This archive contains over three thousand linear feet of material including correspondence, memoranda, speeches, clippings, legislative papers, reports, campaign material, audio and visual tapes, and personal papers. The material spans Morris K. Udall's childhood, World War II service, time as a University of Arizona student, brief career as a professional basketball player, and also includes papers of his father, Arizona Supreme Court Chief Justice Levi S. Udall.[5] The Web exhibit includes finding aids, digital copies of approximately fifty photographs, multiple full-text formats to Udall's speeches, audio clips from speeches, and links to related Web resources.

Access to exhibits in these and many other such projects numbers in the thousands and use has been incorporated into a University of Arizona Honors class and local K-12 classes. Such outreach efforts utilizing emerging technologies are only at an initial stage. One of the objectives of the renovation project is to provide the technological resources and infrastructure necessary to provide World Wide Web access to the collections. The Udall exhibit has proved that the Web facilitates access to information by removing many of the barriers imposed by limited hours of access, geographical distances, and the need to provide access to rare and fragile materials.

NEW COLLECTION AND USER SPACE

The renovation of Special Collections will also enhance outreach efforts by creating new physical spaces for its collections and users. The current building where Special Collections is located was opened in 1977 when the traditional role of libraries was to store, organize, and help users find information. Since 1977, increased enrollments and an expanding collection (approximately ten million items), in conjunction with an evolving Library mission, have required adapting existing and/or providing new Library space to meet new challenges.

The University of Arizona Library Special Collections unit contains the only collection that will continue to grow over time yet the UA Library discovered that storage areas could only accommodate five years of collection growth; the library needed more space. After developing several scenarios, it was decided that the most efficient utilization of space would be through the use of compact shelving whenever possible. It is assumed that the Special Collections will have to be on the first floor because of the floor loading requirements of compact shelving units. This expansion on the lower level will keep the collection in one secure area and allow for future expansion within the building thereby improving service to the University and community user. The collections will also be made more accessible to users by providing the space necessary to accommodate multimedia workstations, video and listening stations, and online catalog stations. The renovation also aims to create and environment that reflects the cultural heritage of the Southwest, that highlights the Southwest and Borderlands collections and that creates a community meeting place. This will be accomplished through the redesign of the reading room, new spaces for exhibits that highlight the collection, and seminar and meeting rooms where the community can gather to learn more about the history and culture of the area.

DESIRED OUTCOMES OF RENOVATION

The renovation of Special Collections is in synch with the broader outreach goal of the University of Arizona "to strengthen University outreach to address societal needs of the community, State, and nation."[6] Several of the ways the UA plans to do this is by focusing on outreach opportunities in which the University can make unique contributions by addressing major social, cultural, economic and public policy needs; and by taking advantage of new and emerging technologies to enhance outreach capabilities. The renovation of Special Collections addresses both of these objectives. Enhancing access to these materials provides the community with the resources they need to understand the social, cultural, economic and political issues of the area and provides the infrastures in which technology, and in particular the World Wide Web, can be used to share resources and information.

As part of a land grant institution, it has always been important to the University of Arizona Library to create programs that benefit the local community in Arizona, the Southwest, and society at large. By enhancing access to our collections through the utilization of new technologies and the renovation of Special Collections, the library is improving outreach efforts and creating for itself a more visible presence in the community.

REFERENCES

1. The University of Arizona Factbook World Wide Web–http://daps.arizona.edu/daps/factbook/factbook.html

2. The University of Arizona Library Outreach Project World Wide Web–http://www.library.arizona.edu/library/teams/outreach9798/reach.htm

3. Glogoff, Stuart and Glogoff, Louise "Using the World Wide Web for Community Outreach: Enriching Library Service to the Community." *Internet Reference Services Quarterly* (The Journal of Innovative Information Practice, Technologies and Resources) Vol. 3 No. 1 (1998).

4. Antelman, Kristin A and Glogoff, Stuart. "Relieving Archival Gridlock: Congressional Archives on the Web," *Internet Reference Services Quarterly* (The Jour-

nal of Innovative Information Practice, Technologies and Resources) Vol. 1, Issue 4 (1996).

5. Glogoff, Stuart; Morales, Micaela and Taleb, Mohamed "Stop the Presses! Electronic Publishing Opportunities for Librarians," College and University Libraries Division, Contributed Papers, Arizona Library Association Annual Conference, 1996. World Wide Web. http://www.library.arizona.edu/users/sglogoff/azlapapr. html

6. University of Arizona Strategic Plan (Feb. 1998). World Wide Web.http://daps. arizona.edu/uaplan/index.html

APPENDIX

Through Our Parents' Eyes: Tucson's Diverse Community
http://www.library.arizona.edu/images/diverse/diverse.html

Mission Churches of the Sonoran Desert
http://www.library.arizona.edu/images/swf/mission.shtml

War Relocation Authority Camps in Arizona, 1942-1945
http://www.library.arizona.edu/images/jpamer/wraintro.html

Bloom Southwest Jewish Archives
http://www.library.arizona.edu/images/swja/swjalist.html

The Promise of Gold Mountain: Tucson's Chinese Heritage
http://www.library.arizona.edu/promise

In The Steps of Esteban: Tucson's African-American Heritage
http://www.library.arizona.edu/esteban

USS Arizona–"that terrible day"
http://dizzy.library.arizona.edu/images/USS_Arizona/USS_Arizona.shtml

Morris K. Udall–A Lifetime of Service to Arizona and the United States
http://www.library.arizonia.edu/moudall

Expanding Outreach
to a Unique User Community:
The Slavic Reference Service
and the Internet

Teresa E. Tickle

SUMMARY. For the past twenty-five years, the Slavic Reference Service has been providing specialized bibliographic and information reference service to the community of students, scholars, and librarians in the field of Slavic Studies. This service includes the verification, location, and acquisition of rare monographs and serials, and answering both ready-reference and in-depth research questions. The Internet and e-mail have provided a new medium by which we are able to expand our services both to our traditional community of users in the Slavic field, and also to the general public. The expansion of our services has cause us to reconsider our methods of providing reference service in a virtual reference environment. *[Article copies available for a fee from The Haworth Document Delivery Service: 1-800-342-9678. E-mail address: getinfo@haworthpressinc. com <Website: http://www.haworthpressinc.com>]*

KEYWORDS. Electronic reference, Slavic Studies, bibliographic services

INTRODUCTION

With the exponential expansion of the Internet, more people than ever are online; surfing, searching, and using e-mail as a primary

Teresa E. Tickle is Visiting Assistant Professor and Reference Librarian, Slavic Reference Service, Slavic and East European Library, 225 Main Library, 1408 West Gregory Drive University of Illinois at Urbana-Champaign, Urbana, IL 61801.

[Haworth co-indexing entry note]: "Expanding Outreach to a Unique User Community: The Slavic Reference Service and the Internet." Tickle, Teresa E. Co-published simultaneously in *The Reference Librarian* (The Haworth Information Press, an imprint of The Haworth Press, Inc.) No. 67/68, 1999, pp. 69-83; and: *Library Outreach, Partnerships, and Distance Education: Reference Librarians at the Gateway* (ed: Wendi Arant, and Pixey Anne Mosley) The Haworth Press, Inc., 2000, pp. 69-83. Single or multiple copies of this article are available for a fee from The Haworth Document Delivery Service [1-800-342-9678, 9:00 a.m. - 5:00 p.m. (EST). E-mail address: getinfo@haworthpressinc.com].

method for communication. The Internet allows communications between people to move at a much quicker and often easier pace than the
more traditional contacts of telephone or mail. For libraries that provide reference service, the Internet has become a way to enhance
outreach services to their user community. The Internet is open 24
hours a day, seven days a week, so questions can be submitted when
libraries are closed, and librarians can answer questions and respond
to patrons more easily. The user can ask a question in a much less
intimidating environment at his/her own pace, and users without access to libraries now have library service open to them. Using the
Internet to expand and enhance reference service is clearly an idea
whose time has come.

The Slavic Reference Service at the University of Illinois has spent
the past twenty-five years providing reference and bibliographic services to the community of students and scholars in the field of Slavic
studies. This free, federally supported service provides a much-needed
resource for the Slavic field and for the library profession as well,
since few university libraries have the staff or resources in this very
specialized field to provide reference services. Scholars and librarians
alike have come to rely on our services to assist them in their research
and provide the bibliographical and reference expertise that is not
freely available anywhere in the United States.

Until the last five years, the outreach of the Slavic Reference Service was generally limited to contact by phone, mail, and interlibrary
loan requests. Scholars learned of us through word-of-mouth, and librarians found us through occasional promotional mailings, but many others
in the field of Slavic Studies or peripheral fields do not know of our
existence. With the advent of the Internet and the demand for greater
online access to information, the Slavic Reference Service has turned
to the new electronic medium to expand outreach service to its community of users. This article explains the type of outreach services that
we have provided to the scholarly community over the past 25 years,
and how the use of the Internet and e-mail has affected these services
to our users.

THE SLAVIC REFERENCE SERVICE:
MISSION AND OUTREACH

The Slavic Reference Service was started in 1973 with a unique
mission: to provide specialized bibliographic and information service

to students and scholars in the field of Slavic and East European Studies. The service is located at the Slavic and East European Library of the University of Illinois at Urbana-Champaign, which currently has one of the largest collections of Slavic materials in the United States. The Doris Duke Reading Room, from which the Reference Service operates, contains a reference collection of more than 15,000 volumes. Additional materials are available in the main Slavic collection, which numbers over 600,000 volumes in the vernacular, 100,000 microforms, 4,000 current periodicals, and over 100 current newspapers. This outstanding collection makes the University of Illinois at Urbana-Champaign a natural location for the Slavic Reference Service.

Although the Reference Service serves the needs of the students and professors on our own campus like any library reference department, our main function is to provide outreach service to students and scholars in the field of Slavic and East European Studies in the United States and around the world, regardless of affiliation. This outreach has become indispensable to those in the field of Slavic and East European studies because of a lack of this type of reference service anywhere else in the United States. In most libraries, even research libraries, there may be only one or two librarians with a knowledge of Russian or Eastern European languages. Many of these librarians have primary responsibilities in cataloguing or acquisitions for Slavic language materials. Slavic studies reference is a peripheral service, often performed by appointment only. Most libraries have budgets that also do not permit them to purchase specifically Slavic reference resources because the affiliated user base is too small. Slavic librarians are, therefore, often isolated in their work and unable to provide in-depth reference service because of a lack of staff and material resources. Other libraries have no Slavic librarian at all and rely on the librarian with some language expertise or the tenacity to tackle the Russian (or Polish, or Hungarian . . .) requests that might come their way. In many cases, scholars in the field find themselves without Slavic reference assistance at all, and rely on their own scholarly networks to accomplish their research. This situation is why the Slavic Reference Service is dedicated to the mission of providing reference service to the students, scholars, and librarians that turn to us for help. No question is too trivial, no search too complicated for our staff to tackle.

BIBLIOGRAPHIC SERVICES

The questions received by the Slavic Reference Service are divided into two types: bibliographic questions and information questions. Bibliographic questions, which make up about 70 percent of the more than 2,000 requests received each year, are those that ask for information on a specific book, journal, or newspaper title in a Slavic or East European language. Most frequently, the information needed is a location for the book or a particular issue of a journal or newspaper. These requests come to the Reference Service largely via the Interlibrary Loan Office of the University of Illinois at Urbana-Champaign. If the interlibrary loan staff cannot locate the item in our collection based on the citation provided, the request is brought to the Reference Service. Often, interlibrary loan departments with fragments of citations or unverified, unclear citations will send such requests to our Interlibrary Loan Office with the knowledge that the item automatically will be sent to the Slavic Reference Service to be researched. Other libraries and individuals bypass our Interlibrary Loan Office and send bibliographic requests directly to us by mail, fax, and increasingly through our web page.

Bibliographic requests are answered using a system of searching and verification laid out in search forms. Search forms have been created for each type of material requested: monographs, serials, and newspapers. When a request comes in, a Reference Service librarian or staff person chooses the appropriate search form for the material and searches those resources listed on the search form, noting the information gathered from each resource. The typical monograph search includes searching the University of Illinois online catalog, the card catalog (for older materials), the Slavic library's "ordered and received" file, OCLC Worldcat, RLIN, the *National Union Catalog* and the *Slavic Cyrillic Union Catalog* (for older materials),[1] and the online catalogs of major Slavic collections in the United States such as the Library of Congress, Harvard University, New York Public Library, and the University of California MELVYL System. Similar search procedures, using both print and online resources, are followed for serials and for newspapers.

If the item is not found at the University of Illinois, on OCLC, RLIN, or the Slavic Cyrillic Union catalog, the citation is verified for accuracy. This verification involves using the Slavic Library's extensive collection of national and subject bibliographies, periodical indexes, and other reference books from Russia and all of the countries of Eastern Europe and the former Soviet Union. Verification often reveals that the citation sent to us is incorrect in some way, and once verified and corrected, the item is often located in our collection and sent to the requesting library. This type of service to the library community seems logical to provide as a common courtesy, but in these days of rising demand and shrinking personnel, it is becoming more rare. In the Slavic field, the service is often non-existent: if the requested citation is incorrect or even incomplete, in many libraries, it will be returned to the requesting library as unfillable, with no further information. The library passes this information on to the patron, who may then believe that a research trip to Russia or Eastern Europe is necessary to obtain the needed material.[2]

The Slavic Reference Service provides verification in order to help scholars find the items that they need, but takes bibliographic service one step further by locating items not found in the library. If an item is requested from the Slavic Library at the University of Illinois at Urbana-Champaign, and we do not own the material, we will search for other locations in North America for the item and suggest them to the patron. Often this means phoning the institutions with holdings of an item to verify both that the item is located in the library and also to be sure that the item can be photocopied or loaned to the patron. This way, the patron is aware of the availability of an item in the West, and if an item cannot be loaned (for example, a long run of a rare periodical), the scholar can plan a research trip in the United States or Canada instead of a much costlier trip to Russia or Eastern Europe. We also regularly search catalogs of the British Library, the Bibliothèque Nationale de France, Die Deutsche Bibliothek and the Helsinki University Library, all of which may be more accessible to scholars than libraries in Russia or parts of Eastern Europe.

What is more, if a scholar is seeking a monograph or a particular issue of a newspaper or journal, and it is found to be inaccessible in the United States, we will offer to order a copy of the item on microfilm from one of our exchange partners in Europe or Russia, providing that we can verify that the citation is correct. The Slavic Reference Service sends sizable orders for microfilm copies to our exchange partners two or three times per year, and when the film arrives, it is processed and cataloged as part of the Slavic collection at the University of Illinois at Urbana-Champaign. Then the institution or patron that originally requested the item is contacted directly and given the option to either borrow the film through interlibrary loan, or to purchase a copy of the microfilm at a modest cost. For each film, we make a microfilm master copy so that there is always a copy of the material available to scholars in the West. This service provides an inexpensive, alternative source of materials from Russia and Eastern Europe for the scholar, and it allows our library to identify rare Slavic language materials and acquire them on microfilm for our collection.

The only drawback to this service is that currently such requests take more than a year to fill, depending largely on the financial situation of the libraries in Russia and Eastern Europe. These libraries often do not have the funds to maintain and operate microfilm processors, and some have been too short on funds to pay for postage to mail exchange orders to us. Orders can take months or years to be delivered to us, and then they must wait to be processed and cataloged in our library. Therefore, ordering from abroad is usually limited to scholars engaged in long-term projects who can wait for such materials. Many of these scholars are from colleges and universities that do not have the resources to enable them to make frequent research trips abroad, and so our service is the only way they have access to such materials. The bibliographic location and ordering services that the Slavic Reference Service provides as part of our outreach to the scholarly community has proved over time to be one of our most important services.

Information Services

The other type of reference service we provide to our user community is information assistance. Information reference services encompass all of the remaining requests we receive for the Slavic field. These types of requests are extremely varied in nature: from ready reference on names, dates, spelling, and word translations to in-depth investigations of persons, places, or events of all kinds. Questions can take a few minutes or even a few days to answer. Ready reference questions tend to be answered very quickly, while in-depth requests are placed in a file and taken in the order in which they are received. Since the Reference Service has only two full-time librarians, two part-time paraprofessionals, and one or two graduate assistants (depending on annual funding levels), this sometimes results in backlogs of six to eight weeks, but any person with a deadline for the needed information is always accommodated.

There are only two types of information request that we cannot answer: genealogy requests and requests for bibliographies or reading lists. Genealogy requests are generally outside of our scope because we do not have a collection of genealogical materials (such as church or city records from Eastern Europe or Russia) for specific information on an individual or family. We will, however, locate towns and villages and trace any name changes for them, and we will search for the origin or meaning of family names or provide biographical information on a person who appears in the major biographical sources of the country of origin. We also collect town and city directories on microfilm which are available for loan. But our resources do not extend to the very specific sources needed by genealogists. For questions of this type that come our way, we refer patrons to organizations within the United States that have such information, or to groups in the country of origin that now provide genealogical services to the international community.

Requests that ask for us to compile bibliographies or reading lists are simply beyond the scope of what our service can do. Often these requests are for students beginning a thesis or dissertation on a specific topic. The time and effort needed to compile such bibliographies would put an enormous strain on the small staff of the Reference Service, and, in addition, we do not have the subject expertise in all fields to compile such bibliographies. Instead we will recommend subject bibliographies that are already in print and periodical indexes either in English or in the vernacular that provide subject access for the patron's topic. This way, we do not turn the user away from our resources, but instead encourage the exploration of the vast number of bibliographic resources in our field that are available but are often overlooked by students and scholars alike.

Our outreach to the scholarly community culminates annually in our Summer Research Laboratory for Slavic and East European Scholars. This unique program, funded by the Departments of State and Education, allows around 300 scholars from all over the United States and around the world to come to the University of Illinois for up to a month to pursue research in their field. Each scholar is given free or reduced-cost housing at the university along with full access to all of the materials in the library of the University of Illinois. In addition, scholars can make use of the Slavic Reference Service available in the Slavic Reading Room. The Summer Research Lab gives the Reference

Service Staff the unique experience of personal interaction with scholars that we normally only contact via e-mail or phone. One-on-one bibliographic service such as this allows us to introduce many of them to the basic Slavic reference sources in the field. For the scholars, it gives them the opportunity to work with librarians that are specifically trained in the field of Slavic Studies in order to further their research goals. This type of outreach service to the scholarly community, although limited to a few weeks in the summertime, has proven invaluable to many researchers in the field.

In the twenty-five years of its existence, the Slavic Reference Service has filled an important gap in the resources for the field of Slavic Studies. Students, scholars, and librarians alike have turned to the Reference Service for questions that cannot be answered without the specialized collection located at the University of Illinois and the librarians who are trained in the field of Slavic bibliography. As more and more people have come to rely on our services, we have worked to make the Reference Service more accessible to our community of users. The new mediums of e-mail and the Internet have presented us with ways to expand our outreach to students, scholars, and librarians who may not otherwise know of our services. This type of virtual reference service comes with new challenges to traditional reference service that must be considered in order to make Internet reference service a successful endeavor.

THE INTERNET AND E-MAIL REFERENCE SERVICES: EXPANDING OUTREACH TO A NEW USER COMMUNITY

In the past several years, e-mail and Internet-based reference service has emerged as a new medium by which to provide better outreach to the user community. The existing literature on Internet reference services shows that these programs have had varying success based largely on the type of service offered. Internet reference can largely be divided into three types of service: reference services provided by university, college, or public libraries; "virtual" reference services–Internet sites devoted to reference service; and Internet reference service by special libraries.

Internet reference service by reference departments in university, college and public libraries is often modeled after telephone reference, ready reference and reference referral services.[3] These services provide quick answers to questions or refer the question to a specific librarian to be answered more extensively within the physical setting of the library. Because of a lack of staffing and/or funding, these services are often limited to very narrow user groups–faculty or students of the university, or residents of the city being served by the public library.[4] Others who attempt to use the service may be turned away or charged a fee for research services.

The limited nature of the service may also be the cause of the limited use many of these services have reported. Patrons looking for quick answers to questions may prefer to call rather than wait for an e-mail response. Unless e-mail is constantly monitored, it will always have a slower response time than telephone reference. Limited use may also be related to the fact that libraries tend to not heavily advertise such services to the community because of the fear that e-mail reference will put an extreme burden on the staff resources of the library and cause service to be lessened in more traditional areas.[5] However, with the exponential growth of the Internet in the past few years, it may be that such services will continue to grow and expand.

"Virtual" reference services have also appeared in the past several years. These services are not based in any one library but instead exist at a virtual reference department located at a website. Internet-based services such as the Internet Public Library or AskEric have extensive websites where any Internet user can submit a question.[6] The thousands of questions that are submitted are then distributed largely to volunteer librarians or library school students at institutions around the country that field the questions individually and respond to the patron. The enormous number of questions received by these services necessarily means that limits must be placed on the services that are provided: in-depth reference service is generally not provided, and some questions simply go unanswered. Plus, these services rely on volunteers for staff which can lead to unpredictable levels of service.

Finally, Internet reference services by special libraries has emerged as a third type of service. This is the group to which the Slavic Reference Service belongs. Libraries that provide this type of service are devoted to a narrow area of expertise: in our case, Russia, the former Soviet Union, and Eastern Europe.[7] Subject specialization helps to limit the questions that are submitted to a number that is manageable for the staff, which in turn allows us to answer almost any question, no matter how complicated or involved. This type of niche service is particularly suited to the environment of the Internet. We may be located in the middle of Illinois, but through the Internet our resources can be shared by persons all over the world. We can be contacted at any hour of the day or night, and we can respond to our patrons quickly and clearly in a way that is simply not possible via telephone or regular mail. Reference transactions that once took weeks to complete are now finished in days or even hours.

The medium of the Internet has also allowed us to reach out to a new group of users. In the past, the information services provided have been mainly to scholars, students, and librarians who come to us by previous experience or by word-of-mouth from others in the field. Today, because of the Internet and e-mail, the number and type of users we serve is expanding at a rapid pace. The changes brought about by this new medium have in turn altered many of the ways that we provide reference service since our user community is now much more difficult to define narrowly as Slavic area studies students and scholars. As we adopted the Internet and e-mail as a new medium for reference service, we were forced to consider a number of issues that arise with "virtual" reference service.

EXPANDING SERVICES TO THE INTERNET COMMUNITY

As with many libraries that provide reference service via the Internet, the Slavic Reference Service began its outreach slowly and expanded gradually. First, e-mail was merely a way to facilitate the reference services provided to our patrons. Sometimes students and scholars that knew of our services asked for the e-mail address of the Manager of the Reference Service, Helen Sullivan, in order to make a request for bibliographic or information reference service. In addition, staff of the Reference Service often ask patrons to send lengthy or complicated questions through e-mail rather than taking such questions over the phone. This is particularly useful for bibliographic queries, since telephone reference can be tricky for foreign language materials. Exact bibliographic citations sent through e-mail help to eliminate telephone misunderstandings.

Our e-mail reference service expanded further as other librarians in the Slavic field began to refer some of the reference questions they received to our service. As mentioned previously, these librarians simply do not have the resources to answer many of the questions that they receive. In one case, the librarian Karen Rondestvedt runs an extensive Internet site for Slavic and East European Studies. The REESWeb site (http://www.pitt.edu/~cjp/rees.html) has become an important resource for students and scholars in the field by directing them to resources now available on the Internet, but the site receives frequent e-mail reference questions as a result of being a central source of information. Since Dr. Rondestvedt does not have the staff resources to answer all of the questions received, many are forwarded to the Slavic Reference Service. The Reference Service currently has a link on the REESWeb page, but those who do not find the link can still submit a question to REESWeb and in many cases have it answered by us.

CREATING A REFERENCE HOMEPAGE

The decision to expand the reach of the Slavic Reference Service by creating an Internet site was not made lightly. Helen Sullivan, consulting with the staff of the Reference Service, considered many factors in creating a homepage. The most important consideration was whether the Reference Service had the staff resources to handle the additional requests we anticipated. Since there is no way to measure the type of response we might receive to our specialized service on the Internet, the decision to expand was something of a risk, but a risk our Manager felt was necessary in order to facilitate greater outreach to our community of users.

The next consideration was what type of Reference Service homepage to create. While we wanted the page to be informative and useful for students and scholars in the field, we knew that we did not have the resources to maintain an extensive homepage and expand our outreach services at the same time. We also felt that there were several other excellent Internet sites (such as REESWeb) that serve the purpose of being central Internet sites for the field of Slavic studies. Most importantly, we did not want to detract from the main purpose of the homepage: to serve as a site that offers reference service to our patrons. Therefore, the decision was made to keep the Slavic Reference Service homepage very simple and limit the information contained in it.[8]

The method of submission of reference questions was the third important consideration, and one that we are still modifying. Our first homepage simply explained our services and provided the e-mail address of the Reference Service Manager. The results of this experiment showed us the importance of a preliminary "reference interview."[9] These early submissions were often fragments of reference questions: some were vaguely worded or otherwise unclear, others lacked important information such as names, e-mail addresses, or when the information was needed. Patrons might have to be contacted a second time to conduct a reference interview via e-mail. In other cases, reference service staff might spend a considerable amount of time on a request, only to find that the e-mail address did not work, or that the patron no longer needed the information.

Our current submission form takes into account the lessons learned in the early stages of our Internet Reference Service by simulating a brief reference interview: the most basic questions we need to know are now included in the submission form itself. Now the user is asked to submit a name, e-mail address, languages known (so that we know whether to suggest English language or other language materials), date needed by and, perhaps most important, whether the user has access to interlibrary loan.[10] This is of great importance because in many cases it determines the type of resource that we recommend. If the requestor does not have access to interlibrary loan, we cannot recommend print sources in our collection or in the collections of other libraries. Where appropriate, we try to find the information needed on the Internet, but sometimes we must recommend a general source that may or may not be available to the patron locally. Our new reference question submission form, by anticipating the questions used in a typical reference interview, has reduced the occurrence of problem reference questions.

NEW PATRONS, NEW QUESTIONS: OUTREACH TO A NEW USER COMMUNITY

The greatest change brought about by the posting of our services on the Internet is the expansion of the type of patrons and questions that come in to our service. Whereas previously we were sought out largely by students and scholars in the field who learned of us through word-of-mouth or professional referrals, now we frequently receive queries from the general public that find us through our own homepage or the links to our homepage that exist on Internet sites in the Slavic field. These questions have broadened the type of services we provide, but they have also forced us to confront the problems of providing reference service to an extremely diverse community of users.

The largest problem we encounter with these requests is the uncertainty that we can provide the resources needed by the requestor. Our answers to queries are often found in print sources in our collection, most of which we will loan to any library that participates in interlibrary loan. Many patrons are affiliated with a university, but if one is not, we ask the patron if a local public library provides interlibrary loan. If the patron does not have access to interlibrary loan (which is frequently the case with international queries), our reply may be severely limited. If the needed information is on a few printed pages, we sometimes photocopy and mail items directly to the patron. In some cases, such as extensive research questions from students and scholars, we can recommend that they come for our Summer Research Lab, at which time they can easily access the materials. For the general public, however, this is not an option. In these cases we often must forget about the "best" source and concentrate on the most accessible source for the patron by suggesting Internet resources or Slavic studies materials that are widely available. Every situation is different, of course, and we make every effort to work with the patron until the needed information is somehow delivered.

The second problem with some of the requests from the general public is that the patron quite often cannot read the language, and is therefore limited in the types of resources that he/she may be able to use. In some cases, we can recommend English-language resources, or even retrieve ready reference facts and figures in the language and translate them for the patron, but we cannot provide any type of extensive translation service. This type of request is most troublesome, because there may be dozens of excellent bibliographies and other sources in Russian, but almost nothing in English. Sometimes patrons do not realize that most of this material has never been translated into English, and they are unhappy when we cannot provide a translation for them. While we have found this type of problem to be relatively rare, it is certainly the most frustrating for the Reference Service staff to handle.

Overall, however, we have had an overwhelmingly positive response to our Internet reference service by students, scholars, and the general public alike. Patrons of the service often reply that they posted their question to several places on the Internet, and that our service was the only one to respond to them. Others express the disbelief that such a service exists for free. The success of the service is shown most clearly by the number of users that find us on the Internet and become "regulars." Many of these patrons are students and scholars that enjoy the convenience of e-mailing an urgent question to us at 2 a.m. in the middle of finishing a publication, and having a response by the time they return to their computer the next day. Our Internet page means that we are always open, even if the staff is only physically available from 8 a.m. to 5 p.m. on weekdays.

In the twenty-five years of the existence of the Slavic Reference Service, the librarians and staff have worked to provide much-needed specialized reference service to the community of scholars and students in the Slavic field. Scholars have come to rely on us to find obscure citations and locate rare items for their use, or to fill in information gaps in their research. Of no less importance is the number of students and scholars who come to learn of a special bibliography or reference book through the efforts of the Reference service that makes their research even more fruitful. The use of the e-mail and the Internet to provide these services now means that we can reach even more of the students, scholars, and librarians that make up our primary user community. It also means that we can now offer our services to more libraries and the general public who find us through our Internet site. This new user community has caused us to rethink and reconsider the way we provide reference service, and continues to challenge us to find new ways to deliver virtual reference service.

REFERENCES

1. The *Slavic Cyrillic Union Catalog of Pre-1956 Imprints* contains information on the holdings of U.S. institutions of materials in the Cyrillic alphabet up to 1980.

2. Unfortunately, restrictions in our funding from the Department of State do not allow us to verify and search scientific and technical citations at this time. We will search for such items in our collection, but we cannot resolve bad citations through verification or refer patrons to other holding institutions.

3. For studies of e-mail reference service in the college or university environment, see Lara Bushallow-Wilber, Gemma DeVinney, and Fritz Whitcomb, "Electronic Mail Reference Service: A Study," in *RQ* 35:3 (Spring 1996), pp. 359-371. Several informal discussions of e-mail reference service have been held on the listserv of reference librarians: LIBREF-L; see the summaries posted on 9 March 1996 and 31 August 1998.

4. Indiana University has noted several dilemmas in attempting to limit e-mail reference service. See Ann Bristow and Mary Buechley, "Academic Reference Ser-

vice over E-mail: An Update," in *College & Research Library News* July/Aug. 1995, pp. 461-62.

5. The experience of the University of South Florida with advertising online services is particularly illustrative: see, Ilene Frank, "E-mail Reference Service at the University of South Florida: A Well-Kept Secret." *Art Documentation* 17:1 1998, p. 8-9.

6. See the articles explaining these services: Sara Ryan, "Reference Service for the Internet Community: A Case Study of the Internet Public Library Reference Division," *Library and Information Science Research* 18 (1996), pp. 241-259. On Ask-ERIC, see Robin Summers, "Meeting Education Information Needs through Digital Reference Service," *Art Documentation* 17:1 1998, pp. 3-4.

7. For example, the National Museum of American Art has an Internet reference service that provides answers for questions specifically on American art. See the description of their services by Joan Stahl, "'Have a Question? Click Here': Electronic Reference at the National Museum of American Art," in *Art Documentation* 17:1 1998, pp. 10-12.

8. Slavic Reference Service homepage: http://www.library.uiuc.edu/spx/srs.htm

9. For an excellent study of methods of conducting e-mail reference interviews, see Eileen G. Abels, "The E-mail Reference Interview." *RQ* 35: 3 (Spring 1996), pp. 345-58.

10. The Slavic Reference Service's submission form can be found at http://www.library.uiuc.edu/spx/newsrs.htm. Another good example of a submission form that attempts to simulate a reference interview is that of the Internet Public Library at http://www.ipl.org/ref/QUE/RefFormQRC.html

II. TARGETING SPECIAL CONNECTIONS: SPECIFIC USER GROUPS AND LIAISON PARTNERS

Ready to Read:
A Collaborative, Community-Wide Emergent Literacy Program

Marge Kars
Mary Doud

SUMMARY. In 1997, Kalamazoo Public Library and Bronson Methodist Hospital along with several other community organizations collaborated to create an emergent literacy program. The program provides volunteer readers at community sites, pediatricians' prescription of reading aloud for healthy child development and giving books to children at well-baby visits, providing a cloth book for every child born in

Marge Kars is Manager, Health Sciences Library and Health*Answers*, Bronson Methodist Hospital, 252 East Lovell Box B, Kalamazoo, MI 49007. Mary Doud is Assistant Director for Public Services, Kalamazoo Public Library, 315 South Rose St., Kalamazoo, MI 49007.

[Haworth co-indexing entry note]: "*Ready to Read:* A Collaborative, Community-Wide Emergent Literacy Program." Kars, Marge, and Mary Doud. Co-published simultaneously in *The Reference Librarian* (The Haworth Information Press, an imprint of The Haworth Press, Inc.) No. 67/68, 1999, pp. 85-97; and: *Library Outreach, Partnerships, and Distance Education: Reference Librarians at the Gateway* (ed: Wendi Arant, and Pixey Anne Mosley) The Haworth Press, Inc., 2000, pp. 85-97. Single or multiple copies of this article are available for a fee from The Haworth Document Delivery Service [1-800-342-9678, 9:00 a.m. - 5:00 p.m. (EST). E-mail address: getinfo@haworthpressinc.com].

Kalamazoo County, offering workshops on reading and book sharing skills for parent groups and providing book collections and volunteer readers to child care centers. This program is unique in its widespread collaboration of twenty community service organizations to provide county-wide services. *[Article copies available for a fee from The Haworth Document Delivery Service: 1-800-342-9678. E-mail address: getinfo@haworthpressinc. com <Website: http://www.haworthpressinc.com>]*

KEYWORDS. Medical community, preschool, immergent literacy, at risk children, ready to read, community outreach

If we could get our parents to read to their preschool children fifteen minutes a day, we could revolutionize the schools. (Trelease 11)

INTRODUCTION

Ready to Read is a community-wide emergent literacy initiative, launched in Kalamazoo, MI in March, 1997, whose primary goal is to assure that children in Kalamazoo County arrive at school, having been read to by parents, ready to read and learn. The target population is at-risk children from birth to five years as well as their families. *Ready to Read* is a collaboration of public libraries, hospitals, human service agencies, schools, businesses and other organizations. Through a host of interventions, *Ready to Read* imparts the message to parents that it is imperative to read to children, beginning in infancy, and to ensure that children have opportunities to be exposed to books before they enter school in order to achieve success in school.

NEED FOR EARLY READING INTERVENTIONS

Brain research attests that reading aloud to children in the first years of life has a critical and lasting impact on their brain and language development. Family reading to young children has recently been named as one of the 25 indicators of the well-being of our nation's children by the Federal Interagency Forum on Child and Family Statistics. The Forum's report, *America's Children: Key National Indicators of Well-Being*, issued in July, 1997 states:

research shows that reading to young children promotes language acquisition and correlates with literacy development and, later, with achievement in reading comprehension and overall success in school. The percentage of young children read aloud to daily by a family member is one indicator of how well young children are prepared for school. (*America's Children* 43)

Many children in Kalamazoo County are not read to or exposed to books as preschoolers. These children often start kindergarten unprepared for reading and learning. They are at risk of falling behind academically throughout their lives and having trouble finding and keeping employment later in life. National studies show that only about 50% of parents read to their children on a daily basis, regardless of income level. The U.S. Department of Education reports that while family reading in the nation's population as a whole increased slightly in 1996, children in families with incomes below the poverty line are less likely to be read aloud to than are children of families with higher incomes. U.S. Census data from 1990 suggest a downward trend in Kalamazoo County's economy. Because of the long-recognized link between economic well-being and educational achievement, the increasing number of families at-risk economically raises concerns about current and future literacy levels among the county's population.

EMERGENT LITERACY

Medical researchers have pinpointed the time between birth and age three as critical for imprinting children with the ability to learn. Reading to infants, along with exposure to music, sights, noises and eye contact, literally makes the brain take shape. Emergent literacy is the idea that literacy, or the use of written and oral language, is a developing process that begins at birth. The Center for the Improvement of Early Reading Achievement (CIERA) in its document "Improving the Reading Achievement of America's Children 10 Research-Based Principles" lists the first principle:

> Home language and literacy experiences that lead to the development of key print concepts are plentiful among children who enter school prepared to learn to read. Joint book reading with family members helps children develop a wide range of knowledge that supports them in school-based reading . . .

> Preschool programs are particularly beneficial for children who do not experience informal learning opportunities in their homes.

These preschool experiences include opportunities to listen and to examine books, say nursery rhymes, write messages, and see and talk about print. Such preschool experience lead to improved reading achievement in the school years, with some effects proving durable through grade three. (CIERA)

READY TO READ *PROGRAM*

The *Ready to Read* program includes local adaptations of national models which have been piloted successfully. By design, most program activities take place at community sites which serve the target population.

- Volunteers read to children and model book sharing techniques for parents at 25 community sites including a pediatric clinic, the Family Independence Agency, Family Health Center, county immunization clinics and several child care centers.
- Pediatricians "prescribe" reading aloud for healthy child development and distribute gift books at well-baby visits at the Michigan State University/Kalamazoo Center for Medical Studies pediatric clinic.
- Bronson Methodist Hospital and Borgess Medical Center distribute a cloth book to parents of each newborn along with a recommended list of books for reading aloud and an invitation to visit their local library, which has a Books-for-Babies program.
- Librarians conduct "Parents as Partners in Reading" workshops for parent groups about effective ways to share books with children regardless of parental literacy level; each parent participant receives a certificate and a gift book to share with young children at home.
- Fifty child care centers serving the at risk population are provided with book collections and regular volunteer reader visits.

A program coordinator and staff assistant were hired in March 1997. The coordinator is responsible for recruiting, and placing volunteers, working with collaborators forging new partnerships, and recruiting new sites for program activities. She also does presentations to local community service organizations to promote the program and recruit volunteers. The staff assistant maintains records of volunteer hours and anecdotal comments from readers.

To date (June 1998), 146 volunteers have logged 2,603 hours reading 12,591 books to 9,134 children with 4,311 observing. Kalamazoo Public Library has conducted Parents as Partners in Reading workshops for approximately 300 parents in 1998 at a variety of locations. Borgess and Bronson Hospitals have distributed books to the parents of 3,100 babies born in Kalamazoo each year. In April of this year, pediatricians began handing out gift books to children who came to the Michigan State University/Kalamazoo Center for Medical Studies for well baby visits. Earlier this year, the pediatricians participated in informal sessions in emergent literacy principles and have added a new question to their protocols asking if parents read daily to their young child. The physicians send the parents home with a developmentally appropriate book at the end of the well baby visit along with some literacy tips. To date, 400 have been handed out. This clinic is also one of the first volunteer reader sites.

The child care centers portion of *Ready to Read* is modeled after a successful pilot project Kalamazoo Public Library started in 1995. The child care centers will be supplied with a collection of multi-cultural children's books suitable for reading aloud. Volunteer readers will visit weekly to present story times for the children and model book sharing techniques for the child care providers. The long term goal is to start this portion of the program in fifty child care centers focused on economically at-risk children. This spring, the program started with five centers; the Kalamazoo Gospel Mission, YWCA Child Care Center, Housing Resources Shelter, Edison Neighborhood Center and Kalamazoo Drop-In Child Care Center.

The first annual Celebration of Children's Literacy was held on April 8th, 1998. This first event focused on providers of services to children. Speakers included physicians, educators and librarians. The half day event focused on ways providers could support and encourage the value of reading to their clients and the children of their clients. Though attendance was small, evaluations from the program indicated that the audience was pleased with the program and that it had reached the goal of showing that the different professions had a common goal of supporting literacy.

Public Information Campaign

Early in the planning process the team discussed ways to keep the program in front of the public. One team member said he hoped that eventually the program would be "So big and so loud they can't ignore it." The team took that statement as a challenge and a goal for the public information campaign.

During a meeting of marketing and public relations professionals representing the collaborators to advise the development of a public information campaign they advised that the use of posters, billboards and PSAs to take the message of the importance of reading out to the community. A local marketing agency, Traver-Rohrback, agreed to provide pro bono creative work for the program. They were approached initially for a logo for *Ready to Read*. They provided the logo and developed three billboards, two posters, two radio PSAs, a car window decal and editing for two television PSAs. They facilitated placing three different billboards in seven areas of the community for three months. The posters were sent to pediatricians' offices and to all the reading sites.The two video PSAs aired on three local television stations. The PSAs featured Bill Cosby encouraging West Michigan parents to read to their children and to call *Ready to Read* for a list of books to read aloud. The radio PSAs are airing on local radio stations. Ready to Read hosted an annual community-wide literacy "summit," featuring national literacy experts is sponsored for community leaders, educators, parents, literacy volunteers and health and human services professionals.

Funding

The projected first year budget for *Ready to Read* was $130,697. Healthy Futures provided $72,000 in start-up funds in November 1996. An additional $10,000 for books was awarded in August 1997. To complete the funding for the 1997-98 fiscal year collaborators sought and received funding from local foundations, the national Reach Out and Read Foundation, Friends of the Kalamazoo Public Library, service clubs, businesses and private citizens. One of the largest budget portions ($42,650) is required to fund the purchase of books for the children who will benefit from the program and for the volunteer readers to take to the reading sites. The two hospitals in the project, Borgess Medical Center and Bronson Methodist Hospital, have agreed to fund the Books for Babies portion of *Ready to Read*. Michigan State University/Kalamazoo Center for Medical Studies have budgeted to support the purchase of the gift books pediatricians present to mothers at well-baby visits. Grant proposals continue to be written to support the project. The Kalamazoo Foundation has recently awarded a two-year grant to the library to support *Ready to Read* operations. We will submit proposals to a national family literacy foundation and other regional foundations for 1999 funding. In the spring of 1998, the Kalamazoo Public Library held a formal gala preview event to celebrate the opening of their newly renovated building. Invitations to the gala included an opportunity for people to donate money to *Ready to Read*. More than $13,000 was raised at the gala. A local bookstore (Athena Bookstore) provides a significant discount to the two hospitals to purchase the cloth books for Books for Babies. One project collaborator, the local Barnes & Noble Bookstore, participates as part of its corporate commitment to the national First Book organization. Barnes & Noble is a cosponsor of a major fund raising event set for September 1998. An Evening of Mystery, featuring two nationally known mystery authors, William X. Kienzle and Lauren D. Estleman, will be a benefit for *Ready to Read*. Kalamazoo Public Library has made the commitment to assume financial responsibility and incorporate *Ready to Read* into its operational budget in the year 2001. Until that time, grant seeking and the garnering of local sustainers will continue by the library and the other collaborators.

Evaluation

In planning for project evaluation, collaborators have developed systems to measure outcomes, track outputs and evaluate the processes used in each program component. One important outcome of the project is to raise the incidence of parents and/or care givers sharing books with children on a daily basis, beginning in infancy. Strategies for measuring family reading habits will include:

- Pediatricians at the MSU/KCMS clinic have added a question about daily reading to their protocol of questions to parents at well-baby visits.
- A pilot study to assess family reading habits was conducted with parents of kindergartners at parent-teacher conferences in Kalamazoo Public Schools in the fall of 1997.
- A questionnaire administered during annual Kalamazoo County Head Start home visits will include questions about the frequency of family reading.

- Each volunteer reader completes a log after weekly volunteer reading sessions. Included in these reports are anecdotal comments about the children being read to and parents' reactions. These comments often reveal information about family reading behavior.
- The Concepts About Print Test (CAPT) will be administered to a sample of children in Kalamazoo County schools. The CAPT is relevant to books and will reveal a child's previous exposure to books.

Another outcome will be improved reading readiness and improved reading performance among elementary school children in Kalamazoo County will be employed.

- A longitudinal study will track a group of 25 children affected by the *Ready to Read* program through the MSU/KCMS pediatric clinic from their infancy or preschool years through kindergarten. The performance of these children would be compared with a control group of children not involved with the program.
- In the long term, the program hopes to be a contributor to improved MEAP scores of fourth grade students in Kalamazoo County. Mean scores will be tracked year to year.

A third outcome of *Ready to Read* will be its capacity to engage new collaborators, recruit and retain volunteers, establish new sites for program activities, and raise funds to support the project. Sustained community engagement and ownership of this grass roots endeavor will be an important measure of success.

Another feature of evaluating the success of the program is the progress made toward the impact targets for each program component. Tracking outputs, i.e., the numbers of children and families reached by each aspect of the program in relation to the stated goals will supply a scale of effectiveness.

Each program component of *Ready to Read* includes an evaluation strategy. For example, pre and post-workshop surveys are administered to parents attending Parents as Partners in Reading workshops. Surveys are conducted to assess the use of books distributed through the Books for Babies program. Child care providers will be surveyed about their satisfaction with the use of the book collections, and their assessment of the benefits of volunteer readers visiting their facilities.

Volunteer readers are surveyed about the effectiveness of the library's training and orientation program.

Collaborators

The leaders of this collaboration, Kalamazoo Public Library and Bronson Methodist Hospital, are among a growing number of service organizations that recognize the value and effectiveness in collaborating in order to further their respective missions and achieve institutional goals. Having enjoyed a history of cooperation and joint ventures, these two partners came together again as participants in Healthy Futures. Affiliated with the national Healthy Communities movement, Kalamazoo's Healthy Futures is a grass-roots, county wide project aimed at improving the quality of life of county residents by addressing four areas of community concern; poverty, crime, domestic violence and teen pregnancy. The authors work with other community volunteers as members of the initiative to reduce or eliminate poverty.

Illiteracy or low literacy was identified repeatedly as a causal factor in poverty by participants in over 40 public forums conducted by Healthy Futures in 1996. Inspired by this community input, Kalamazoo Public Library, Bronson Methodist Hospital and other literacy stakeholders joined forces to develop an action plan. After surveying 42 local literacy service providers to identify gaps in service and opportunities for cooperation, the library, Bronson and other partners developed *Ready to Read* as an upstream means to break the intergenerational cycles of illiteracy and ultimately reduce poverty.

As in any true collaboration, the partners of *Ready to Read* regard the shared vision for what can be accomplished through *Ready to Read* as compelling and consistent with their own missions for meeting the needs of their constituents and/or the community-at-large. They bring to the table financial resources, in-kind contributions, or important non-financial resources such as technical expertise, political influence or community trust. Following the collaborative model, they are willing to put aside turf issues and corporate cultural differences for the greater good of the collaboration, its goal and its target population.

Kalamazoo Public Library stepped forward to assume the role of employer, administrator and fiscal agent for this endeavor because the goal of *Ready to Read* is closely aligned with the library's mission and core values. One of the library's core values states that the library believes in the value of reading and that an informed, literate community leads to societal well-being. It follows, then, that the library has a long history of leadership and involvement in local literacy efforts as one of the first libraries in Michigan to offer services to children (1997 marked the library's 100th anniversary of service to children). The library views children, parents, care givers and other adults who influence children as a primary service constituency. While the library regularly conducts many children's programs at library facilities, programs and activities at remote sites are now the focus of an expanded emphasis. The library houses the *Ready to Read* office, trains volunteer readers, selects and acquires children's books used in program activities and leads fund development efforts.

Through outreach programs such as *Ready to Read*, the collaboration engineers an effective means of reaching children and families whose life experiences might not otherwise have included or valued books and reading. The library's leadership of *Ready to Read* offers evidence of its commitment to collaborative efforts that will promote literacy and build a library without walls for the community.

Bronson Methodist Hospital is a not for profit, acute care community hospital that places a high priority on re-investing in the community. In 1997 Bronson provided $11.4 million in direct benefits to the community through several external efforts which foster the health and well-being of local citizens. Bronson is a collaborator in ventures such as county-wide immunization clinics, school and community-based clinics which expand access to health care, and various housing and economic development programs which serve families at risk. The hospital's vision of a healthy community led it to become one of the four charter collaborators of Healthy Futures. With Bronson's support of *Ready to Read*, the hospital underscores the belief that literacy and health are closely linked. Bronson provides human resources for administration of the project and monies for the purchase of books for the Books for Babies. Additionally, Bronson provides meeting space and marketing services.

Other collaborators include other health care organizations, human service agencies, educational institutions, physicians, businesses and private citizens. One of the benefits the collaborators have gained through *Ready to Read* is the opportunity to make connections with other organizations which share the objective of promoting emergent literacy. For example, Kalamazoo County Head Start now links with a private venture called The Children's Book Bank to acquire books for distribution to Head Start children. The Ladies Library Association finds new avenues for its book distribution program through *Ready to Read* reading sites. A local reading program sponsored by Kalamazoo Rotary Clubs now join forces with *Ready to Read* to share exhibit spaces at local festivals. A list of collaborators is included in the appendix.

FUTURE PROJECTS

An important measurement of the success of *Ready to Read* will be its ability to engage establish new sites for program activities. Currently we are recruiting additional child care centers in Title One school neighborhoods to work towards our goal of serving fifty child care centers with volunteer readers and book collections.

We have contacted another community agency that provides early intervention for high-risk infants and their parents. This program involves intervention specialists doing home visits and assessing parents for different skills, including literacy. This organization typically works with 500 families a year. They are interested in working with *Ready to Read* by talking to the parents about the value of reading to their child beginning at birth, referring parents to the Parents as Partners in Reading program and providing a gift book for the child during their visits.

Ready to Read is working with the Kalamazoo County Sheriff's Department to extend the program services to the Kalamazoo County Jail. Female inmates who are parents would participate in a series of Parents as Partners in Reading workshops presented by librarians from Kalamazoo Public Library. As an incentive to complete the program the prisoners would be allowed face to face family visits to read with their children. Face to face family visits are currently prohibited at the jail. The parent would also be provided with a choice of books for their children to keep and take home.

It is hoped that with this new program component *Ready to Read* will reach a population that did not previously have access to the library, and introduce a population of at risk preschool children to books and reading.

In January 1998, Michigan Governor John Engler announced the

State of Michigan Reading Plan to help children in Michigan reading at grade level by the time they reach fourth grade. The plan is being developed by the Michigan Department of Education. In June of this year representatives from the Michigan DOE visited *Ready to Read* and are considering this program as a model for the birth to age five component of the state plan.

The true success of *Ready to Read* cannot be determined for several years. The evaluation components of the program, the longitudinal study tracking 25 children and improved MEAP scores, will take time. Some early outcomes, like the number of times volunteer readers share books with children or the gift books provided to children at pediatric visits are positive easy demonstrations of the positive impact of the program. Perhaps the most important aspect of *Ready to Read* is its unique collaboration among a public library, a community hospital and several community organizations to work toward a common goal.

REFERENCES

America's Children: Key National Indicators of Well-Being. (Washington, D.C. Federal Interangecy Forum on Child and Family Statistics, 1997), 43.

Improving the Reading Achievement of America's Children. 10 Research-Based Principles. CIERA. (1998). Available: http://www.umich.edu/~ciera/about-ciera/principles/principles.html.

Jim Trelease, *The Read-Aloud Handbook.* 4th ed. (New York, Penguin Books, 1995), xi.

APPENDIX

READY TO READ COLLABORATORS

Kalamazoo Public Library
Bronson Methodist Hospital
Borgess Medical Center
Western Michigan University
Michigan State University/Kalamazoo Center for Medical Studies
Kalamazoo County Human Services Department
HeadStart
Child Care Resources
Kalamazoo Area Rotary Clubs
Kalamazoo Public Schools
Kalamazoo Public Education Foundation
Portage Public Schools
Rambling Road Pediatrics
Children's Book Bank
Senior Services
Portage Public Library
Hispanic American Council
Edison Neighborhood Center
Barnes & Noble Bookstores
Ladies Library Association

Pressing the F1 Key–
And Retrieving Each Other

Leslie Kahn

SUMMARY. At 3:30 any afternoon of the week, public librarians may feel confident of serving students. Indeed, students comprise a significant portion of public library users, and they require a good deal of attention. Unless librarians work with the schools, though, we do not truly complement the curriculum. The Newark (NJ) Public Schools and the Newark Public Library have therefore embarked on a program of library orientation for teachers. Synergy with instructors has taught public librarians new means of reinforcing learning. *[Article copies available for a fee from The Haworth Document Delivery Service: 1-800-342-9678. E-mail address: getinfo@haworthpressinc.com <Website: http://www.haworthpressinc.com>]*

KEYWORDS. Cooperation, cooperation–continuing education, public libraries, public libraries–services to schools, school and public library relationship, school libraries

PURPOSE

What a golden opportunity! Most public services librarians have been confronted with countless student assignments that lack clarity ("Who invented the clock?") or that cannot be satisfied because of

Leslie Kahn is Supervising Librarian, Arts and Humanities Division, Newark Public Library, 5 Washington Street, Newark, NJ 07101.

The author gratefully acknowledges the editorial support of her wonderful colleagues, Heidi Lynn Cramer and Jane Seiden.

[Haworth co-indexing entry note]: "Pressing the F1 Key–And Retrieving Each Other." Kahn, Leslie. Co-published simultaneously in *The Reference Librarian* (The Haworth Information Press, an imprint of The Haworth Press, Inc.) No. 67/68, 1999, pp. 99-110; and: *Library Outreach, Partnerships, and Distance Education: Reference Librarians at the Gateway* (ed: Wendi Arant, and Pixey Anne Mosley) The Haworth Press, Inc., 2000, pp. 99-110. Single or multiple copies of this article are available for a fee from The Haworth Document Delivery Service [1-800-342-9678, 9:00 a.m. - 5:00 p.m. (EST). E-mail address: getinfo@haworthpressinc.com].

99

limited resources ("Everyone is to bring in a copy of *Anynovel* tomorrow.") or that are not well considered ("Name the elementary school
attended by Harriet Tubman."). Adding to these frustrations are
hordes of students needing to prepare research papers but lacking
proper instruction in the process. Wouldn't we love to give teachers a
piece of our minds (in the gentlest, noblest sense of the expression).[1]
A contract negotiated with the Newark Public Schools has allowed the
Newark Public Library staff to present three-day workshops about
library resources and services along with information about report
writing from a librarian's vantage point.

The Newark Public Library has long served school-aged children
and teenagers in those traditional, nominal ways common in many
communities.[2] Summer reading and activities programs thrive at both
the main library and at the ten branches. Throughout the year, youth
services librarians arrange for programs of educational entertainment
in dance, drama, film, science, and sports. Branch librarians visit
classrooms in their neighborhoods, and teachers make appointments
for their classes to tour public library facilities and to conduct research
under the guidance of reference librarians.

Three innovations have been prized by the public library's school
constituency. First, an instructional video collection available exclusively to teachers resides in the public library's two largest branches.
The very popular Club Success is an after-school walk-in homework
help program; in every Newark Public Library children's room on
Mondays through Thursdays during the academic year, professional
teachers, sometimes assisted by high school student volunteers, work
with youngsters on problem questions. Finally, in early 1998, branch
libraries restored Saturday hours, thereby increasing access to the
city's residents; for years, because of fiscal difficulties, only the Main
Library was open on Saturdays. All three programs receive generous
funding assistance from the Newark Public Schools, and the Pruden-
tial Insurance Company Foundation has been a principal partner in
opening branch doors on Saturdays.

What teachers note, however, is more what the public library no
longer provides than what it does offer to schools. In the past, a
division of six to twelve full-time public library employees constituted
a Newark Public Library Schools Division that prepared cases of
books for classrooms. These books remained in the schools from
September through June, and teachers could request additional materi-

als to enrich lessons. In addition, teachers and pupils looked forward to regular visits by the public library bookmobile, which traveled throughout the city. Unfortunately, as funding for the public library declined, this institution could not alone afford these expensive programs and turned to the school board for help in paying for them. Although the school board at the time recognized that these services benefited students, it was unused to the idea of giving financial aid to or contracting with another agency.[3] Cooperation necessitates mutuality,[4] and, by 1991, the public library had ceased maintaining either a schools division or a bookmobile.[5] Since many parents do not allow their children to travel alone, even to community library branches, loss of those classroom cases of books and of bookmobile services means that some students are deprived of access to library resources.

An experiment in joint facilities was attempted for a number of years. From 1954 until 1997, one public library branch existed in a school.[6] During school hours, the library was open exclusively to students and teachers, and a school librarian helped them. At three o'clock, the community was welcomed by the public librarian. In a time of fiscal crisis, the public library, unable to justify retaining a facility for what was an active but quite small number of patrons, gave its collection to the school and transferred its staff to other services.

The Newark Public Library in the past proved itself so helpful that many schools did not develop their own libraries . . . and school libraries in Newark today generally remain inadequate to the needs of students.[7] Not all Newark schools have libraries. Particularly in elementary schools (pre-kindergarten through grade 8), school librarians serve more as "prep period" providers than as information literacy educators. While classroom teachers are creating lesson plans or marking papers, school librarians, a number of whom do not have an MLS degree and none of whom works with clerical assistance, may, with limited materials, give instruction in library use. At the end of the day, these librarians have not had time to answer reference questions or to order catalog materials. In any case, many school media specialists tell the public librarians that their budgets allow few new acquisitions, although 1997 brought the Newark district a one-time windfall grant that improved automation and collections.

High school librarians work in facilities that vary widely through the city. One school's library shares a space in which mathematics classes are conducted simultaneously with library operations. Another of Newark's elite high schools was the first to obtain Internet and other computer technology . . . and is, unfortunately, presently manually checking out books and waiting for essential upgrades to its circulation system, while other schools, until recently with few or no computers, receive equipment.

As in most cities and towns, Newark school libraries close at the end of the school day,[8] possibly because teacher and school media specialist salaries tend to be relatively high (higher than those of public and university librarians).[9] During an occasional school media center visit of thirty to fifty minutes, with classmates vying for the same resources, a student cannot accomplish in-depth research. For accessibility and often for quality of materials, students at all grade levels therefore rely heavily on the Newark Public Library.

Unfortunately, many of their teachers have not used the Newark Public Library in a long time. Some have never visited the public library in Newark, and some who live outside the city do not make great use of their local libraries.[10] Over the years, the Newark Public Library attempted outreach; but tours, teas, and other events failed to attract teachers. When, in 1994, the public schools launched a broad initiative of requiring term papers of students from the fifth through the twelfth grades, an overwhelmed public library reference staff wondered again how to interest teachers in preparing their students for the public library experience. Newark's is the largest public library in New Jersey and therefore offers much to its patrons–but the massiveness of the collections intimidates new users, as well as some teachers with advanced degrees.

Fortunately, Rosa Ramos, who now administers Title I programs for the Newark Public Schools, was aware of the need for children and teachers to use well equipped libraries. Knowing that students could not wait for improvements to the schools' media centers, she sought grants to finance public library based Library Research and Writing Institutes for teachers. The funding, which goes directly to the public library, supports salaries of public library personnel involved in the programs as well as the expenses of materials and supplies. Each year, at the invitation of the Newark Public Schools, the public library's teachers' institute coordinator and her assistant director write a proposal detailing the costs of the program. After each workshop, a bill for that session goes from the public library to the Title I office of the school district. The money received allows the production and purchase of materials for the next scheduled institute.

Rosa Ramos gave the public library a relatively free rein to design the program, asking only that the public library staff instruct teachers in catalog and periodical index use and that teachers receive some writing skills along with term paper guidance.[11] The writing skills requirement initially gave the public librarians pause. Writing skills are discussed in the context of research so as to reduce the possibility of embarrassment. In their role as knowledge brokers, teachers can be proud, and librarians do not wish to undermine their confidence but, rather, to add to its substance.

WORKSHOP ORGANIZATION

The three-day institutes are presented five or six times annually, and each group of registrants includes twenty people, generally selected by their school principals. Basic skills teachers of sixth through eight graders comprised the first groups. Participants are now largely drawn from regular classroom teachers for those grades, although one program was designed for teachers of primary grades, and three were for school librarians. One of the institutes for school librarians extended for five days, with the last two days concentrated on electronic resources, especially the Internet. Because of the school system's fiscal cycle, it is necessary to present the workshops during the latter half of the academic year.

Every group exhibits a unique "chemistry," with individual needs and interests. The presenters from the public library listen carefully during introductions at the start of each session and continue to "take pulses" throughout the program in order to remain responsive to special explicit and implicit needs and wishes. A goal for public librarians is to demonstrate the generosity of our profession, even as we must articulate certain limits to what teachers can expect of our institutions. For strict attention to curriculum requirements, we refer teachers to the school library system, since the public library budget must allot resources to demands of constituencies other than students.[12]

With the conclusion of introductions and a brief overview of what participants may expect of the workshop, teachers tour the main library, finishing in the Children's Room, which serves patrons through the eight grade (although youngsters are welcome to use adult materials . . . and adults to use children's). A children's librarian informs the group of services such as the Club Success homework program and discusses selected reference tools as well. Throughout the tour, we offer special tips, such as the interest students take in examining the microfilm of the *Newark Star Ledger* for events that occurred on their birth dates; the availability of free library cards to anyone who lives, works, or attends school in the city; and the advisability of students bringing some money when they visit the library so that they can make copies from reference, microform, and electronic media.

Having provided some physical orientation, we move on to language. Library jargon is treated first. Public librarians try not to use too much of it, but specialized vocabularies creep into discussions, and library and school administrators agree that students and teachers need familiarity with terms like "periodical" so that they understand the purpose of sources such as the *Reader's Guide*; "verso," so they know a good place for locating the date of a book; and the differences between autobiographies, biographies, and bibliographies. Conducted in a twenty-questions game format, this vocabulary lesson appeals to participants with interactive learning styles and allows the teachers to display newly acquired knowledge and skills.

In this same spirit, we pair participants during the "communications" segment. Teachers are invited to report what they do not care for about their school libraries (if they have them), the Newark Public Library (generally they miss those book cases and the bookmobile), and libraries in general. Remarks vary but often offer the opportunity of correcting misperceptions. The partners next present skits illustrating principles in our "How to Win Friends and Influence Librarians" brochure.[13] This handout contains ideas that help teachers to plan library assignments. Principles that may seem obvious to librarians steeped in realities of information seeking can elude teachers, so this communications training offers such advice as that not all topics lend themselves to bibliographies requiring three reference sources, three periodicals sources, three circulating books, three pamphlets, three Internet sources–and no encyclopedias. Explaining that we applaud teachers' wishes to expose students to types of materials beyond *The World Book Encyclopedia*, we also express remorse over what young people miss when they decline the *International Encyclopedia of Dance* and instead seek pamphlets.

Just as some people are sensitive to being taught about writing, so may some teachers feel offended by librarians presenting instruction about term paper presentation. To reduce any affront, librarians remind the teachers that we are offering the perspective of our profession; in addition, we proceed within the context of efficiently using the Newark Public Library for research purposes. This approach permits the logical segmenting of the term paper process into three distinct sessions.

Day One of the program concludes with the initial "term paper clinic." Here we refer to research by scholars like Kulthau[14] and Small,[15] who emphasize the affective aspects of the term paper project, and, work together to brainstorm means of overcoming feelings of overload, confusion and frustration. We also touch on concerns teachers have over loss of control: when they conduct lessons, they can teach to standardized tests or work toward other necessary goals, but when students conduct their own research, teachers cannot so closely steer them. By the end of this first day, we hope that we have established a secure and relaxing but stimulating environment for the participants, many of whom may have arrived in the library with misgivings about library instruction.

Resource rich is what we endeavor for Day Two. After a review, the second term paper clinic commences with the importance of topic selection, of reading widely before determining a thesis statement, of note-taking, and of the value of an outline or other organizing device. The subject of note-taking often evokes teachers' difficulties with plagiarism, and we work on means of eliminating mere copying by choosing age appropriate topics and sources, writing for one's younger cousin, and hearing teacher encouragement. Practice in taking notes from a dry text underscores the messages. We also emphasize that note-taking and other skills need development in advance of the term paper assignment.[16] The group also develops an outline kinesthetically, with teachers standing and holding numerals and letters in outline formation to represent various elements in the outline structure; subjects outlined have ranged from the O.J. Simpson trial to the medical uses of leeches.

Participants move on to learn how best to employ the functions of the Newark Public Library's Dynix catalog and of the *SearchBank/ InfoTrac* index of periodicals delivered over the Internet from the Gale Group. Brochures about how to use each tool are in the thick packet of handouts, and we elucidate instruction in these pamphlets; we also show a video about *SearchBank*. Many of our teachers come to us unaware of the concepts like truncation and Boolean logic, while some have little experience with computers. More than a couple have indeed imagined that pressing the F1 key summons a librarian from behind the reference desk.[17] We employ two or three librarians to work with the teachers while they operate the machines and work on basic exercises. Telling teachers the limitations of these tools is also essential; otherwise some expect to find individual poems listed in the library catalog, and some expect articles from the 1960s to be included in *SearchBank* indexing.

After lunch sessions consist of book talks about arts, humanities, science, and social science reference materials. Librarians pull from the reference shelves the volumes most likely to appeal to the academic and personal needs and interests of students and teachers, and we point to their various features. To practice finding information in these sources, teachers work on a sampling of students' questions. We are not seeking to create amateur librarians but, rather, to acquaint these patrons with a sense of what they can find in the reference sections of the Newark Public Library. Many participants tell us that leafing through the books is their favorite portion of the workshop.

Most, though, declare learning about the Internet the most valuable benefit of the institute, and they enjoy this opportunity at the start of the third day. At least once weekly, the Newark Public Library presents introductory and advanced Internet classes for the general public, and what we offer to the teachers is much like the introductory class but with a focus on education and information for students. Because the Internet's ease, variety, and vastness so dazzles people, librarians balance their enthusiasm by providing site evaluation standards and by pointing to cases in which print materials and commercial databases currently outperform the Internet. Everyone, even the experienced Internet user, tends to indicate on the workshop evaluation form a desire for more time with the World Wide Web.

We do nonetheless drag the group out of the library's public technology center, a computer laboratory established for training and for wider public access to word processing and other computer applications. At this point, the final term paper clinic is offered to cover the organization of various sorts of reports. Much of this material derives from Baugh,[18] Garrett,[19] Robinson,[20] Vandergrift,[21] and Wesley.[22] At the conclusion of this segment, the group divides into three or four sections, and each team works on a five-paragraph mini-paper on some aspect of topics ranging from cross-racial adoption to ebonics to same-sex marriage to school vouchers. These subjects strongly resemble the ones chosen by the teachers' students, and gathering information and writing about these issues allows workshop registrants to encounter something of what their students experience at the public library and in the writing process. The exercise initially provokes groans but invariably results in a sense of accomplishment and of having proven learning what the institute is supposed to teach. In addition, everyone finds that the teachers gain enormously from networking with each other, and this activity enhances exchanges from previous partnering and team work.

RESULTS

Evaluation forms completed by participants at the end of the last day have shown universally positive marks for this program. The teachers discover that they like the public library, its staff, its resources, and its services. Many remark in a postscript that this was one of the most outstanding workshops they have been to, that every Newark teacher and administrator should attend the institute, and they would appreciate regularly scheduled refresher classes.

Both partners in this venture endeavor to accomplish the greatest possible quality of learning from the institutes, but, unfortunately, neither the school system nor the public library make additional or subsequent evaluation studies.[23] Any improvements to the program have been at the initiative of its public library coordinator, who, for example, has increased handouts from an original packet of some twenty items and two books to over thirty pieces along with two new books, one about report writing, the other about the Internet for students. Members of the public library staff observe a decreasing number of assignments that only the librarian, not the student, can handle. Twice the number of appointments for class visits to the public library have come from schools since the inception of the teachers' institutes. Relatively few teachers or school librarians visit in person without classes, but more are telephoning with reference queries. Most importantly, school and public librarians alike report that the students appear more able to use their libraries. While the young people do not always arrive with complete understanding of how to employ resources, they are more fully evidencing the essential expectation that the library and its staff will contribute significantly to their academic and personal success. A study to investigate the areas and degree of change in students' library literacy is desirable.

These small but steady achievements have caused a rise in our expectations. Those at the public library would like to see the teacher institutes extended to make them available to high school teachers. Almost as much as the students, we long for stronger school libraries and for clearer definitions of the similarities and differences between the roles of school and public librarians in regard to students and teachers.

Quite a few teachers have expressed the wish for personnel dedicated as liaisons between the schools and the public library. More joint meetings of school and public librarians, use studies, and even cooperative purchasing and access programs have been recommended by school librarians.[24] Specialization, with each library in Newark sharing its strengths with all the others, would involve coordinated resource and equipment collection development.[25] Longer library hours are natural goals for both the public library and for the school system.

In the future, Teachers' Research and Writing Institutes at the Newark Public Library will develop into five-day programs, with an enriched electronic resources component. As it progresses, this joint school/library effort can serve as a basis for further collaboration in elevating library services. When some in our profession are fearing that the public may view the Internet as replacing libraries, continuing education that includes consulting with people working on issues similar to ours makes for alliances that spark new ideas. Together we can advance the purposes and visibility of school, public, and other types of libraries.

Information literacy has come to incorporate an element of social responsibility:

> The student who contributes positively to the learning community and to society . . . recognizes the importance of information to a democratic society [and] participates effectively in groups to pursue and generate information.[26]

As students coordinate their endeavors to cultivate and to share information, so must librarians. Budget reductions and the resulting curtailment of time and resources make collegiality more difficult to achieve–and more compelling than ever.

REFERENCES

1. Caywood, Carolyn "Caught in a Trap: School and Public Libraries Are Wasting Time Bickering Instead of Zoning in on Real Problems." *School Library Journal* 44 (Jan. 1998): 51.

2. These nominal and more ambitious programs are elaborated in various sources, such as Bell, Anita C. "A Term Paper Resource Center." *School Library Journal* 38 (Jan. 1992): 34-36; Branner, Mary Ann. "The ACCESS PENNSYLVANIA Resource Center: Swartara Junior High School's 'Biggest Bang for the Buck!'" *Computers in Libraries* 14 (March 1994): 12-16; Callison, Daniel. "Expanding Collaboration for Literacy Promotion in Public and School Libraries." *Journal of Youth Services in Libraries* 11 (Fall 1997): 37-48; Commings, Karen. "Public/School Library Cooperation Highlights Two Automation Projects." *Computers in Libraries* 16 (Jan. 1997): 14, 16; Fitzgibbons, Shirely, and Verna Pungitore. "Educational Role and Services of Public Libraries in Indiana." *Indiana Libraries* 8 (1989): 3-56; Olson, Renee. "'Big Easy' Schools, PL Address Race in Collection." *School Library Journal* 43 (June 1997): 15; Ristau, Holly, "Suggestions for Public Library and School Library Cooperation." *Illinois Libraries*, 72 (Feb. 1990): 185-187.

3. Ford, Barbara "All Together Now." *School Library Journal* 42 (Apr. 1996): 48

4. Killock, Peter "Transforming Social Dilemmas: Group Identity and Cooperation." In *Modeling Rational and Moral Agents.* Ed. By Danielson, Peter. Oxford: Oxford University Press, 1997.

5. Schuyler, Michael "Libraries and Schools–The Technology of Cooperation." *Computers in Libraries* 16 (Jan. 1996): 43-45. Schuyler notes that school libraries rarely share their resources with public library constituencies and that academic librarians believe that public library collections do not have reciprocatory value to their college and university patrons; the Newark Public Library, however, hosts many college and university students, who appreciate the hand-holding provided in the public library setting; in addition, the Newark Public Library collections are quite large and therefore more adequately than other public libraries do serve college students.

6. Earlier, another Newark school contained a library jointly operated by the school and the public library, but security difficulties terminated that collaboration

7. Alaya, Ana M., and Jesse Drucker. "Libraries in 5 Newark Schools Still Closed for Renovation." *Newark Star Ledger* (Sept. 9, 1998), Essex ed.: 37.

8. Killock, Peter "Transforming Social Dilemmas: Group Identity and Cooperation." In *Modeling Rational and Moral Agents.* Ed. By Danielson, Peter. Oxford: Oxford University Press, 1997.

9. Gregory, Vicki, and Kathleen de la Pena McCook "Breaking the $30K Barrier." *Library Journal* 123 (Oct. 15, 1998): 38.

10. Public librarians learned these facts during teacher institutes.

11. Useful guidelines for a joint or independent planning process are outlined in Farmer, Lesley SJ. *Creative Partnerships: Librarians and Teachers Working Together.* Worthington, OH: Linworth Publishing, 1993.

12. Goldberg, Beverly "Public Libraries Go Back to School." *American Libraries* 27 (Dec. 1996): 54-55.

13. Similar to our brochure is Houdyshell, Mara L. "First Contact: Reaching out to Local Schools Before Their Students Reach Your Library." *Public Library Quarterly* 16 (1997): 57-63.

14. Kulthau, Carol C *Teaching the Library Research Process.* Metuchen, NJ: Scarecrow Press, 1994.

15. Small, Ruth V. "Designing Motivation into Library and Information Skills Instruction." *SLMQ Online* (1998), http://www.ala.org/aasl/SLMQ/small.html. Accessed 12 September 1998.

16. McGregor, Joy H, and Denice C. Streitenberger. "Do Scribes Learn? Copying and Information Use." *SLMQ Online* (1998), http://www.ala.org/aasl/SLMQ/scribes.html. Accessed 12 September 1998.

17. Nahl, Diane "What Are They Doing: Understanding Patron Behavior in Digital Environment." Responses to panelists at program by RUSA Machine Assisted Reference Section, American Library Association annual conference, Washington, D.C., June 28, 1998.

18. Baugh, Sue *How to Write Term Papers and Reports.* Linwood, IL: VGM Career Horizons, 1997.

19. Garrett, Linda J *Teaching Library Skills in Middle and High School: a How-to-Do-It Manual. New York:* Neal-Schuman, 1993.

20. Robinson, Adam *What Smart Students Know.* New York: Crown, 1993.

21. Vandergrift, Kay E *Power Teaching: A Primary Role of the School Library Media Specialist.* Chicago: American Library Association, 1994.

22. Wesley, Threasa L *Thinking and Learning Through Library Research: Your Guide to Successful Research Projects.* Dubuque, IA: Kendall/Hunt, 1993.

23. Recommendations in Gnage, David *Strategic Considerations to Be Used to Evaluate Joint Ventures.* ERIC, 1995. ED385329.

24. Similar visions are articulated in DelNegro, Janice M "In Unity, Strength: School/Library Cooperation at the Chicago Public Library." *Illinois Libraries* 72 (Feb. 1990): 132-136; Garland, Kathleen. "Children's Materials in the Public Library and the School Library Media Center in the Same Community: a Comparative Study of Use."" *Library Quarterly* 59 (Oct. 1989): 326-338; Kachel, D.E. "Improving Access to Periodicals: a Cooperative Collection Management Project. *School Library Media Quarterly* 16 (Winter 1996): 93-103; Rockfield, Gary. "Beyond Library Power." *School Library Journal* 44 (Jan. 1998): 30-33.

25. Hendricks, Susan "Re: How Do We Do It?" PubLib-L (Posted 17 Oct. 1998). Accessed 18 Oct. 1998. Publib@sunsite.berkeley.edu. Her description of the program conducted by five schools and six public libraries in rural Iowa is part of a thread in which subscribers discuss working with individual teachers and school systems; see the PubLib Archive, http://sunsite.berkeley.edu/PubLib/archive.html.

26. "Information Power: The Nine Information Literacy Standards for Student Learning" http://www.ala.org/aasl/ip_nine.html. Accessed 21 October 1998.

Orienting Neighborhood Youth to an Academic Library: Creating Campus-Community Connections

Robert Kudlay

SUMMARY. Early in 1997, full Web access was added to Babson Library's public workstations. In a few short months, library computers became a mecca for neighborhood youth. The library's "open door" philosophy and Springfield College's strategic vision to strengthen campus/community ties brought the library to the forefront of actively developing services for community youth. An outreach program for community youth was designed to address the issue of computer access. The development of the program involved the entire library and provided an opportunity for collaborative interaction among the library, related campus programs, and community agencies. Its impact on the library brought to the forefront the debate between "academic service" and "community service." *[Article copies available for a fee from The Haworth Document Delivery Service: 1-800-342-9678. E-mail address: getinfo@haworthpressinc.com <Website: http://www.haworthpressinc.com>]*

KEYWORDS. Community outreach, youth programming, campus-community relations

INTRODUCTION

At the beginning of the spring 1998 semester, Babson Library at Springfield College launched a community outreach initiative to pro-

Robert Kudlay is Reference Librarian, Babson Library, Springfield College, Springfield, MA (E-mail: rkudlay@spfldcol.edu).

[Haworth co-indexing entry note]: "Orienting Neighborhood Youth to an Academic Library: Creating Campus-Community Connections." Kudlay, Robert. Co-published simultaneously in *The Reference Librarian* (The Haworth Information Press, an imprint of The Haworth Press, Inc.) No. 67/68, 1999, pp. 111-130; and: *Library Outreach, Partnerships, and Distance Education: Reference Librarians at the Gateway* (ed: Wendi Arant, and Pixey Anne Mosley) The Haworth Press, Inc., 2000, pp. 111-130. Single or multiple copies of this article are available for a fee from The Haworth Document Delivery Service [1-800-342-9678, 9:00 a.m. - 5:00 p.m. (EST). E-mail address: getinfo@haworthpressinc.com].

vide computer training and library orientation to neighborhood youth. The program was the culmination of months of staff discussion and planning. Its focus was the creation of a structure to manage and provide service to a growing number of neighborhood youth during after-school and weekend hours using the library's public computer workstations with Internet access. This paper chronicles how Babson Library addressed the issue of creating a service structure to accommodate community youth using the library's computer resources.

"Outreach" may not be the most appropriate term to use in this context. Babson Library did not seek out or extend a formal invitation to community youth to use its facilities. Rather, they appeared in the library and continued to appear in increasing numbers. What attracted them to Babson Library was the library's proximity to their neighborhood and the library's resources, an attraction common to many urban academic libraries. "Compared to public libraries, their [academic library's] collections are strong; their facilities are usually accessible to handicapped individuals; their online bibliographic databases are accessible to many who have no affiliation with the institution; and the public perceives libraries as free for everyone to use" (Russell et al., 1992). Additionally, the sophisticated and extensive use of readily available technology, in particular, Internet access, at academic libraries frequently outstrips similar resources at either local public or school libraries. Given these resources and their attraction for community users, are there ways that academic libraries can adopt service options developed from more traditional outreach programs to address the issue of library use by external, non-affiliated users?

OUTREACH SERVICES

Much of the literature related to academic library outreach activities focuses on the expansion of services to faculty and students. Library/ faculty liaison activities, library-sponsored instruction, collection development initiatives, and relationships with campus technology and information service departments are examples of ways academic librarians develop new service strategies to enhance their ties within the academic community. All of these services share a common core. Whether they are based on personal or electronic contact, whether they are delivered in classrooms or residence halls, whether they are formalized in service manuals or policy directives, these services are designed for the benefit of an existing, traditional campus population: faculty, staff, and tuition-paying students.

Another category of outreach programming reaches beyond these traditional campus clients and is based on wider links between institutions. Here service is based on partnerships and cooperative inter-institutional arrangements. One of the most common examples of this linkage is in the relationship between academic communities and other educational entities. "Our whole educational system is inextricably linked. Education is a long-term process without artificial boundaries" (Stewart quoted in Watkins, 1990). This sentiment is rephrased and reiterated in both library administration and reference literature (Jesudason, 1993; Simon, 1992). Examples of these types of outreach alliances range from sharing technological resources (Garretson, 1994); developing wider community service initiatives (McCann and Peters, 1996; Bennett and others, 1993); participating in existing programs such as Upward Bound (Garcha and Baldwin, 1997); to creating new service alliances such as the Boston urban education collaborative (Davidson, 1998). President Clinton's 1998 State of the Union address reemphasized the goals common to all educational institutions with his resulting "High Hopes for College for America's Youth" initiative (Office of Postsecondary Education, 1998). Where the client population is not an integral component of the campus community, these outreach and partnering programs present new service and resource challenges for academic librarians (Miller and Russell, 1985). "Formal college/school partnerships create a need for organizational change and new communication structures" (Simon, 1992).

A third category of outreach programming–and one neglected in much of the professional literature–focuses on users with no formal ties to the library or institution. These are the "walk-in" patrons. Seldom can their resource or service needs be anticipated or predicted. If meeting the needs of inter-institutional alliances is problematic, then efforts to identify service options available to a wider, non-affiliated community can be almost insurmountable. For the non-affiliated library user, there are seldom any formal support structures at academic institutions available to define the scope or content of service options. "Among the problems facing urban university libraries are those caused by users who have no affiliation with the institution" (Verhoeven et al., 1996). These external users just happen to be geographically situated where educational and community resources are inadequate and where a healthy academic institution and library is available (Heath, 1992). It is with this group–urban youth–that Babson Library at Springfield College was challenged to develop innovative outreach options.

SPRINGFIELD COLLEGE AND BABSON LIBRARY

Springfield College is an inner city institution with an undergraduate population of about 2,800 students and a graduate population of about 700 students. Major areas of study fall under three of the College's schools: School of Arts, Sciences, and Professional Studies (about 39%), School of Human Services (about 29%), and School of Physical Education and Recreation (about 29%). Adjacent to the campus is the Upper Hill and Old Hill neighborhoods of Springfield. The two neighborhoods share several demographic characteristics that distinguish them from many of the city's other neighborhoods: race and ethnicity (Table 1); age (37% of Old Hill and 26% of Upper Hill residents are under the age of 18, demographically making these two neighborhoods among the "youngest" in the city); and recent population shifts (both neighborhoods have witnessed a significant increase in minority residents since 1980). In addition, Old Hill is one of the poorest neighborhoods in Springfield with the second highest percent of persons below the poverty line and the second lowest per capita income level (Springfield Planning Department, 1995 and 1996).

Springfield College supports a variety of partner alliances with local schools; several campus departments, notably Recreation and Leisure Services, have strong ties with city agencies such as the Parks and Recreation Department. There is also an expanding number of curriculum-based, service learning components offering after-school

TABLE 1. Race/Ethnicity of Adjacent Neighborhoods

	Old Hill	Upper Hill
Non-Hispanic Blacks	62.2%	59.2%
Non-Hispanic Whites	10.1%	30.6%
Hispanics	25.3%	9.1%

Source: Springfield Planning Dept., 1995, 1996

and weekend reading, tutoring, and mentoring opportunities for local grade school students. The College's long association with the YMCA (until 1953, Springfield College was known as the International YMCA Training College) has traditionally attracted a student body whose career goals are focused on human service professions. Springfield College's Vision Statement reiterates the College's central theme to be a "leader in educating people committed to a life of service through its programs in physical education, allied health sciences, and human and social services."

In November 1997, a campus-wide Institutional Priorities Committee was created to "identify the initiatives that are most central to the realization of our mission." Among the priorities was a goal to "undertake activities to build a community, both internally and with external neighbors." This initiative stated that the "college has much to gain from a closer interaction with its neighbors" and for the campus to "provide resources to implement the initiatives with the external neighborhood" (Odierna, 1998).

During the spring and summer of 1997, the topics of community access to Babson Library and the library's relationship with the campus neighborhood were discussed at staff meetings, supervisor meetings, and reference meetings. The library is a member of the Cooperating Libraries of Greater Springfield (CLGS) consortium, providing a framework to offer circulation privileges to students from other area colleges and to city residents holding a Public Library card. Access to Babson Library's open stack collection has always been available to any youth accompanied by an adult. One area of library resources not covered by these policies was the recently networked bank of public access computer workstations featuring full Web access, the library's online catalog, and a growing number of bibliographic and full-text databases. By the end of the 1997 spring semester it was apparent that neighborhood youth had discovered the library's public workstations and were using the computers in increasing numbers and with increasing regularity.

The question of staff responsibilities in dealing with youth who were using the library's public workstations became one of the most discussed and debated topics in the library. An exploratory meeting of the Library Director, Senior Reference Librarian, and the Reference Instruction Coordinator was scheduled to meet with the campus Director of Student Volunteer Services to review the impact and possible

service options related to the use of the library's computer workstations by neighborhood youth. At this meeting four broad strategies
were outlined:

1. collect data on the number of youth using the library's computer
   workstations;
2. formulate a plan to address the needs of these youth that was
   consistent with the library's vision and service goals;
3. address the issue of library staff awareness with respect to community youth using library facilities;
4. find ways to identify these youth: were they local, what schools
   did they attend, why were they using the library, and did they
   have access to other computer resources?

COLLECTING DATA ON YOUTH USE

The reference desk was the logical place to begin collecting user
data. The bank of public workstations is immediately in view of the
reference desk and reference staff ordinarily rove in order to answer
questions and intercept possible technical problems arising from patrons using the workstations. Usage statistics for ready-reference and
research-oriented questions are kept at the reference desk in an hourly
log. With this log already in place, the reference desk became the
logical place to track youth activity at the computer workstations.

The log sheet is an hourly tick-check of patron interaction in two
categories: (a) questions asked that are identified as "ready reference"
and (b) questions asked that are "research oriented." Two additional
columns were added to the reference log: (c) questions asked by
"youth," and (d) an hourly "youth headcount." For the purpose of the
youth headcounts, "youth" was defined as anyone under 18 who was
neither a student at Springfield College nor a participant registered in a
Springfield College program. Reference staff was not required to
check identification of computer users. Rather, it was by way of non-
intrusive observation that computer users were identified as "youth."
The headcounts, like the other entries in the reference log, were kept
on an hourly basis.

Youth counts were added to the reference log at the end of May
1997. Use of the computer workstations by youth was fairly regular
during the summer, beginning in the mornings and lasting throughout

the day. A total of 258 youth were counted during the first month (Table 2a). Use patterns shifted when the fall semester began and public schools were back in session. Weekends and the hours between four and seven on weekdays saw the heaviest traffic. Although youth were at the computers for fewer hours per day in the fall as compared to the summer, their numbers continued to increase (Table 2b).

TABLE 2a. Hourly Youth Headcount: June 1997

	Mon.	Tues.	Wed.	Thurs.	Fri.	Sat.	Sun.	Total
8:00 am	0	0	0	0	0	n/a	n/a	0
9:00	1	3	0	0	0	n/a	n/a	4
10:00	3	1	0	1	7	2	n/a	14
11:00	1	1	0	1	7	2	n/a	12
12:00	3	1	1	1	14	0	0	20
1:00 pm	4	4	4	11	17	3	6	49
2:00	9	4	3	13	7	2	11	49
3:00	3	0	0	11	0	2	4	20
4:00	5	4	0	7	n/a	6	2	24
5:00	8	9	1	2	n/a	2	2	24
6:00	4	11	4	8	n/a	n/a	n/a	27
7:00	7	5	1	2	n/a	n/a	n/a	15

Total for June 1997: 258   n/a = library not open

TABLE 2b. Hourly Youth Headcount: October 1997

	Mon.*	Tues.	Wed.	Thurs.	Fri.	Sat.	Sun.	Total
8:00 am	0	0	0	0	0	n/a	n/a	0
9:00	0	0	0	0	0	0	n/a	0
10:00	0	0	0	0	0	8	n/a	8
11:00	3	0	0	0	0	8	n/a	11
12:00	3	0	0	0	0	7	11	21
1:00 pm	5	0	0	0	0	7	13	25
2:00	5	0	0	0	0	6	16	27
3:00	0	0	4	1	0	13	13	31
4:00	9	8	9	6	5	16	10	63
5:00	9	15	12	10	5	22	15	88
6:00	4	12	15	8	0	15	12	66
7:00	0	0	0	6	0	5	4	15
8:00	0	0	0	0	n/a	n/a	2	2
9:00	0	0	0	0	n/a	n/a	0	0
10:00	0	0	0	0	n/a	n/a	0	0
11:00	0	0	0	0	n/a	n/a	0	0

Total for October: 357   n/a = library not open
* Monday morning use can be attributed to public school holidays.

FORMULATING A PLAN FOR YOUTH

Data collected from the headcounts verified library staff opinion that youths were using computers in the library and that few, if any, library procedures existed to provide service to them. Compounding the lack of library service options, there seemed to be few campus programs or resources available to provide an alternative for youth frequenting the library. In fact, requests from other campus programs were being made for the library to provide instruction to area high school classes, to participate in programs teaching teachers how to integrate electronic resources into classroom activities, and to offer computer orientation sessions for local community center groups.

Various library departments explored separate but interrelated avenues related to providing uniform service to youth. The library administration investigated the possibility of making available a campus "guest" identification card for participants in a variety of campus programs (including youth) to provide a common and recognizable identification and tracking mechanism for facility access to campus guests. The library circulation staff reviewed its policies regarding library users not directly affiliated with Springfield College, particularly in relation to existing reciprocal borrowing arrangements with the Springfield City Public Library. There is no charge or other financial impediment to get a public library card, and anyone with a public library card could obtain a Babson Library card to borrow books. The only real obstacle for getting a public library card is that youth had to request a card at the main library or one of its branches. Youth who attended schools and participated in community programs but had never been to the main library or one of its branches would not have a public library card. This information needed to be communicated to youth in the library and, if they did not have a public library card, provisions for them to get one needed to be incorporated into any youth program.

The reference department, however, felt the greatest impact of youth use. Its background in resource and computer instruction needed to be translated into a service program that would address the need for youth to learn about using the library's networked computers as well as gain a greater appreciation about using the Internet and related electronic information tools.

Invited to attend these early discussions were the Director of Volunteer Services on campus, the Outreach Coordinator at the Springfield City Public Library, and the Youth Services Coordinator at the Western Massachusetts Regional Library System (WMRLS). Topics addressed at these meetings included: availability of additional student staffing in the library to work with youth; cooperative arrangements with the city library to provide information to youth about getting a city library card and about resources and programs available through the public library system; and, WMRLS-sponsored workshops appropriate for library staff to learn more about youth services and resource development.

A final component in the development of a preliminary youth service initiative was the question of computer access. An underlying concern was that the implementation of any youth program in the library would increase rather than decrease youth demands on the workstations and on the public service staff. Reference, library administration, and the College Information Technology Services Department met and scheduled the computer training lab in the library for youth sessions to be held two days a week: on a weekday afternoon between four and seven p.m. and on Sundays between two and six p.m. The lab would provide a non-public area for youth activities and offer a classroom environment for youth instruction.

By late fall 1997 a basic outline for a "model" library youth program was in place: student staffing dedicated to youth services; interlibrary cooperation; future staff training options; and availability of computer classroom space.

STAFF AWARENESS

Although computer use by youth was a fact of life in the library, there was little agreement among library staff about its desirability. Staff attitudes ranged from observations about the library becoming a "local hangout" (one comment suggested that the library was beginning to look like a shopping mall) to concerns that the library had neither adequately trained staff or appropriate resources to deal with youth (a common refrain was "I chose to be an academic librarian, not a children's librarian or babysitter"). In an informal survey of library staff regarding youth access and service, diversity of opinion was readily apparent. Below are the first three questions on the survey and a sampling of the responses:

1. What is your opinion about youth under the age of thirteen using Babson Library?

I think that no matter what their age may be, as long as they act in a mature manner and abide by the rules of the youth program, that they should have access to the services provided by the library.

I don't enjoy policing little kids, asking them to be quiet, etc. I also do not like to see a lot of printing of cartoons, rap lyrics, etc.

I have more mixed feelings on this group than the teenagers. But my bottom line is–better Babson Library than hanging out on the street. We may have a chance to turn these children on to learning and will never be able to measure the impact on their lives. . . . It's not as much the content of what they are researching but the comfort level they have in a library and working with librarians and computers.

This is a thoroughly wretched idea.

Mixed. Part of me thinks that it's wonderful that kids that age want to come to the library and that they should be encouraged. The other part of me is stressed, feeling like I have to watch them and may have to intervene if any problems come up.

2. What is your opinion about young adults between the ages of 13 and 18 using Babson Library?

When they are trying to do homework, I'm generally pleased to try and help them (they're looking for information as opposed to the younger ones who are mainly amusing themselves, even though they may be learning in the process) although I often have to refer them to the public library for more appropriate resources.

The YAs [Young Adults] have proved to be more "rowdy" than the younger kids. At times it seems more difficult to quiet them down. There are times I feel like our students may be intimidated by a group of Young Adults.

I have less problems with them in the library since they've had more schooling (perhaps even had to write a research paper) and are theoretically more able to take care of themselves.

For the most part I'm seeing older kids doing more in the way of research than recreational surfing and I feel better about that. That's what I lean towards believing academic libraries are for. They are also closer to the age group I've been trained to work with, and so I'm more comfortable talking to them.

3. What impact do you think offering services to these age groups has on the library?

I believe it is a good way to share our resources with the community.

Morale has suffered to a certain extent. Some staff members and librarians have been gruff with the kids which does not do the library's image any good. . . . On the plus side, I do think what we are doing has enhanced our image in the community which I believe is important. I think we may have already had a positive effect on inner-city kids' lives.

Most academic librarians didn't sign on to deal with children and I think the advent of this program has had an impact on the public services staff that deal with them.

I think that providing supervision is very time consuming, and as a result our students get poorer reference service when there are several youth in the library.

. . . it takes energy and resources away from other areas and increases the stress on employees–after all this is work we neither chose nor trained for.

Although literature focusing on the role of academic libraries serving external users is relatively sparse and serving nonaffiliated youth almost non-existent, staff attitudes at Babson Library reflected wider professional concerns about library security, limited resources, and service priorities. Extending services to local neighborhood residents is frequently based on public relations strategies and a philosophical commitment to service in general regardless of primary clientele (Johnson, 1984) rather than as a natural extension of traditional on-campus library services. To a large degree, staff attitudes echoed this conflict between "academic service" and a philosophical commitment to "community service."

To address some of the concerns expressed by library staff and to help focus staff attention on the broader issue of library-community relations, the Director of Volunteer Services worked with the library to arrange a meeting with community leaders. The Youth Development Coordinator from the Martin Luther King Community Center, which serves the neighborhoods adjacent to campus, was invited to partici-pate in a library staff meeting where the issue of youth access to the library and library service options were aired. At this October 1997 meeting the topic of youth services shifted away from narrow proce-dure-based discussions and began to center on issues such as youth/staff interactions and understanding youth needs.

FINDING WAYS TO IDENTIFY YOUTHS

The library's "open door" philosophy regarding access to public services and computer resources prohibited identification of youth users except informally during personal contact. Were the youth from neighboring communities? Did they attend schools where the college already had a partner or other program relationship? Were they public library users? What were their interests? Why were they using Babson Library? Although not strictly analogous to the type of information (such as subject discipline, extent of library training, computer litera-cy) about campus users appropriate in designing and implementing on-campus outreach programs, this type of information about youth users could help in structuring appropriate programming as well as help identify other campus programs addressing similar areas.

Simply registering individuals to use the public workstations (simi-lar to requesting a reciprocal borrowing card to check-out books) would have supplied this basic information without jeopardizing the library's open access philosophy. But registration alone would not have addressed any of the other service-related concerns. Instead, a compulsory library orientation session was designed as part of an overall youth program. Registration from this orientation session would provide information about youth users and the session itself would help guarantee that youth using the library received basic instruction about the library, its staff, its resources, and its policies.

The registration form was made available at the reference desk along with a schedule of orientation dates and computer lab times set aside for youth programming. The information requested on the form included name, address and telephone number of the youth as well as school attended and whether the youth had a city library card. Two general questions were also asked: what hobbies and interests the youth had, and the reasons they were using Babson Library. With the absence of a generic campus "guest" card, the library prepared a Library Youth Card (later to become known as the "yellow card" because it was printed on canary card stock). Youth attending one of the orientation sessions would receive the youth card. A copy of the library's new policy was printed on the registration form and posted in the public service area. The policy was a brief, one sentence statement: "Computer use by youth will be restricted to those who have a Library Youth Card, or are registered in a Springfield College Program, or are accompanied by an adult."

BABSON LIBRARY YOUTH PROGRAM

After the various discussion and planning meetings during the summer and fall of 1997, the Library Youth Program was scheduled to begin in January 1998. Funds from the Office of Student Volunteer Services were made available to the library to hire a Student Youth Assistant who would be responsible for offering the orientation sessions. A student already working in the reference department was hired as the Student Youth Assistant. Her knowledge about library resources and policies and her computer coursework made her an ideal candidate to offer the orientation sessions and training in the computer training lab. The Instruction Coordinator from the reference staff was named as the Youth Program Coordinator to supervise the Student Youth Assistant and to oversee the program. The library supplied basic supplies for the program, such as paper, printing, and computer disks.

A final decision before the program's start in January concerned promotion of the program. It was obvious that there was sufficient youth traffic in the library to justify the program, but there was considerable hesitancy about its promotion outside the library. A generally expressed concern was that promotion of the program would increase rather than stabilize youth traffic and require additional library resources to maintain the program. Thus, during the spring semester, information about the program and registration for the orientation sessions was limited to in-library contact. As the program developed, the young people spread the word about the program to their friends and neighbors.

The first part of the Youth Program consisted of a required one-hour orientation session when library policy, expected in-library behavior, roles of various library staff, review of library services, and computer use policies were presented. Information about City Library services was also distributed at the session. Two positive outcomes grew out of these orientation sessions. First, youth came to know the Student Assistant as well as a number of library staff on a more personal level. Second, there was gradual reduction of the number of times when library staff intervention was required on the floor to explain or enforce library policy. Registration for the orientation session also provided library staff with an option for dealing with new youth coming into the library. Instead of being forced into a role of reciting policy and procedures to newcomers, staff had the opportunity to invite youth to register for one of the orientation sessions.

In addition to the orientation sessions, the Student Assistant prepared and offered regular activities in the computer training lab. When the computer lab was not available for the program because of conflicts with other library instruction classes, alternate activities were scheduled, including help-with-homework sessions, tours of the library's open stacks for youth to select books to read and share with each other, walking tours of the campus, and visits to the campus snack bar. The campus tours proved to be very popular. Many of the youth wanted to see what a dorm room looked like and what college students did in their spare time. Eating at the campus snack bar was, in the words of one youth, "as good as McDonalds." These tours helped to develop a bond between the youth and the Student Assistant and to build in the youth a sense of belonging to the campus community as a whole.

Over the course of the semester, the activities designed for the computer lab focused on four general areas: enhanced computer literacy; instruction on appropriate online resources (such as Web access to the Encyclopedia Britannica); creative design activities using paint, presentation, and word processing software; and introduction to Web sites based on a bibliography of youth-oriented sites prepared by library staff. These activities were geared toward younger users under the age of 12. Older youth (Table 3) who attended the orientation session but for whom these activities would have been inappropriate, were able to use the computer lab and were monitored by the Student Assistant.

The basic framework for the Youth Program was outlined in a memo distributed to library staff:

> The Library's Student Youth Assistant will be offering four 1-hour Orientation sessions for youth using Babson Library. Youth interested in attending must register for these sessions. There are registration forms at the Reference Desk. The sessions are scheduled for the Training Center.

> Youth attending one of the sessions will receive a 'Babson Library Youth Card.' After February 4, only youth with one of these cards may use the library computers. It is up to library staff to ask to see the card and to inform youth of the Orientation sessions if they do not have a card. Having one of these cards does not give youth borrowing privileges or any other library privileges.

> Additional Orientation sessions can be scheduled after February 4 (at the same Wednesday and Sunday times) for youth who were not aware of the first four scheduled sessions.

> The Orientation sessions will provide information about getting a Springfield City Library card and a librarian from the City Library will be presenting additional information.

> Throughout the semester, the Student Youth Assistant will be able to use the Training Center during her hours working as Youth Assistant (Sundays and Wednesdays) unless the Training Center has been booked for other uses. During these times, the Youth Assistant will act as a monitor for youth using the Training Center and will be preparing youth-oriented activities using the Training Center computers and other library resources.

TABLE 3. Ages of Youth Registered for Orientation Session

AGE	under 9	9-10	11-12	13-14	15-16	17-18	Total
NUMBER	8	21	33	23	14	2	101

January 1998 to May 1998

AFTERWARDS AND AFTERTHOUGHTS

As the Youth Program continued throughout the semester, library staff, the Youth Coordinator, and the Student Youth Assistant kept in regular contact, reexamining the progress of the program and fine tuning it as new issues arose. One noted concern was the knowledge of library staff in designing youth-oriented activities. To address this issue, the Youth Coordinator attended several youth service workshops sponsored by the Western Massachusetts Regional Library System. At one of these workshops (Braun, 1998) a checklist of twelve items useful in the implementation and evaluation of interactive youth projects was discussed.

1. enough computers for hands-on training;
2. a good (stable and fast) Internet connection;
3. a published and clear Computer Use Policy;
4. interaction with non-computer library resources and program options;
5. knowledge of computer use and Internet resources by the instructor;
6. a connection (either formal or informal) with curriculum activities;
7. enough staff time to prepare and implement the program;
8. age-appropriate activities;
9. skill level of youth (how much computer instruction do they need?);
10. availability of experts outside the library for special projects;
11. clearly understood goals for the program;
12. commitment by the library to the program.

For items 1 through 5 library resources were available to meet the demands of the Program. Item 6, connection with curriculum activities, was met incidentally when youth themselves brought in their homework assignments. Item 7, sufficient staff time, was partly solved by the hiring of a Student Assistant, but the student's part-time status proved inadequate to monitor lab use, provide orientation sessions, and prepare weekly activities. In addition, nearly one-quarter of a reference librarian's time was devoted to oversight and management of the program as its Coordinator. Items 8, 9, and 10 were met by training workshops available from WMRLS and cooperation from city library staff.

Overall, several of the principal goals that the drove initial discussions leading to the implementation of the Youth Program were met in part if not fully:

- ☒ The Program maintained with minor modification the library's open access policy;
- ☒ It reduced (though not eliminated) tensions in staff/youth interaction;
- ☒ It provided a structure for youth to participate in the use of library resources with greater awareness and understanding;
- ☒ It brought the library staff into direct contact with other programs on campus and in the community that shared concerns about the local resources available to local youth;
- ☒ It offered students working in the library a unique opportunity to apply their service skills to a broader, more diverse group of library users;
- ☒ As a model program, it provided a kind of litmus test by which future programming efforts could be compared.

One original concern about the implementation of the program was that it would attract more youth into the library, bringing additional congestion to the library's workstations. Although the number of youth who registered for the orientation session exceeded expectations (30 to 40 had been anticipated, and over 100 eventually participated), the headcount of youth at the public workstations actually decreased as the programs in the computer lab became available. During the seven months in 1997 before the program began, the average monthly youth headcount was 289 (Table 4a) while for the five months in 1998 when the program was offered, the average dropped to 178 per month (Table 4b).

Regarding item 12, library resources devoted to the program were

TABLE 4a. Monthly Youth Count in 1997

June	July	Aug.	Sept.	Oct.	Nov.	Dec.	Total
258	397	243	218	357	356	186	2,015

Average per month: 289

TABLE 4b. Monthly Youth Count in 1998

Jan.	Feb	Mar.	Apr.	May	Total
237	273	173	114	95	892

Average per month: 178

provided on an as-need basis. This included additional staff time, computer resources, and incidentals such as printing and paper supplies.

In the Program's final month of May, the library submitted a grant proposal to a local community agency for funds to continue the Program in the fall of 1998 and spring of 1999. The grant request highlighted resource needs and future program development ideas. Funds for additional staffing, acquisition of age-appropriate software, and a promotional budget were requested. For program design, the request focused on increased community input and involvement, stronger ties with existing campus programs, and staff awareness and training activities. The grant was successfully funded in the summer of 1998.

With the grant, Babson Library was able to continue and expand its Youth Program in October, 1998 by hiring additional student youth assistants to organize and run the orientation sessions and to monitor and supervise scheduled computer lab hours. The grant also provided funds to hire a half-time staff member to work with the Reference Department to develop additional program efforts. Computer training lab scheduling was increased from 2 days a week to 4 days a week. A campus photo ID replaced the original library-produced Youth ID. The campus ID also provided access to other campus facilities and resources to youth participants in the library youth program.

The Program, however, did not settle with any finality some of the more critical concerns embedded in one of the first questions asked by a member of the reference staff: Why even bother having kids in a college library? The core conflict between "academic service" and "community service" was never put completely to rest either in the library or on the campus as a whole. And at the root of it all were the youth themselves. Were they served well at Babson Library because of the implementation of the Youth Program? Or were they served well by the Program because of the absence of equivalent programs available to them in the public sector?

REFERENCES

Bennett, J. A., Fowler, M. L. and Ankerson, N. (1993). Town & gown: partners in educational services. Jekyll Island, GA: Georgia Council of Media Organizations. (ERIC Document Reproduction Service ED364165).

Braun, L. W. (1998). Internet projects in schools and public libraries. Hatfield, MA: Western Massachusetts Regional Library System. Workshop presented on May 15, 1998.

Davidson, P. S. (1998). The Greater Boston urban education collaborative. *Education 118(3)*, 353-358.

Garcha, R., and Julia B. (1997). Bibliographic instruction for the Upward Bound residential students. *The Reference Librarian 58*, 135-141.

Garretson, A. L. (1994). A Cooperative CD-ROM network: school libraries and Mansfield University. *Computers in Libraries 14(2)*, 42-46.

Heath, F. (1992). Conflict of mission: The midsize private university in an urban environment. In Gerald B. McCabe (Ed.), *Academic Libraries in Urban and Metropolitan Areas* (pp. 15-23). New York: Greenwood Press.

Jesudason, M. (1993). Academic libraries and outreach services through precollege programs: a proactive collaboration. *Reference Services Review 21(4)*, 29-36,96.

Johnson, B. L. (1984). A Case study in closing the university library to the public. *College & Research Libraries News 45(6)*, 404-407.

Kudlay, R. (1998). *My Diary: Chronology of the Babson Library Youth Program from the Beginnings of the Library Network to Future Funding Options.* Unpublished Project Report, Springfield College, Springfield, MA.

McCann, R. and Peters, C. D. (1996). At-risk youth: the Phoenix phenomenon. *JOPERD 67(2)*, 38-41.

Miller, R. and Russell, R. (1985). Implications of high school student use of academic libraries. (ERIC Document Reproduction Service ED269024).

Monsour, M. (1996). Getting connected at a local level to benefit the community. *American Libraries 27(8)*, 58-60

Odierna, J. (1998). Priority Initiatives for Springfield College. Memo to the college community. Springfield College, February 26.

Office of Postsecondary Education. *High hopes for college for America's youth.* (1998). Online: http://www.ed.gov/offices/OPE/PPI/highhopes.html. (Accessed March 19, 1998).

Russell, R. E, Robison, C. L., Prather, J. E., and Carlson, C. E.. (1992). External user access to academic libraries in urban/metropolitan areas. In Gerald B. McCabe (Ed.), *Academic Libraries in Urban and Metropolitan Areas* (pp. 27-32). New York: Greenwood Press.

Simon, M. (1992). Forging new organizational and communications structures: The college library school library partnership. *Library Administration & Management 6(1)*, 36-40.

Springfield Planning Department. (1995). *Old Hill Neighborhood.* Springfield, MA: Springfield Planning Department.

Springfield Planning Department. (1996). *Upper Hill Neighborhood.* Springfield, MA: Springfield Planning Department.

Ury, C. J. (1996). Value-added: high school research projects in an academic library. *The Clearing House 69(5)*, 313-315.

Verhoeven, S., Cooksey, E. B., and Hand, C. A. (1996). The Disproportionate use of reference desk service by external users at an urban university library. *RQ 35(3)*, 392-397.

Watkins, T. W. (1990, June 27). Collaboration between schools and colleges called best strategy for reform. *The Chronicle of Higher Education (36)*, A15, A18.

Providing Library Outreach
to Student Athletes

Maureen Puffer-Rothenberg
Susan E. Thomas

SUMMARY. Student athletes' schedules can be very tightly structured around classes, homework, study, practice, and athletic events. As a result, they do not have the same freedom with their schedules as the average student. A library outreach program was developed at Valdosta State University to target the Department of Health, Physical Education and Athletics, and specifically the student athletes. The goals of this program are: (1) to provide the Department faculty and staff with a library contact or liaison, (2) to help student athletes learn to use the Library more effectively under pressure, thus relieving some of the stress they face with their demanding schedules, and (3) to make the library a less intimidating, more welcoming environment. The Library's outreach program is incorporated into the Department's NCAA CHAMPS (Challenging Athletes' Minds for Personal Success) program and includes tailored library instruction sessions. CHAMPS, as designed by the NCAA, does not currently include a library skills component.[1] Library outreach may be defined as any activity or program such as tailored library instruction that is created "to meet the information needs of an unserved or inadequately served target group."[2] Outreach activities often focus on a specific user population such as high school students, off-campus students, international students, non-traditional students, and even faculty, and are often a method of promoting the use of the library.[3] Providing outreach to student athletes is not well documented, however, there are a handful of universities with some type of outreach program to student athletes in

---

Maureen Puffer-Rothenberg is Catalog Librarian, and Susan E. Thomas is Reference Librarian/Facilitator, both at Odum Library, Valdosta State University, Valdosta, GA 31698.

[Haworth co-indexing entry note]: "Providing Library Outreach to Student Athletes." Puffer-Rothenberg, Maureen, and Susan E. Thomas. Co-published simultaneously in *The Reference Librarian* (The Haworth Information Press, an imprint of The Haworth Press, Inc.) No. 67/68, 1999, pp. 131-146; and: *Library Outreach, Partnerships, and Distance Education: Reference Librarians at the Gateway* (ed: Wendi Arant, and Pixey Anne Mosley) The Haworth Press, Inc., 2000, pp. 131-146. Single or multiple copies of this article are available for a fee from The Haworth Document Delivery Service [1-800-342-9678, 9:00 a.m. - 5:00 p.m. (EST). E-mail address: getinfo@haworthpressinc.com].

131

place.[4] *[Article copies available for a fee from The Haworth Document Delivery Service: 1-800-342-9678. E-mail address: getinfo@haworthpressinc.com <Website: http://www.haworthpressinc.com>]*

KEYWORDS. University libraries, outreach to athletes, library instruction

INTRODUCTION

Valdosta State University's Odum Library began an outreach program to student athletes in September 1996. The program is primarily a library instruction program for the Department of Health, Physical Education and Athletics where the Librarians work with the Department Faculty and Coaches to provide orientations, tailored library instruction, and one-on-one contact with all student athletes. The Librarians also provide research assistance to the Department Faculty in their use of the library. The overall goal of the program is to assist with the academic success of the student athletes.

HISTORY

Valdosta State University is one of two Regional Universities within the University System of Georgia offering a Bachelor's, Master's, or Doctoral degree in 94 programs covering Education, Business, Arts and Sciences, Nursing, and Social Work. The University was established in 1906 as an all-women's college and became co-educational in 1950; in 1995 the College became Valdosta State University. The current enrollment is approximately 9,800 students.[5]

Collegiate athletics began at VSU during the 1954-55 academic year with the establishment of a men's basketball program. Currently, "11 sports, six for men: football, cross country, basketball, tennis, baseball and golf, and five for women: cross country, basketball, fast-pitch softball, tennis and volleyball"[6] are offered. Cheerleading and the basketball dance troupe are also coordinated through the Department of Health, Physical Education, and Athletics. Valdosta State University "competes on the NCAA Division II level and is a member of the Gulf South Conference."[7]

WHY ATHLETES?

As there are many student populations that can benefit from a library outreach program, why choose to target student athletes? Student athletes have very demanding schedules and as a result, they do not enjoy the same freedom and flexibility with their schedules that the average student enjoys. For example, a student athlete may come in to use the library at 8:00 p.m. after having been in class all day, practice after classes, and finally supper. He has come to the library to find articles he needs for his paper and it may be his first time in the library. He may attempt to find the information he needs on his own which will take him awhile if he is unfamiliar with using the library. He may ask a librarian for simple directions or assistance believing he has some idea of what he is looking for. Two hours later, he may still be attempting to find the articles he needs even after assistance from a librarian or library employee. If he had been more familiar with the library and how to find information in the library, he would have been able to come to the library and locate his articles in half the time it took him to find what he needed in an unfamiliar setting. This example is based on an actual encounter one of the Information Services Librarians had with a student athlete and was a motivating factor in establishing the outreach program.

The academic success of student athletes or lack thereof is a common issue on many college campuses. It is not uncommon to find newspaper and magazine articles discussing the inability of student athletes to succeed academically. Student athletes are pushed by coaches and trainers to excel at their sport with little notice given to their academic ability. Collegiate sports generate a significant percentage of yearly revenue for many colleges and universities; when this is the case, the institution must focus on putting together a winning team regardless of whether individual students can compete off the playing field: " . . . many student athletes are recruited by college and universities solely for their excellence in sports, while the educational side of their college experience is often ignored. Thus many of these students are encouraged to apply for admission not on any academic basis, but with the focus solely on their athleticism. Not surprisingly, such students are often ill-prepared for the academic rigor that leads to graduation. In the extreme, there have been instances where enrolled athletes were unable to read a newspaper, balance a checkbook or write a simple expository paragraph."[8]

The National Collegiate Athletic Association (NCAA) enacted Proposition 48 in 1983, to put the focus back on education by requiring all first year incoming student athletes to have earned a grade-point average of 2.0 or better in eleven core college preparatory courses. In addition, students are required to have a minimum score of seven hundred on the SAT or fifteen on the ACT to be eligible to play sports their first year. "The intent of the legislation was to create standards for academic preparation at the high school level that would insure a student athlete of a fair chance to earn a college degree."[9] In 1992, Proposition 48, was revised to require a grade point average of 2.5 or better. While Proposition 48 has received a fair amount of criticism it has forced both high school and college coaches to focus not just on the game, but on the classroom as well.

With so much emphasis placed on excelling in sports, academic achievement and preparation for life after college can become secondary to the development of athletically based relationships and abilities, unless the student is offered specifically targeted guidance and support. Odum Library's outreach program is designed to provide targeted academic support. The Library's efforts are geared towards helping student athletes become familiar with using the library so that when they are trying to complete an assignment under pressure to meet class deadlines, with physical fatigue as a compounding factor, they are not faced with the added stress of learning how to use the library. Another factor in providing outreach to student athletes is the issue of retention. Retention of students, especially minority student athletes, is a concern on many campuses.[10] By assisting student athletes with their use of the library we are making it easier for them to successfully complete assignments in order to pass their classes and remain in school.

GETTING STARTED

The outreach program was started by making personal contacts, reviewing the literature, and conducting a discussion list survey. The Library contacted the Director of Athletics at VSU to discuss the possibility of such a program. He was able to refer the librarians to several faculty members to work with to develop tailored library instruction. The faculty approached were agreeable and enthusiastic about the proposal.

The literature specifically addressing library outreach to student athletes is sparse and it was difficult to find information about outreach programs aimed at student athletes that might be running at other institutions. A search of *Library Literature* from 1984 to the present yielded only two articles specifically addressing library education programs for student athletes, one at the University of Central Florida and the other at the University of Wisconsin.

The University of Central Florida's program involves two one-hour class sessions for Freshmen. During the first session, students work in pairs to develop topic sentences for possible theses, and in the second session identify journal articles on a topic, locate journals in the online catalog, and identify different journal formats.[11] The University of Wisconsin's outreach program schedules two one-hour sessions whenever possible for student athletes. In the first session students are introduced to the campus libraries and to the use of subject dictionaries and encyclopedias. Students complete an exercise in online searching. Smaller classes are given a demonstration of online searching, while larger classes receive an explanation of search types. The University of Wisconsin utilizes a second session when possible to provide instruction on using the *Reader's Guide to Periodical Literature*, understanding citations, and finding journals. In the assignment for the second session, students are asked to locate one journal or magazine article on a specific subject.[12] Melba Jesudason, a Public Services Librarian at the University of Wisconsin asserts that many student athletes are so unprepared to use a college library that bibliographic instruction classes designed for athletes "must start with basic concepts . . . [and] be more slowly paced" than those designed for other students.[13]

In September 1997, the librarians posted an inquiry to BI-L, an Internet discussion list for bibliographic instruction librarians, stating their intention to start a new instruction/outreach program aimed at student athletes and asking whether other libraries had similar programs in place. The posting led to an online debate over whether "special" library instruction or services should be offered to student athletes, or to any other group set apart from the rest of the campus population[14] Several librarians questioned the logic of developing bibliographic instruction programs based on students' involvement in a non-academic extracurricular activity. Were we discriminating against other students by offering instruction specifically to athletes–or against the athletes themselves by targeting them as a group needing special help? Were we setting a precedent that would require us in the future to create instruction programs for other groups of students linked only by non-academic activities?

Some respondents felt that the tight schedules imposed on student athletes (particularly due to frequent attendance at out-of-town games) placed them in a uniquely challenging position academically and therefore made them a logical choice for targeted, intensely focused group instruction. Others expressed their eagerness to work with any group requesting and willing to receive library instruction; for these respondents, targeted group instruction programs were not incompatible with their goal of providing service to the student body overall.

THE FIRST SESSION

The first library outreach activity designed for student athletes was a course-integrated library instruction session for one of the CHAMPS classes. CHAMPS, Challenging Athletes' Minds for Personal Success, is a NCAA program for student athletes. The program provides student athletes with life skills training they may not receive in college such as etiquette and proper nutrition.[15] Schools interested in participating in the CHAMPS program must apply with the NCAA. CHAMPS is composed of five sections: academic, athletic, career development, personal development, and commitment to service. Each section focuses on a specific aspect of a life skill such as personal/health issues or study skills.[16] The academic section focuses on study skills, time management, and goal setting, but as discovered after some review, the program does not specifically cover use of the library. Working with the Valdosta State University Coordinator for CHAMPS, a course-integrated library instruction section is being developed for each section.

The first CHAMPS library orientation was conducted in February 1997. It was scheduled for two hours during the regular class time. This particular CHAMPS class was for Freshmen and Sophomores and focused on an aspect of the academic section. The librarians tailored their instruction to include use of the online catalog, GALILEO databases, and print indexes.

GALILEO is an acronym for Georgia Library Learning Online. It is a state funded Web based database system allowing Georgia colleges and universities to share resources.[17] Over 150 databases are available in GALILEO, some with full-text information. Most of the databases in GALILEO have the same graphical user interface making it easy to learn how to search not one, but many of the databases offered.

Sports related topics such as salaries of professional athletes were used as search examples to keep the students interested in the presentation. The students were given a demonstration on searching the online catalog by author, title, or subject. Keyword searching was demonstrated with an explanation of Boolean searching. The physical layout of Odum Library was explained, as well as the location and arrangement of periodicals and books. Obtaining materials not owned by Odum Library through Interlibrary Loan was covered. A brief explanation on using print indexes, such as *SportSearch*, was included.

After the instruction session, students were given an in-class assignment (Appendix 1) on using the various resources shown to reinforce what had been presented. The assignments were collected at the end of the class to provide feedback on the effectiveness of their instruction efforts. If a student answered a question incorrectly, it suggested that the presentation was either ineffective or so boring that the student had not paid attention. Efforts are made to modify and improve instruction efforts where teaching weaknesses are noted.

VSU 101 ORIENTATION

The next outreach activity offered was course-integrated instruction for a section of a VSU 101 class specifically reserved for student athletes. The VSU 101 course provides students, usually Freshmen, with an introduction to life at the University. Working with the instructor for the class, the librarians developed a special two-session library orientation for the student athletes. The goals of the augmented orientation were to provide students with a introduction to Odum Library, provide basic instruction and demonstrations of library resources, and to introduce students in a positive way to some of the people with whom they would most often interact as they used the library.

Instructors of the VSU 101 classes often ask for a tour of the library as part of the orientation, however, the classes are usually too large to be taken through the Library as a group, and staffing limits prohibit offering tours to several smaller groups. For this special VSU 101 Library Orientation, the librarians designed a self-guided tour for the student athletes that overcame our obstacle of touring Odum Library with fifty students.

The self-guided tour helps the students become familiar with the resources available in different locations of the library. To overcome the staffing problem, Library personnel were recruited for the tour activity through a combination of email and personal requests. Three Information Services Librarians, one Technical Services Librarian, the Coordinator of Media Services and two Technical Assistants from Circulation volunteered to participate in the tour. In a standard library orientation, students would interact only with one or two Information Services Librarians. Involving all levels of staff resulted in students having an introduction to some of the people they would see often as they used the Library.

During the first VSU 101 library orientation, the class of fifty students was divided into groups of ten and each student was given a map of the Library with large "X's" marking various service points and resources, such as print indexes and circulation, available in the Library (Appendix 2). A Library employee was stationed at each "X" on the map ready to describe the resources and/or services available there. The students were instructed to work together in locating each "X" on the map where a Library employee was waiting to tell them about that area of Odum Library. Many of the locations marked with an "X" required the Library employee to cover several different service points or resources. For example, one of the Library employees stationed at an "X" on the third floor covered Media Services as well as a brief introduction to the Library of Congress classification system. After the students received a description or instruction of the service point or resources available, the Library employee initialed each student's map at the appropriate "X" and the students, using the map as a guide, located the next "X" designation in the library. After the students had been to all designated locations in the library and had obtained initials from each library employee at an "X", they were finished with the first orientation session. The instructor for the class greatly assisted our self-guided tour efforts by remaining stationed at the exit of the Library to check each student's map before they left to make sure they had completed the tour.

In a standard VSU 101 library orientation, students complete a vocabulary exercise in which they are invited to describe or use in a sentence library related terms which may not be familiar (Appendix 3). The vocabulary exercise is designed to make students more familiar and comfortable with terms and jargon they will hear when they use the Library. During the second day of the VSU 101 library orientation, students were given a printed guide to Odum Library and asked to complete the standard VSU 101 library vocabulary exercise. After the students completed the exercise, the librarians went through the different terms listed and provided brief demonstrations on searching the online catalog and GALILEO. Students are asked to volunteer their definitions to provide them with an opportunity to share their answers and receive immediate feedback on how well they know library vocabulary. In-class participation also keeps interest levels high. At the close of the second session, refreshments of cookies and soda were provided to the student athletes, and the Library employees who had met the students during the tour were invited to partake and to mingle with the students.

WHAT WE LEARNED FROM THE FIRST TWO SESSIONS

Active learning techniques such as class participation and in-class assignments reinforce what is taught and can also provide an evaluation of the library instruction. By seeing how the students answered the questions on the in-class assignment, we could evaluate the effectiveness of our presentation and look for ways of improving the next session. Course-integrated instruction that relates to a specific assignment or topic being covered in class helps to keep the interest level high during a presentation. Sometimes, the most important thing to leave with the students with is the knowledge that there is a familiar face they can go to if they need help in using the Library.

THE RESPONSE

The Athletic Liaison program has thus far been very well received by teaching faculty in the Physical Education Department, the Athletic Director, and both Library and University Administration. The VSU 101 Faculty Instructor whose students completed the first instruction session was very enthusiastic and believed the approach developed, particularly the self-guided tour and introduction to library staff, would reduce the intimidation students often feel when they begin using the library. Librarians are currently working with the same Instructor to schedule another repeat session for his new VSU 101 class.

FUTURE ACTIVITIES

VSU will continue to develop and teach NCAA CHAMPS course-integrated library instruction sessions in collaboration with the CHAMPS coordinator. They are considering submitting a proposal to the NCAA asking the organization to include a library and research skills section in the academic component of the CHAMPS program.

VSU's Physical Education Department has challenged the Library to provide further library instruction and orientations that will not duplicate the material students typically cover in other classes, such as VSU 101 library orientations or introductory English classes. The librarians are also working with the Director of Athletics to have a brief library orientation become a part of the summer orientation VSU provides to new student athletes.

As evaluation is important in assessing whether or not goals and objectives are being met, the librarians are looking at more formal methods of evaluating their instruction efforts. Current feedback looked only at the results of in-class exercises and verbal response from Faculty. It would be beneficial to implement other evaluation tools such as pre- and post-tests, surveys, and possibly a review of grade point averages and retention rates.

Several other Information Services Librarians at Valdosta State University are working on similar outreach programs to other student populations. One Librarian has started offering library orientations to new international students at the beginning of each term. His focus in these orientation sessions is to introduce international students to American library jargon, but he also includes demonstrations on searching the online catalog and GALILEO. He has found, as we did, that one of the most important things the students may leave the orientation session with is the knowledge that there is a contact person in the Library they can go to if they need assistance.

NOTES

1. National Collegiate Athletic Association. *NCAA & 1A Directors, CHAMPS Life Skills*, [A Brochure], nd.

2. Young, Heartsill (ed.). *The ALA Glossary of Library and Information Science.* (Chicago: American Library Association, 1993), 160.

3. Davidson, Nancy M. "Innovative Bibliographic Instruction: Developing Outreach Programs in an Academic Library." *The South Carolina Librarian* 29:1 (Spring 1985), 19-20.

4. Jesudason, Melba. "Proposition 48 and User Education for Athletes." *Reference Services Review* 17:1 (1989), 17.

5. Office of the Registrar and MIS/Information Technology of Valdosta State University. *Quarterly Enrollment Analysis, Fall 1997* (Valdosta, GA: Valdosta State University, 1997).

6. Valdosta State University Athletic Department. *1998-99 Valdosta State University Student Athlete Handbook.* (Valdosta, GA: Valdosta State University, 1998).

7. Ibid.

8. Ibid, Jesudason, 15.

9. Rhoden, William C. "Sports Industry 101: A Standard Proposal." *The New York* (Jan. 9, 1996), 43.

10. Ibid, Jesudason, 14.

11. Ruscella, Phyllis L. "Scoring: Bibliographic Instruction Helps Freshman Athletes Compete in the Academic League." *The Journal of Academic Librarianship* 19 (Sept. 1993), 232-236.

12. Ibid, Jesudason, 16.

13. Ibid, Jesudason, 15.

14. "Student Athletes and Library Instruction." Multiple responses posted to BI-L discussion list, BI-L@BINGVMB.CC.BINGHAMPTON.EDU, Sept. 1997).

15. Ibid, National Collegiate Athletic Association.

16. Ibid, National Collegiate Athletic Association.

17. GALILEO, Georgia Library Learning Online. [Internet,WWW]. ADDRESS: http://www.galileo.peachnet.edu.

REFERENCES

Blandy, Susan Grisworld. "Keeping Library Instruction Alive." *The Reference Librarian* 51/52 (1995), 425-447.

Davidson, Nancy M. "Innovative Bibliographic Instruction: Developing Outreach Programs in an Acadmeic Library." *The South Carolina Librarian* 29:1 (Spring 1985), 19-20.

GALILEO, Georgia Library Learning Online. [Internet,WWW]. ADDRESS: http://www.galileo.peachnet.edu.

Gawrych, Elaine. "Academic Library Outreach To Special Student Population." *Library Instruction Conference, Working with Faculty in the New Electronic Library* (Ann Arbor, Michigan: Pierian Press, 19992), 129-141.

Helms, Cynthia Mae. "Reaching Out to the International Students Through Bibliographic Instruction." *The Reference Librarian* 51/52 (1995), 295-307.

Jesudason, Melba. "Proposition 48 and User Education for Athletes." *Reference Services Review* 17:1 (1989), 13-20+.

Moeckel, Nancy and Presnell, Jenny. "Recognizing, Understanding, and Responding: A Program Model of Library Instruction Services for Internatioanl Students." *The Reference Librarian* 51/52 (1995), 309-325.

National Collegiate Athletic Association. *NCAA & 1A Directors, CHAMPS Life Skills*, [A Brochure], nd.

Office of the Register and MIS/Information Technology of Valdosta State University. *Quarterly Enrollment Analysis, Fall 1991.* (Valdosta, GA: Valdosta State University, 1997).

Rhoden, William C. "Sports Industry 101: A Standard Proposal." *The New York* (Jan. 9, 1996), 43.

Ruscella, Phyllis L. "Scoring: Bibliographic Instruction Helps Freshman Athletes Compete in the Academic League." *The Journal of Academic Librarianship* 19 (Sept. 1993), 232-236.

"Student Athletes and Library Instruction." Multiple responses posted to BI-L discussion list, BI-L@BINGVMB.CC.BINGHAMPTON.EDUSept. 1997).

Valdosta State University Athletic Department. *1998-99 Valdosta State University Student Athlete Handbook* (Valdosta, GA: Valdosta State University, 1998).

Young, Heartsill (ed.). *The ALA Glossary of Library and Information Science.* (Chicago: American Library Association, 1993), 160.

Zaporozhetz, Laurene E. "Fifteen Ways to meet Your User: Public Relations and Outreach Suggestions for Bibliographic Instruction." *The Reference Librarian* 24 (1989), 289-296.

APPENDIX 1

CHAMPS Library Orientation Exercise

CHAMPS
LIBRARY ORIENTATION
IN-CLASS EXERCISE
WINTER 1997

NAME_____

1. Where would you look to find a book in Odum Library?_____

_____

2. Where would you find the current Rolling Stone magazine? Is it on the shelf?_____

_____

3. What is the Odum Library Periodical Holdings List and what do you use it for?_____

_____

4. Where would you ask for last month's issue of *Time* magazine?_____

_____

5. Please list a few things you can find using GALILEO?_____

_____

6. Using the journal citation given to you in class, please complete the following:

    a) Write down the name of the journal listed in the citation._____

    b) Does the library own the journal listed in the citation?_____

    c) If the library does not own the journal what are some other ways to obtain the article?

_____

_____

    d) If the library owns the journal, find the journal on the shelf, locate the article from the citation and show to the instructor.

    e) If the library does not own the journal, obtain an interlibrary loan form and fill out the form. Show the form to the instructor.

APPENDIX 2
Odum Library Self-Guided Tour–First Floor
VALDOSTA STATE UNIVERSITY
ODUM LIBRARY
FIRST FLOOR

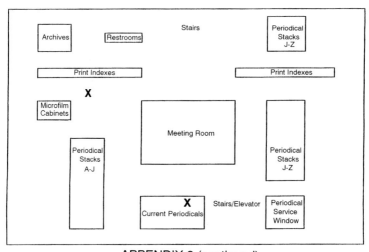

APPENDIX 2 (continued)
Odum Library Self-Guided Tour–Second (Main) Floor
VALDOSTA STATE UNIVERSITY
ODUM LIBRARY
SECOND (MAIN) FLOOR

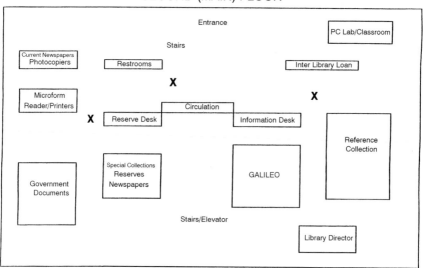

APPENDIX 2 (continued)
Odum Library Self-Guided Tour–Third Floor
VALDOSTA STATE UNIVERSITY
ODUM LIBRARY
THIRD FLOOR

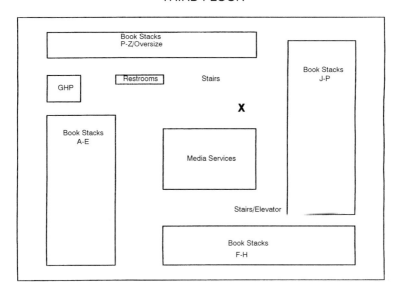

APPENDIX 3
VSU 101 Vocabulary Exercise

VSU 101   **ODUM LIBRARY**   **ORIENTATION**

NAME_____   LIBRARIAN'S NAME _____

DATE_____   PROFESSOR'S NAME _____

AT THE BEGINNING OF CLASS   **AT THE END OF CLASS**

WHATIZIT?	HAVE HEARD OF	CAN EXPLAIN	HAVE USED	USE?	LOCATION?
ONLINE CATALOG					
DRAGON					
LIBRARY OF CONGRESS CLASSIFICATION					
STACKS					
PERIODICAL					
PERIODICAL INDEXES					
READERS GUIDE					
CD-ROM					
LAN					
PERIODICAL HOLDINGS LIST					
MICROFILM					
INTERNET					
GALILEO					

Developing Proactive Partnerships: Minority Cultural Centers

Elaina Norlin
Patricia Morris

SUMMARY. Enhancing diversity programs and initiatives has been a challenge for higher education and academic libraries. Financial constraints at colleges and universities have made it essential to develop academic partnerships with other departments on campus to exchange ideas and combine resources. One academic diversity program, which has been around for approximately 30 years, is Minority Cultural Centers. Minority Cultural Centers provide an invaluable support service for minority students. This article provides background and current knowledge about Minority Cultural Centers and obstacles these centers face as we head into the 21st century. A sample proposal, outreach ideas and marketing strategies will help librarians get started into developing a long lasting relationship with Minority Cultural Centers. *[Article copies available for a fee from The Haworth Document Delivery Service: 1-800-342-9678. E-mail address: getinfo@haworthpressinc.com <Website: http://www.haworthpressinc.com>]*

KEYWORDS. Academic libraries, diversity, outreach, partnerships, minority cultural centers, and marketing

Elaina Norlin is Assistant Librarian, Undergraduate Services Librarian, Main Library, University of Arizona, Tucson, AZ 85721. Patricia Morris is Associate Librarian, Science & Engineering Librarian, Science & Engineering Library, University of Arizona, Tucson, AZ 85721.

[Haworth co-indexing entry note]: "Developing Proactive Partnerships: Minority Cultural Centers." Norlin, Elaina, and Patricia Morris. Co-published simultaneously in *The Reference Librarian* (The Haworth Information Press, an imprint of The Haworth Press, Inc.) No. 67/68, 1999, pp. 147-160; and: *Library Outreach, Partnerships, and Distance Education: Reference Librarians at the Gateway* (ed: Wendi Arant, and Pixey Anne Mosley) The Haworth Press, Inc., 2000, pp. 147-160. Single or multiple copies of this article are available for a fee from The Haworth Document Delivery Service [1-800-342-9678, 9:00 a.m. - 5:00 p.m. (EST). E-mail address: getinfo@haworthpressinc.com].

147

INTRODUCTION

Colleges and universities look very different today than they did 50 years ago. Currently, higher education is receiving applicants from a pool far wider than the traditional 18-year-old white middle class student. The new undergraduate population differs greatly in terms of age, ethnic background, race, career goals and academic preparation. Multiculturalism and diversity have consistently remained on the front burner for most academic institutions strategic planning efforts. As federal funding for academia slowly decreases, minority recruitment and retention rates play an even more active part to secure monetary support. For example, the Arizona Board of Regents (governing body over all Arizona universities) has a website for its "Strategic Directions and Goals." One of the goals states to improve achievement of underrepresented students by attaining the five-year recruitment and graduation goals identified in the Minority Student Progress Report (ABOR, 1995). The University of Arizona continues its efforts to attract a wide range of diverse students.

Higher education has made significant strides to increase minority enrollment numbers, but often continues to miss the mark when it comes to minority retention. Most colleges and universities have trained professionals who effectively recruit students from diverse backgrounds. However, higher retention rates are essential, one reason being that the government and concerned parents are not only looking at how well institutions recruit top candidates, but retain them through graduation. In "A Comprehensive Model for Enhancing Black Student Retention in Higher Education," Credle confirms that low minority retention rates can be attributed to a multitude of complex factors including academic, financial and/or personal. Institutional barriers are also cited as another reason for low retention rates. Institutional barriers result from the campus homogenous environment geared toward the traditional dominant culture. Underrepresented students usually have to quickly assimilate into a new lifestyle or begin to feel isolated and alienated from their own culture (Credle, 1991). According to the National Statistics for Higher Education, by the time students reach college only 46% Asian, 34% African American, 32% Hispanic will go on to obtain a bachelors degree (Credle, 1991). From the above numbers, over 50% of minority students will drop out before graduation.

One solution to combat minority student's feelings of alienation and isolation was the development of cultural/resource centers for diverse students. These cultural centers became an initial haven for minority students slowly adapting to a new world called academia.

MINORITY CULTURAL CENTERS

Carolyn Prince's, "A Precarious Question of Black Cultural Centers Versus Multicultural Centers" and Melvin Terrell's "The Emergent Role of Multicultural Education Centers on Predominately White Campuses" provide a comprehensive historical look at Cultural Centers. Minority Cultural Centers emerged during the civil rights movement. At the time, the federal government was offering incentives to increase minority enrollment numbers. In the late 1960s, it was the Higher Education Amendments to the 1965 Higher Education Act, Title IV, which assisted in helping minority students enroll in higher education through liberal enrollment standards (Terrell, 1988). However, minority students who were admitted through "open door policies" did not have the preparation skills to remain successful in higher education. Moreover, culture shock, isolation and discrimination were added obstacles to keep diverse groups off-balance. Cultural centers and/or houses surfaced to help build a transition between home and college life (Princes 1994). For the first few years, Cultural Centers supported students dealing with alienation and preserved cultural pride and identification. More importantly, the initial research numbers concluded that these centers played a role in increased minority retention rates for incoming groups (Terrell, 1988).

CURRENT ANALYSIS

While higher education continues its uphill battle for adequate funding, most departments on campus are forced to become more "accountable" and show tangible outcomes. Minority Cultural Centers have also taken a beating during the past few years. Minority Cultural Centers normally provided excellent social programs, but sometimes became isolated from the rest of campus life which hinders the development of successful academic partnerships. These scholastic programs were the added component to help minority students achieve academic excellence. Therefore, some centers folded while

others had to adapt to the university's minority student retention policies. Carolyn Princes, director of a Multicultural Center, states that
over the years Black Cultural Centers folded while others survived and
thrived. Ed Riley III, former director of the Latino House at the University of Illinois Urbana-Champaign, conducted a survey and found
many cultural centers were faltering. He further states that the new
minority students want to hang out at the centers but really needed
guidance to help them accomplish educational and eventually financial prosperity. The centers that survived took on expanded services to
include educational activities with social programming.

EDUCATIONAL AND SOCIAL PROGRAMS: SUCCESSFUL MINORITY CULTURAL CENTERS

During the new era of limited funds, Minority Cultural Centers
need to combine academic programming with social activities. Several
universities have stepped up to the challenge and continue to "survive
and thrive."

The University of Arizona has four minority cultural centers, His-
panic/Chicano, African American, Asian/Pacific and Native American. Each center is housed at a different location and offers new
students social activities and cultural identification. In addition, reading materials, tutoring and computers are available to help students
with their classes. This semester, all of the centers have decided to pull
together its resources in order to become more strategic. They have
also aligned themselves with Minority Student Services. Minority
Student Services currently provides several educational programs targeted to minority and financially disadvantaged students.

Forming a partnership with Minority Student Services creates a
balance between social and educational programming. In the University of Arizona's, "Program in Support of Student Diversity and
Achievement White Pages," retaining Minority Resource Centers is
essential because the centers support the scholastic and cultural activities of minority students on campus (Knott, 1993). Each unique center
helps the student feel a sense of belonging and enriches an environment for learning. Multicultural Education Center at the University of
Wisconsin (Oshkosh) (http://wilson.mio.uwosh.edu/tour/content/mec.
html).

The Multicultural Education Center (MEC) promotes cultural diversity through a combination of social, cultural and educational activities. During the 1980s, 80% of the MEC programming was devoted to Asian, African American, Hispanic and Native American, 20% of the scheduling was devoted to women and European ethnic groups. During the late 1970s, the MEC voluntarily linked itself administratively to the College of Education. The center also began to link three other populations: academic departments, student service programs and community agencies. From this alliance, they were able to collaborate with a wide variety of groups to secure funding and help increase minority graduation rates.

Wisconsin Multicultural Center in Madison-Wisconsin (http://www. wisc.edu/imcc/imcc.html) The Interim Multicultural Center was founded in 1988. This center has also combined educational, social and cultural activities. Their facilities include a lounge/study area and a computer center. According to the website, the Multicultural Center utilizes a variety of vehicles for programming including scholarly lectures, seminars, discussions and video viewing. Some sample programs on the calendar include, writing instruction classes, career advising, diversity education, film festivals and academic counseling.

WHERE ARE THE LIBRARIES?
LIBRARIES, OUTREACH AND DIVERSITY

Libraries are no strangers to diversity initiatives. Academic libraries, mirroring higher education, continue to site diversity as one of its strategic goals. In *Enhancing Ethnic and Racial Diversity: A New Challenge for Libraries*, Mary Lenox states "as we move toward the 21st century, libraries and other information agencies are challenged to develop and implement new ways to strengthen practices that ensure the integration of diversity into the mainstream of information services" (Lenox, 1993). She further states that in order to enhance diversity libraries need to promote access, maintain an attitude of service, and provide programming opportunities for different ethnic and racial groups on campus (Lenox, 1993). These programming opportunities create attention for librarians who are taking on leadership roles within their institutions. Thriving outreach programs confirm that the library not only embraces diversity but also is proactive in helping the recruitment and retention of minority students.

When librarians at the University of Arizona contacted several minority cultural centers across the country, no one responded that they had enough assistance. Most centers were very grateful for any suggestions but every one of them wanted additional computer technological support. The wave of the Internet, increased electronic access and current career opportunities demanding computer expertise does not make this fact surprising. In *Academic Libraries and Outreach Services*, Melba Jesudason states "one-third of the projected work force will be from so called minority groups in the year 2000. It is necessary for librarians to join hands with other on campus to help the nation prepare these people for their part in maintaining a competitive edge in the global marketplace" (Jesudason,1993).

RESULTS FROM PARTICIPANT INTERVIEWS WITH MINORITY CULTURAL CENTERS AND ACADEMIC LIBRARIANS

The authors contacted 20 Minority Cultural Centers directly through phone calls and e-mail and went on the African American Cultural Center listserv which reaches over 100 members to ask specific questions about partnerships with academic libraries. Overall they contacted and communicated with 40 people who were either directors, staff members or affiliated with Minority Cultural Centers. During the course of these participant interviews with Minority Cultural Center directors and staff, it was consistently asked if librarians were collaborating to develop educational programs for minority students. The answer for 85% of those surveyed was an overwhelming no and the remaining 15% said librarians occasionally helped with some form of collection development or cataloging. However, when asked if the librarians approached them or offered assistance outside the library, the answer remained negative. Over 90% of people we contracted through the listserv stated that librarians did not support Minority Cultural Centers or, if they did, it was with collection development or cataloging activity. The other 10% were not sure about what their academic libraries did except shelve and organize books.

The same questions were posed to five librarian e-mail listservs. The Academic Librarians who responded did not work with Minority Cultural Centers. A few librarians (20%) said they used to work with the centers, but usually with negative results.

Some overall librarian barriers/obstacles mentioned were:

- Not knowing how to get started;
- Not knowing what the Minority Cultural Center needs;
- Time restraints (overwhelmed at work);
- Did not know a Minority Cultural Center existed;
- Financial restraints;
- Assume they need a minority librarian to "tackle" this issues.

TURNING OBSTACLES/BARRIERS INTO CHALLENGES

The road to building a mutually beneficial partnership between a Minority Cultural Center and a library can be lined with numerous obstacles; however, these challenges are opportunities for growth and development. Some of these challenges are self imposed or avoidable while others may be structural and or inherent to the academic environment. These potential barriers can range from personal discomfort to organizational or institutional agendas influenced by national politics. The discussion, which follows will describe some of the most common issues which tend to hinder the initiation and or development of partnerships between university libraries and student cultural centers on campus. Each discussion will also offer suggestions that can be used as starting places for developing solutions locally.

The circumstances under which this potential partnership begins can also strongly influence the emotional high or low and subsequent success associated with the initial interaction. The first step is to clearly outline individual expectations as well as the organizational vision, mission and level of support for this particular project. In addition, it is essential that these expectations as well as outcomes be in line with the larger institution goals.

Building Cultural Understanding

Just contemplating beginning a relationship with those from an unfamiliar culture can be emotionally challenging. It can be positively and or negatively stimulating depending on the depth of encounters, experiences and or misinformation with which one is operating. One essential first step before approaching any of the student cultural centers is to gain an overview of that cultural group. This will help to alleviate anxiety due to unknowns as well as possibly illuminate areas of misinformation. There are several books which provide positive and informative approaches to understanding other cultures such as *Increasing Multicultural Understanding: A Comprehensive Model* (Locke, 1998) and *Breaking The Ice: A Guide to Understanding People From Other Cultures* (Kabagarama, 1997). After reviewing some of the literature, conversing with colleagues who have had first hand experience dealing with other cultures could be a next step. This potential partnership will be beneficial not only for the students but also a learning experience for those from the library.

Partnerships Within the Library

Minority librarians are essential in creating a multicultural environment for minority students, scholars and faculty members, who can benefit any diversity outreach initiatives. However, minority librarians are not the only people who can develop minority partnerships. An optimum scenario would have a diverse group of librarians working together and presenting information as a team. This shows harmony within the library organizational structure and strengthens the library's stance on diversity and developing partnerships within the campus community.

Obstacles

The issue of time to initiate, build and maintain such partnerships is another important concern. Like most workers, a Librarians' to-do list always seem to be much longer than any 8-hour or even 10-hour workday. Outreach projects do not have to incorporate tremendous energy and time. For example, developing five targeted workshops in one semester and slowly adding more activities might be all the partnership requires to be successful. Yet, in order for this type of project to succeed one must be personally committed to the idea that this is a significant partnership, which should not be thought of as the low priority activity. So when developing this partnership, be realistic and up front about the amount time that will be available to invest in building and maintaining this activity. When it is necessary to increase or decrease the initially agreed upon time, make sure to adjust other activities accordingly or delegate others to assist in maintaining a positive and proactive level of interaction. If it should become necessary to cut back on the quantity of interactions, never diminish the quality of those interactions and remember never to promise that which cannot be delivered. It is much more difficult to rebuild a trusting relationship after broken promises than to increase the interaction of a relationship that has been on a slow but qualitative track. The important part is to start small and remain consistent.

Limited resources available from the library to support this type of project can also be a challenge. Usually the biggest issue surrounds the question of personnel. As mentioned before, the goal is to start with a realistic amount of programming. This programming can best be handled by a team of librarians who can share the work and responsibility. This also provides a person who should be ready to step in if another team member is unable to fulfill an obligation. A team approach will insure not only the delivery of promised activities but also help to avoid competition with other work assignments.

The question of whether there is appropriate technology available at the Center's site may also prove to be a challenge. If the Center lacks the right type of computer equipment, then this is a great opportunity to assist them in preparing a proposal or grant to acquire it from the Institution or some other source. Remember this may include wiring for the building too. Hopefully your library will have portable computer equipment that can be used in the meantime for activities such as workshops scheduled at the Center. If the Library lacks a "take-it-on-the-road" set-up, you are again presented with a great opportunity to either request such equipment be purchased or seek out local or national grant funding.

Outreach and the Tenure Process

In many academic institutions, librarians are classified as faculty and are in a "tenure" or continuing status track wherein they are required to achieve this status in six years or are required to leave their positions. They are constantly coached to carefully choose and be involved in those activities, which will support their case to be granted "tenure." The question or dilemma therefore arises as to whether building these types of partnerships will be acknowledged with substantial credit towards their case for gaining this status. There are at least two parts to consider regarding this issue. The first is the quantity and quality of personal satisfaction to be gained in initiating or becoming involved in this type of undertaking. Building positive interpersonal relationships with a key customer group is a very significant motivating factor in increasing job performance. Positively enhanced job performance will definitely contribute towards achieving "tenure" status.

Leaving the Library Walls

Last but certainly not least is combating the view that "it is the students responsibility to come to us (the library) for assistance." The library, as with other campus areas, can be quite an intimidating place. This was a comment repeated several times in student focus groups held at the University of Arizona Libraries in the Fall of 1998. These focus groups were asked questions about reference services and even though the staff received high marks for approachability, the size and complexity of a research library were viewed as intimidating barriers particularly for new students. The shockingly low retention and graduation rates of racially diverse students informs us that we need to develop new ways of reaching and creating an opportunity to assist in improving these numbers. We can increase the quality and quantity of interactions with students, who avoid the library or do not know how to utilize library services, at Minority Cultural Centers, which provide a more relaxed environment for them. This is an opportunity to transform those feelings of intimidation regarding the library into feelings of confidence provided by our positive interactions and supportive services that assist them in succeeding in their academic careers.

Plan of Action

How do you approach the Minority Cultural Center now that you have decided that this would be a mutually positive and strategic partnership to build? The steps outlined below are suggested components of the approach that best fits your local situation.

Step 1: Investigate the history of the Cultural Center at your institution. Try to find out about past successes and unsuccessful ventures.

Step 2: Find out the goals, resources (personnel, financial and technology), existing partnerships and other supporters.

Note that Steps 1 and 2 may be accomplished by researching past annual unit reports, campus wide reports, campus newspaper archives, etc. Interviewing the administrator over the center's supervisor may provide information from another perspective. The more information in hand before proceeding to Step 3 the better. This process, however, should not be a barrier to initiating contact with the Center. There may exist the situation where most of this information will have to be obtained from personnel within the center. The main objective here is to get started with an informed positive attitude to build a mutually strategic partnership that is academically beneficial to the students.

Step 3: Generate a list of ideas to present to the center staff that you can realistically assist them with to address some of their needs. This should not be presented as a "this is what you should do list." This list may include suggestions that require the co-operation of other units.

Step 4: Discuss these ideas and others that may be presented by the Center staff. Reach consensus on those ideas which can be realistically accomplished. If other units will need to be involved, they will have to be contacted first before agreeing to proceed.

Step 5: Get started by putting together a plan with specific tasks to be accomplished by specific dates with specific contact names and best contact method. Also plan a regular meeting time so that activities and communication can be kept on track. An email distribution list of all key players should also be created if possible for frequent ease in communicating.

Step 6: Evaluate the partnership on a regular basis. Decide on an evaluation schedule. It is optimum to discuss and document this after each program. However it may be more manageable logistically to create this "report" every two months, three months, etc. Use these assessments to improve the programs as well as the partnership.

You Made a Connection . . . Now What?

Developing an outreach proposal requires a lot of detail, planning, organization and communication skills. Another skill, which might make or break your project, is marketing an effective publicity campaign. Although library instruction sessions, PowerPoint presentations, interactive websites and/or impressive bibliographies may be a work of art, they will not be successful if the target audience does not acknowledge your expertise. Librarians have other obstacles because we are not commonly known for outreach, creativity or being assertive. A targeted marketing campaign will start you on your way towards accomplishing your objective.

Target Market–Goals and Objectives

In *Academic Libraries and Outreach Services*, Melba Jesudason states that "marketing efforts achieve more efficient and effective results when they are directed to a subgroup of the general population" (Jesudason, 1993). To maximize impact for the proposal, specific target markets/audiences should be defined. Target market or audience helps one remain focused throughout the initial time frame. Examples include:

- The "Fantastic" Proposal will specifically target African American, Latino and Asian incoming students who attend Multicultural Cultural Center activities.
- The Proposal will help students learn how to create home pages or searching the catalog, or how to develop their research paper.
- The "Brand New" Proposal will specifically target the Minority Cultural Center staff members to develop their library research skills.
- The "Creative" Proposal goal is to design, implement and evaluate five library research workshops for Native American students during the Spring Semester 1999.

The proposal does not have to be this specific, yet the caution is against making the goals and objectives too broad. Keep in mind that the smaller goals and objectives usually can be obtained more successfully than broad unfocussed plans.

Another point to mention is to not get discouraged. At one cultural center, the director said the library did reach out one semester with assigned office hours. The students did not show up during the office hours, and the center never heard from the library again. When you approach a new project, which is new and different, expect a slow gathering for the first few months. Word of mouth usually remains the most effective way at building a strong campaign or project. Even if only five people attend your instructional session but they really enjoyed and appreciated the help, these five students can tell their friends and so on and so on.

Proactive Persistence

At the University of Arizona, library staff are currently developing partnerships with the Multicultural Resource Centers on campus. When we initially called and e-mailed the centers, they were surprised and happy for the assistance. However, we had to remain persistent and assertive during the initial proposal development. For this particular example, the Minority Resource Center directors did not know all the wonderful technological expertise and knowledge librarians already had at their fingertips. Therefore, we listened closely to some of the problems and concerns, and then suggested mini-projects and a time frame. Once the plan was completed, we negotiated for additional projects during the course of the year.

As librarians we had to conduct the initial phone calls, initiate e-mail messages, follow up and continue to follow up and make suggestions. If we did not remain persistent, the partnership would have remained just a nice idea. Although the multicultural or African American, Native American, Latino, Asian or international center on your campus might be more assertive, most centers probably will still have the old-fashioned views of librarianship and librarians. Moreover, most centers are also very busy trying to educate, enlighten and entertain its clientele to get them ready for four to five years of higher education.

CONCLUSION

In the next millenium the environment on college campus' across the nation is projected to provide more challenges than opportunities for fewer and fewer minority students. The deterioration of affirmative action gains such as scholarship funding and targeted internship opportunities have already contributed to greatly decreased numbers of minority students in higher education institutions in places like California and Texas. Other factors such as the ever widening gap between the technology haves and have-nots are also contributing to this loss of human potential in post secondary academics.

What does the future hold for library-minority cultural center partnerships? Challenging opportunities to increase the retention rate of these minority students by collaborating on creative ways to aid in their educational endeavors. This is an opportunity as well as a responsibility to develop more customized services, which aid in the retention rates of all students.

REFERENCES

Arizona Board of Regents (1995) "Strategic Directions and Goals" *http://www.abor. asu.edu/planning/dirgoals.html* pg. 1.

Credle, Joann O. "A Comprehensive Model for Enhancing Black Student Retention in Higher Education." Journal of Multicultural Counseling and Development 19,4, 158-165, October 1991.

Gerhard, Kristin H. and Jeanne M.K. Boydston. "A Library Committee on Diversity and Its Role in a Library Diversity Program." College & Research Libraries 54,4, 335-343. Jesudason, Melba. "Academic Libraries and Outreach Services through Precollege Programs: A Proactive Collaboration." RSR Reference Services Review 21,4, 29-36, January 1993.

Kabagarama, Daisy. *Breaking the Ice: A Guide to Understanding People from Other Cultures*. Boston: Allyn and Bacon, 1997.

Knott, J. Eugene and Laura I. Rendon. Renewal of Commitment: An Assessment of the University of Arizona's Programs in Support of Student Diversity and Achievement, February 17, 1998.

Lenox, Mary. "Enhancing Ethnic and Racial Diversity: The New Challenge for Libraries." Illinois Libraries 75, 292-295, Fall 1993.

Locke, Don C. *Increasing Multicultural Understanding: A Comprehensive Model*, 2nd edition. Thousand Oaks, CA: Sage Publications, 1998.

Princes, Carolyn D.W. "The Precarious Question of Black Cultural Centers Versus Multicultural Centers, Eric Document ED383273, March 1994 56 pages.

Smith, Thomas M. *Minorities in Higher Education* Washington, DC: National Center for Education Statistics, U.S. Department of Education, Office of Educational Research and Improvement, 1997.

Terrell, Melvin C. "The Emergent Role of Multicultural Education Centers on Predominately White Campuses" *From Survival to Success: Minority Student Retention* Washington D.C.: National Association of Student Personnel, 1988, 133pgs.

Smith, Thomas M. *Minorities in Higher Education* Washington, DC: National Center for Education Statistics, U.S. Department of Education, Office of Educational Research and Improvement, 1997.

Wiley, Ed III. "Educator Stresses Role of Cultural Centers in Survival." Black Issues in Higher Education 5,21, 18, January 1989.

Expanding the Learning Community:
An Academic Library Outreach Program
to High Schools

Keith Gresham
Debra Van Tassel

SUMMARY. While educational partnerships between academic libraries and public schools have taken many forms throughout the later half of the century, a less common approach to building learning communities is coordinated outreach visits by academic librarians to secondary schools to provide active-learning, hands-on workshops that include remote access to the wide range of information technologies and electronic resources available in academic libraries today. This article reviews the concept and practice of learning communities, establishes a connection between learning communities and information literacy, and offers an outreach model that promotes information literacy and expands the academic learning community to college-bound high school students. *[Article copies available for a fee from The Haworth Document Delivery Service: 1-800-342-9678. E-mail address: getinfo@haworthpressinc. com <Website: http://www.haworthpressinc.com>]*

KEYWORDS. Learning communities, library instruction, information literacy

Keith Gresham is Assistant Professor and Central Reference Librarian, and Debra Van Tassel is Instructor and Central Reference Librarian, both at the University of Colorado at Boulder Libraries, Campus Box 184, Boulder, CO 80309-0184.

The authors wish to thank Betty Astle, Librarian at Evergreen High School, for her commitment to and participation in the outreach program described in this article.

[Haworth co-indexing entry note]: "Expanding the Learning Community: An Academic Library Outreach Program to High Schools." Gresham, Keith, and Debra Van Tassel. Co-published simultaneously in *The Reference Librarian* (The Haworth Information Press, an imprint of The Haworth Press, Inc.) No. 67/68, 1999, pp. 161-173; and: *Library Outreach, Partnerships, and Distance Education: Reference Librarians at the Gateway* (ed: Wendi Arant, and Pixey Anne Mosley) The Haworth Press, Inc., 2000, pp. 161-173. Single or multiple copies of this article are available for a fee from The Haworth Document Delivery Service [1-800-342-9678, 9:00 a.m. - 5:00 p.m. (EST). E-mail address: getinfo@haworthpressinc.com].

Educational partnerships between academic libraries and public schools have taken many forms throughout the latter half of this century. Documented projects and programs include circulation and borrowing agreements for high school students, librarian referral agreements, workshops for secondary school librarians and teachers, pre-visit orientations, and instruction sessions for student groups visiting academic libraries (Craver 1987; Kemp et al. 1986). Less common have been outreach visits by academic librarians to secondary schools to provide active learning, hands-on workshops that allow high school students off-site access to the wide range of information technologies and electronic resources found in academic libraries today.

For the past four years, the University of Colorado at Boulder Libraries has experimented with such an approach as part of a larger library instruction outreach program that helps secondary school students acquire an understanding of the library research process and develop the critical thinking and evaluation skills important to their academic success. The networked learning environments now being built in school libraries and media centers have allowed the University Libraries to extend both its information literacy programs and library collections beyond traditional user groups and campus boundaries. More than just an exercise in enhanced community relations, this outreach workshop program has succeeded in creating collaborative partnerships that contribute to the building of statewide learning communities.

LEARNING COMMUNITIES: AFFECTING POSITIVE CHANGE

The learning community concept is central to the discussion of contemporary educational partnerships between secondary and higher education. Although precise usage of the phrase varies widely throughout the field of education, "learning community" typically refers to diverse individuals and groups purposefully united in a shared educational mission to affect long-term positive change on the student learning process. In both K-12 and higher education, the concept is closely associated with pedagogical theories of active and collaborative learning, problem-solving, critical thinking skills, lifelong learning, team teaching, and interdisciplinary themes (Sergiovanni 1994; Gabelnick et al. 1990).

In higher education, the idea of learning communities draws upon the works of educational theorists and philosophers John Dewey and Alexander Meiklejohn (Gabelnick et al. 1990) and is used to describe an undergraduate curriculum reform movement that closely links courses and academic disciplines around a unifying theme "so that students find greater coherence in what they are learning as well as increased intellectual interaction with faculty members and fellow students" (Matthews et al. 1996, 6). Typical models of this movement include linked courses, learning clusters, freshman interest groups, and coordinated studies programs.

In elementary and secondary education, the learning community concept has seen a much broader application and operates at three levels: the student level, the professional level, and the community level (Wallace et al. 1997). The concept is used to describe a wide range of initiatives, including active learning curricula; team learning; organizational structure and performance; shared leadership; teacher empowerment; collective responsibility; and collaborative involvement that includes a "broad engagement of parents, community members and community leaders in building and achieving the school's vision" (Wallace et al. 1997, 181).

A frequently cited model of an ideal learning community in practice–one in which public school students, teachers, administrators, parents, and community leaders all united around a common educational goal–is the Denali Project in Fairbanks, Alaska (Hagstrom 1992). In this case, the common goal was to transform an old and outdated school into a new math-science learning center that emphasized student exploration and teachers as learners.

LEARNING COMMUNITIES AND THE INFORMATION LITERACY CONNECTION

Learning communities, the anecdotal evidence suggests, can provide both the initiative and synergy to enhance learning opportunities for our students. In as much as learning communities help create a nation of lifelong learners/explorers–a valuable citizenry in the constantly changing environments that will characterize the 21st-century world–the core tenets of information literacy provide the foundation upon which these learning communities originate and grow.

Information literacy, loosely defined as the ability to identify, locate, evaluate, and use information effectively, has been a defining issue in the professional lives of librarians, teachers, administrators, and policy makers for much of this decade (National Forum on Information Literacy 1998). As the Internet and other computer networks become integrated into the daily lives of learners at all levels of education, information literacy standards and guidelines have been developed to help librarians and teachers modify curricula in ways that allow students to both develop information searching skills and conceptually understand the nature, role, and uses of information.

In 1994, the State of Colorado issued K-12 information literacy guidelines based upon the belief that students should "actively engage in the world of ideas" by constructing meaning from information, creating quality products, learning independently, participating effectively as group members, and using information responsibly and ethically (Colorado Department of Education 1994, 1). These guidelines also implicitly emphasize many core learning community concepts, such as collaborative activities among librarians, teachers, staff, administrators, and community members. Within such a context of information literacy, the learning community model:

> suggests that all of us–students, teachers, administrators, and parents as well as our local, regional, state, national, and international communities–are interconnected in a lifelong quest to understand and meet our constantly changing information needs. This new learning community is not limited by time, place, age, occupation, or disciplinary borders but instead is linked by interest, need, and a growing array of telecommunications technology. (American Association of School Librarians 1998, 2)

THE UNIVERSITY OF COLORADO
AT BOULDER EXPERIENCE

Answering this call for greater statewide connections to the K-12 community, the University of Colorado at Boulder, Colorado's flagship research university, has developed an extensive network of collaborative outreach programs. The central administration of the university system maintains a searchable database on the World Wide Web providing descriptive information about more than 500 outreach programs and services provided to the citizens of Colorado by the University's faculty and staff. Many of these outreach programs take advantage of the technological infrastructure of the campus in the design and implementation of outreach programs. Such use of technology "testifies to the power of these partnerships in harnessing the resources of the University of Colorado in service to the growth and development of [the] state" (University of Colorado 1998).

The proliferation of information-sharing networks and cooperative resource sharing agreements throughout Colorado have allowed the University of Colorado at Boulder Libraries to provide outreach activities that aid in the growth and expansion of statewide learning communities. Since 1994, the state's largest research library has sponsored the Secondary Schools Outreach Program, an information literacy project that has provided more than 3,500 students, teachers, and librarians from approximately 25 partner schools with process-oriented, hands-on instructional workshops, many of which take place from within the students' own school library (University of Colorado at Boulder Libraries 1997).

Through their participation in the outreach program workshops, students and teachers from outside of Boulder are discovering the value of information technologies. Instruction and application in the use of these technologies permit the formation and growth of collaborative learning communities between secondary and higher education, independent of distance or geography. Although the specific content and structure of an outreach workshop session may vary depending upon the information needs and learning facilities of the secondary school group in question, the following description of one recent off-site outreach visit provides a useful design and implementation model for other academic libraries wishing to expand their own learning communities.

OUTREACH TO THE REMOTE COMMUNITY

Evergreen High School, situated in the rapidly growing community of Evergreen, Colorado, is located in the foothills of the Rocky Mountains, 45 minutes west of downtown Denver and 40 minutes southwest of Boulder. The residents of Evergreen are solidly upper-middle class and well-educated: more than 75 percent of the adult population has attended college, and 70 percent of the working residents are employed in professional, technical, sales or administrative positions (Jefferson County Public Schools 1998).

Evergreen High School students consistently score well above the national average on standardized tests, and a majority of graduating seniors continue on to college. As such, the school's curriculum includes a variety of advanced placement, honors and accelerated classes for the approximately 900 students enrolled in the school each year (Colorado Department of Education 1998).

In the spring of 1998, instruction librarians at the University of Colorado at Boulder were invited to provide an off-site information literacy workshop to 90 students enrolled in three different 12th-grade advanced placement literature classes at Evergreen High School. Students enrolled in the literature courses that semester had been reading a variety of English and American literary works and were expected to write a formal research paper as the culminating project of the class. The literature teachers wanted their students to understand the research process as it exists at the college level and experience the full range of literature-related resources available in academic libraries.

Because Evergreen High School possesses a large, recently renovated, and technically sophisticated library managed by a professional librarian and two highly skilled computer support technicians, the school proved to be an ideal location for the collaborative and technology-driven nature of the outreach program.

SESSION STRUCTURE AND CONTENT

Evergreen High School operates on a block schedule in which classes meet every other day, with three periods of 95 minutes each day. Because the schedules for the three advanced placement literature classes varied not only by time but by day, the decision was made to meet with the students for one 95-minute period, which was scheduled as an internal "field trip" for all three classes. To allow for travel and preparation time prior to the session, the last school period of the day (12:55-2:30 p.m.) was selected for the workshop.

Providing meaningful learning experiences for 90 students in 95 minutes, although challenging, can be achieved by incorporating the concepts of information literacy with available information technologies into active learning sessions. Gedeon (1997, 302) notes that "when planning active learning sessions it is appropriate to consider expected learning outcomes in light of their placement on several learning continuums." With that in mind, desired student learning outcomes for the workshop were developed:

- Students will understand the complementary nature of academic and school libraries.
- Students will develop a sense of the size and scope of academic libraries.
- Students will comprehend the full range of information sources and research tools available to literary scholars.
- Students will demonstrate a working knowledge of the research process.
- Students will experience hands-on searching of an electronic index appropriate to their research topics.
- Students will understand criteria and techniques for evaluating information sources.
- Students will cultivate a connection to the larger community of academic scholars.

Evergreen High School's library consists of three distinct physical spaces. Separated in the middle by the reference and circulation desk, the library has two well-defined reading and study areas, east and west, that can accommodate large groups. An attached computer room consisting of fifteen Internet-connected workstations adjoins the east end of the library. Playing to the strengths of this physical layout, the 95-minute outreach session was divided into five segments: a 15-minute introductory session for all 90 students, three 20-minute breakout sessions in the three separate physical spaces through which each class of 30 students would rotate, and a concluding 15-minute question-and-answer session at the end of the rotation period (see Table 1).

The introductory session was designed to demonstrate the similarities and differences between academic and school libraries, to present the range of information resources available in academic libraries, and to provide an introduction to the academic research process. The school librarian introduced the visiting academic librarians as colleagues, stated the purpose of the workshop, and outlined the day's schedule. The academic librarians distributed a printed guide to the

TABLE 1. Outreach Session Schedule

Evergreen High School Outreach Session Schedule				
Time	**Activity**	**Instructors**	**Participants**	**Location**
1:00-1:15	Introduction	Academic Librarians	90 Students	East
1:20-1:40	Session I	High School Librarian	30 Students	West
1:45-2:05	Session II	Academic Librarian #1	30 Students	East
2:10-2:30	Session III	Academic Librarian #2	30 Students	Lab
2:30-2:45	Followup Q&A	All	As Needed	As Needed

University Libraries and briefly discussed the role of academic libraries using the University Libraries as a model. Using an Internet-connected computer and projection system, the librarians introduced students to the University Libraries web site and discussed the focus, organization, and size of the various library collections. A demonstration of CHINOOK, the library's web-based online catalog, displayed the scope and size of the collections. Because the pricing levels of many academic databases are beyond the reach of most high school libraries, a remote connection to the OCLC FirstSearch system was established to illustrate the number and range of electronic databases accessible in an academic environment. The *MLA International Bibliography* was introduced as the primary research tool used by academic literary scholars. Using topics volunteered by the participants, several searches of *MLA* were performed so that FirstSearch commands, record structure, and search statements could be demonstrated. The students were then given instructions for moving to the breakout sessions.

Session I, led by the Evergreen librarian on one side of the library, familiarized students with the array of print and CD-ROM sources available in their local school library. Students used dictionaries, encyclopedias, and biographical sources such to obtain a broad overview of their subjects, focus their topics within a specific context, and identify key dates, facts and terminology.

Session II, held on the opposite side of the library, focused on the electronic search strategy process. The 30 students were divided into six small groups. The session began with a discussion of the types of electronic databases and the information found in each type (Figure 1). Next, using a process-oriented worksheet, students were asked to articulate their research topics, consider the academic discipline(s) related to the topics, and select appropriate periodical indexes from a list of databases available through the FirstSearch system. Students were also asked to identify the key concepts for their topics and write down specific keywords that could be used for searching. The students were instructed how they would use the process worksheets in Session III to search the online databases and record the results of their searches. The session ended with a small-group activity in which each group was asked to examine the elements of four bibliographic records and evaluate the sources based on a pre-defined topic (Figure 2). Evaluation criteria such as relevancy, currency, language, and source were discussed.

Session III allowed hands-on application of the search strategy process using the library's computer room. Working in pairs, the students connected remotely to the FirstSearch web site using a combination of passwords supplied by the high school librarian and the visiting academic librarians. Using *Humanities Abstracts*, *Periodical Abstracts*, *ArticleFirst* and other databases appropriate for literary research, the students conducted searches using the terminology and search statements formulated in Session II. Retrieved searches were evaluated using appropriate criteria, and relevant sources were recorded on their worksheets. Students were encouraged to find at least three sources of information. Procedures for obtaining complete articles from some of the full-text databases were also practiced. For those retrieved items that were not full-text, students were taught to use CHINOOK to find out which academic or public libraries in the Denver metro area owned their needed sources. Students were also encouraged to visit the University Libraries in Boulder to make use of the wide variety of literature-related books, journals, and bibliographic databases.

In the short concluding session, librarians and classroom teachers

FIGURE 1. Electronic Research Databases: Basic Types

Bibliographic: provides full citations to articles, books, reports, etc.

TITLE:	Scientist Cech wins presidential medal
SOURCE:	Denver Post
SEC,PG:COL:	B, 7:1
DATE:	SEP 28, 1995
ABSTRACT:	Nobel laureate Thomas Cech, a University of Colorado at Boulder biochemistry professor, is one of eight winners of the prestigious National Medal of Science for 1995. Cech and other winners will be presented with the medals by Pres. Clinton on Oct. 18.
ARTICLE TYPE:	News
DESCRIPTORS:	Awards & honors; Science; Educators

Full-Text: provides full-text of articles, reports, etc., typically *without* accompanying photographs, tables, and other graphics.

AUTHOR:	Zaslowsky, Dyan
TITLE:	The Battle of Boulder
SOURCE:	Wilderness
VOL/ISSUE NO:	v58n209
PAGE(S):	25-33
DATE:	Summer 1995
COPYRIGHT:	Copyright Wilderness Society 1995
TEXT:	The South Boulder Creek Trail's Bob-O-Link segment is the pastoral route between subdivisions blanketing the tan prairie of the southeast side of Boulder, Colorado, and the city's grandest community center. The flat trail, situated by the creek and on the edge of a pasture, meanders through a narrow corridor of tall cottonwoods. . . .

Numeric: provides statistical data from a variety of sources, usually presented in tabular form.

USA COUNTIES 1994

Geographic Area: Boulder, CO (013)

Table: GENERAL PROFILE

POPULATION (Census)

Total resident population:

1992	238,196
Per square mile	20.8
1990	225,339
Percent under 18 year	23.0
Percent 65 years and over	7.6
1980	189,625

FIGURE 2. Evaluating Citations: Small Group Exercise

Goal: Evaluate article citations in relation to the stated paper topic.

Instructions: Examine the information elements contained in each of the following four article citations. As a group, evaluate each citation as to the article's usefulness or appropriateness as a <u>research source</u> for the paper topic. After evaluating each citation, decide which <u>one citation</u> the group finds to be the <u>most</u> useful or appropriate. Be prepared to report the group's findings, including why certain citations were not chosen.

Paper Topic: **Exploration of the concept of "self-identity" in the novels and short stories of Charlotte Perkins Gilman.**

CITATION 1

AUTHOR: Rose, Jane Atteridge
TITLE: Images of Self: The Example of Rebecca Harding Davis and Charlotte Perkins Gilman
YEAR: 1992
SOURCE: English Language Notes (ELN), Boulder, CO. Article in: vol. 29 no. 4, 1992 June
PAGES: 70-78
LANG: English
PUB TYPE: journal article
DESCRIPT: American literature; 1800-1899; Davis, Rebecca Harding; treatment of self-identity; compared to Gilman, Charlotte Perkins

CITATION 2

AUTHOR: Anderson, Linda
TITLE: At the Threshold of the Self: Women and Autobiography
YEAR: 1986
SOURCE: Monteith, Moira (ed.). Women's Writing: A Challenge to Theory. Sussex; New York: Harvester; St. Martin's, 1986. viii, 196 pp.
PAGES: 54-71
LANG: English
PUB TYPE: book article
DESCRIPT: genres; autobiography; by women writers; relationship to fictional self; sexual identity; especially in Woolf, Virginia

CITATION 3

AUTHOR: Boyles, Mary
TITLE: Woman: The Inside Outsider
YEAR: 1990
SOURCE: Crafton, John Micheal (ed.). Selected Essays from the International Conference on The Outsider 1988. Carrollton: West Georgia Coll., 1990. 174 pp.
PAGES: 117-25
LANG: English
PUB TYPE: book article
DESCRIPT: Canadian literature; 1900-1999; Munro, Alice; "The Office"; short story; and Lessing, Doris; "To Room Nineteen"; Gilman, Charlotte Perkins; "The Yellow Wall Paper"; treatment of women; inner self

CITATION 4

AUTHOR: Hong, Sung-joo
TITLE: Charlotte Perkins Gilman's "The Yellow Wallpaper": The Wallpaper as a Split Self and a Disruptive Text
YEAR: 1995
NOTES: in Korean; Eng. sum.
SOURCE: The Journal of English Language and Literature (JELL), Seoul, Korea. Article in: vol. 41 no. 3, 1995
PAGES: 697-719
LANG.:   Korean
PUB TYPE: journal article
DESCRIPT: American literature; 1800-1899; Gilman, Charlotte Perkins; "The Yellow Wall Paper"; short story; treatment of wallpaper; relationship to split personality; interruption

were available to answer questions and provide feedback on the learning activities.

EXPANSION OF THE LEARNING COMMUNITY

Evergreen High School students, through their participation in the outreach program, began a process of joining the larger community of academic learners. Their knowledge of literary criticism as an integral part of academic scholarship was enhanced through conceptual links to and practical application of the information resources and technologies of higher education. Information literacy strategies were incorporated into the students' understanding of the university-level library research process. Collegial relationships between the school and the university were reinforced, and opportunities for sustained communication between high school students and academic librarians were created. One such opportunity was realized when one of the three literature classes made an on-campus visit to the University Libraries in the weeks following the outreach program. The creation of such educational partnerships in Colorado and elsewhere contributes to the expansion of learning communities and cultivates a citizenry of lifelong learners.

REFERENCES

American Association of School Librarians. 1998. *Information Power: Building Partnerships for Learning.* Chicago: American Library Association.

Colorado Department of Education. 1994. *Model Information Literacy Guidelines.* Denver: Colorado State Library and Adult Education Office, Colorado Dept. of Education.

Colorado Department of Education. 1998. *Jefferson County R-1 School District: Demographics: High Schools* [report online]. Denver, Colo. [cited 31 August 1998]. Available from Internet: <http://cde.state.co.us/dist1420.htm#High>.

Craver, Kathleen W. 1987. "Use of Academic Libraries by High School Students: Implications for Research." *RQ* 27, no. 1 (Fall): 53-66.

Gabelnick, Faith, Jean MacGregor, Roberta S. Matthews, and Barbara Leigh Smith. 1990. *Learning Communities: Creating Connections Among Students, Faculty, and Disciplines.* New Directions for Teaching and Learning, no. 41. San Francisco: Jossey-Bass.

Gedeon, Randle. 1997. "Enhancing a Large Lecture with Active Learning." *Research Strategies* 15, no. 4: 301-09.

Hagstrom, David. 1992. "Alaska's Discovery School." *Educational Leadership* 49, no. 5 (February): 23-26.

Jefferson County Public Schools. 1998. *Jefferson County Public Schools: Guide for Newcomers: Evergreen High School* [guide online]. Jefferson County, Colo. [cited 31 August 1998]. Available from the Internet: <http://204.98.1.2/profiles/high/evergreen.html>.

Kemp, Barbara E., Mary M. Nofsinger, and Alice M. Spitzer. 1986. "Building a Bridge: Articulation Programs for Bibliographic Instruction." *College and Research Libraries* 47, no. 5 (September): 470-74.

Louis, Karen Seashore, Sharon D. Kruse, and associates. 1995. *Professionalism and Community: Perspectives on Reforming Urban Schools.* Thousand Oaks, Calif.: Corwin Press.

Matthews, Roberta, Barbara Leigh Smith, Jean MacGregor, and Faith Gabelnick. 1996. "Learning Communities: A Structure for Educational Coherence." *Liberal Education* 82 (Summer): 4-9.

National Forum on Information Literacy. 1998. *A Progress Report on Information Literacy: An Update on the American Library Association Presidential Committee on Information Literacy: Final Report.* Chicago: Association of College and Research Libraries. Also available online at <http://www.ala.org/acrl/nili/nili.html>.

Sergiovanni, Thomas J. 1994. *Building Community in Schools.* San Francisco: Jossey-Bass.

University of Colorado. 1998. *Outreach On Line.* Boulder, Colo. [cited 31 August 1998]. Available from the Internet: <http://www.cusys.edu/outreach/>.

University of Colorado at Boulder Libraries. 1997. *Secondary Schools Outreach Program* [description online]. Boulder, Colo. [cited 31 August 1998]. Available from the Internet: <http://www-libraries.colorado.edu/ttp/ser/outreach.htm>.

Wallace Jr., Richard C., David E. Engel, and James E. Mooney. 1997. *The Learning School: A Guide to Vision-based Leadership.* Thousand Oaks, Calif.: Corwin Press.

III. A DIFFERENT APPROACH: NEW USER PROGRAMS AND OUTREACH SERVICES

The "Open House," an Effective Library Public Relations and Instruction Tool

Dennis G. Odom
Alexia C. Strout-Dapaz

SUMMARY. This article presents the Open House as a viable public relations and instruction technique to introduce incoming students to basic library facilities and services in a fun and relaxing atmosphere. An overriding goal of the Open House is to empower participating students with the self-sufficiency skills that will allow them to smoothly navigate the library on their own. Includes a comprehensive blueprint for detailing successes, innovations, and pitfalls. Outlines the specific steps to take regarding fundraising and donation solicitation. Ultimate-

Dennis G. Odom (E-mail: d.odom@tcu.edu) is Acquisitions Librarian and Alexia C. Strout-Dapaz (E-mail: a.stroutdapaz@tcu.edu) is Business/Reference Librarian, both at the Mary Couts Burnett Library, Texas Christian University.

[Haworth co-indexing entry note]: "The 'Open House,' an Effective Library Public Relations and Instruction Tool." Odom, Dennis G., and Alexia C. Strout-Dapaz. Co-published simultaneously in *The Reference Librarian* (The Haworth Information Press, an imprint of The Haworth Press, Inc.) No. 67/68, 1999, pp. 175-186; and: *Library Outreach, Partnerships, and Distance Education: Reference Librarians at the Gateway* (ed: Wendi Arant, and Pixey Anne Mosley) The Haworth Press, Inc., 2000, pp. 175-186. Single or multiple copies of this article are available for a fee from The Haworth Document Delivery Service [1-800-342-9678, 9:00 a.m. - 5:00 p.m. (EST). E-mail address: getinfo@haworthpressinc.com].

175

ly, an Open House event can strengthen a library's outreach potential;
an important–yet often neglected–facet of academic librarianship.
[Article copies available for a fee from The Haworth Document Delivery Ser-
vice: 1-800-342-9678. E-mail address: getinfo@haworthpressinc.com <Website:
http://www.haworthpressinc.com>]

KEYWORDS. Open House events-academic libraries, public rela-
tions-academic libraries, fundraising-public relations, outreach-aca-
demic libraries, bibliographic instruction-academic libraries

Academic libraries, in general, have not pursued grandiose or out-
of-the-ordinary public relations events that both highlight their services and serve as an efficient, effective way of educating their customers in the library "basics." Instead, with traditional "bibliographic
instruction," libraries, more often than not, tax their valuable human
resources by plunging directly into research skills when what is most
needed are answers to "How do I check out a book?", "How do I
make photocopies?", and "Which magazines do you own?". Only
after those basic skills are mastered is it possible to effectively move
on to more sophisticated library research skills.

The overriding goal of the Open House was to "mass educate"
freshmen and other students new to campus about basic library services in a fun and relaxing atmosphere. A priority was to provide them
with self-sufficiency skills that would allow them to smoothly navigate the library on their own. The intent was to get students familiar
with both the layout of the building and where to go to perform basic
tasks and much thought was given to the presentation of these survival
skills. Too many facts to remember would overload the students with
too much information, which they would immediately tune out. The
reason basic directional information was stressed, instead of more
formalized library research skills, went back to a student survey done
by the Library the previous spring semester. Students mentioned anxiety and even fear when using the Library for the first time. As a result
of this perceived fear and anxiety, some felt the Library was a place to
be avoided at all costs. The Open House was seen as an efficient
vehicle to introduce timid users to the building in a fun, nonthreaten-
ing way. To ensure the Open House goal was effectively met, an Open
House committee was formed which was later expanded into a Library-
wide Public Relations committee.

The "fun" component to the Open House was seen as crucial since the target audience was the student body. As the perception these days is that college students expect instant gratification, rewards and added incentives would make it all the more meaningful to them. Also, it was critical to rid these new and vulnerable students of many of their unrealistic fears regarding the Library by presenting it as a location that was as "with it" as other campus organizations. Additionally, this extravaganza was seen as a means to persuade Texas Christian University (TCU) freshmen that the Library is a crucial component to their success in school and having some basic navigational skills would make academics easier. Furthermore, executing this type of event was an opportunity for the Library to spotlight itself and to blow its horn to other campus organizations and to administrators controlling the budgetary purse strings. It was also a unique opportunity to break out of the perception, one existing even within the Library, that an academic library cannot market itself in such an extravagant fashion and be successful.

Planning for an event of this magnitude requires focus, time, innovation, persistence, logistical coordination, community partnering, and above all, a fresh mindset allowing for new and different possibilities. While it is impossible to cover all of these planning components in great detail, an outline of the steps involved will be included, with useful how-to's and tips and tricks that can be modified to fit other libraries and the campus communities they serve.

PLANNING CONSIDERATIONS

First and foremost in the planning process is establishing a public relations committee to establish the goals, objectives and desired outcomes of an Open House event. In selecting committee members, it is beneficial to have a diverse group of experience within the committee membership. For instance, it is advantageous to include colleagues with fundraising expertise, others with educational/instructional expertise, and yet others with organizational skills. Of particular importance is communicating well with the Administration, since there will be budget requests and involvement from other service organizations on campus; such as facilities services and/or housekeeping.

Once the library commits itself to stage an Open House, the date, time, and target audience needs to be determined. The schedule of the event must be coordinated with other campus activities to ensure proper attendance. An Open House scheduled during mid-term exams will not attract as many students as one scheduled during the first weeks of school. Look at campus traffic patterns to determine the optimum times and places for hosting the event. Are the majority of students in class during the morning hours? Is there a large student body of commuter students who are not on campus during the evenings? The event will be most successful when the majority of students are on campus with some free time. Lastly, the target audience to be reached by the event needs to be determined. As previously mentioned, the Open House at TCU was geared towards freshmen and other students new to campus.

FUNDRAISING BLUEPRINT

The all important job of collecting donations begins as soon as the basic elements delineated above are set. The door prizes and snack food items donated are incorporated as the event's "hook" and for many students are the primary incentives for attending. The alluring power of food and prizes needs to be played up as much as possible. For this particular event, over $3,000 of food and door prize donations were contributed by area businesses with prizes ranging from free zoo passes to expensive high-end sunglasses, and year-long gym memberships. In order to solicit this level of donation, it is necessary to allot enough "lead time" to this specific task. For this particular event, four months were focused on the fundraising/donation process; from database creation of targeted businesses to the final assemblage of all Open House contributions. The first step in soliciting donations is to compile an extensive list of businesses to target. More positive feedback will be achieved by soliciting donations from businesses that view the college community as a desirable market for their products and services.

The second action item is constructing a database file with contact names, fax number(s), phone number(s), and address(es), e-mail and postal, of the primary donation decision makers. Data entry accuracy and verification is of primary importance since this database file may potentially be recycled for future Open House events.

Very often a business will have a designated donations manager. In other instances, the business owner makes the decision. Regardless of who makes the contribution decision, there is usually a keen interest in contributing. Remember, the solicitation request is giving a particular business the opportunity to contribute to the ultimate success of the event, in addition to giving them the opportunity to market their products and services to potential future consumers. Never consider it to be begging; it is not.

If resources are available, provide the businesses being solicited with donation incentives. For example, let the businesses know that free web advertising on the library's homepage will be provided for a month prior to the event, or, for some other limited time which the Public Relations committee determines beforehand. Even for companies with current web pages, this is an enticing exchange because it helps to widen their web presence.

The third action item is to phone the donations contact and give a brief description of the planned event. Often, a definite commitment will be given over the phone. The next step is to send documentation, on the organization's letterhead, so the business can be assured the request is legitimate while providing documentation for auditing purposes, inventory, and charitable contributions recordkeeping.

If an immediate verbal commitment to contribute is not given, let the contact person know that a follow-up letter containing additional details will be sent. Make the letter as succinct as possible. Use assertive language and get to the point. A sample letter is provided in the Appendix.

The first paragraph will give an overview of the event including its purpose, expectations (results, number of students attending) along with the dates, times, etc. Use bold typeface for critical pieces of information such as *date* and *time*, in addition to anything else that is crucial. In the second paragraph state the request. Briefly, emphasize how the donation will contribute to the ultimate success of the event and the marketing opportunity this will provide their business/service. The third paragraph will indicate the deadline for receiving all donations. Bold the *deadline date* to increase the likelihood the donation(s) will be received prior to the event. A good deadline is two weeks from the moment you send the request. Allowing for more than two weeks increases the likelihood it will be lost, misplaced, or unintentionally discarded. The goal is to have all donations committed to and accounted for at least a week prior to the actual event day.

In the fourth paragraph, illustrate the benefits the organization is able to offer the business donating. As mentioned previously, offer free Web advertising on the library's homepage. Another incentive is to offer to display their marketing/promotional materials in a prominent location such as an Information or Circulation Desk. If web advertising is offered as a donation incentive, let them know the number of hits the web page gets per day. This will give them a "hard fact" to consider and can help in their making a decision to contribute. Finally, the last paragraph thanks them for considering the request and lets them know who to contact in the event there are any further questions.

After faxing or mailing the requests, document all solicitation activity in the database file. Include the date the mailing went out and the deadline established so it is always clear which businesses need to be followed up with. If the deadline passes and no donation is received, the possibilities are: the original request was not received; it was misplaced; or, the person making the decision has been deluged with donation requests. Persistence, tact and follow-up are required at this point. It is best to follow-up with a phone call to determine what the delay might be. As with any type of request, there will be times when the answer is no. The business may have already exhausted its donation funds for the year, or it does not foresee any marketing benefit in donating.

Once a donation has been received, it is imperative to immediately follow-up with a thank you note. It is important to acknowledge, in a timely fashion, receipt of, and excitement over, the donation. It is also important to record receipt of the donation, the type of donation, and when the thank you was sent in the event's database. Another excellent relationship-building strategy is to send pictures or a newsletter article post-Open House. That these businesses have donated is an indication of their support of these type of events and they may be good prospects to approach for future projects. It is vital to continue building relationship ties for future event support.

ADVERTISING

The advertisement phase of the Open House began as soon as the date and times for the event were set. The first advertising attempts were aimed at the summer freshman orientation seminars in which the Library had a 20-minute presentation. Students were given a description of the event and told it was a fun and stress-free way to be introduced to the Library's facilities. As soon as the fall semester began, University departments of interest to incoming students were visited by committee members. They were given the details on a specially designed flyer and offered departmental booth space to showcase their particular department's offerings. Additionally, they were asked to advertise the Open House to their student clients and encourage participation. Fraternity and Sorority pledge trainers were contacted and asked to send their new pledges. Fliers and posters were distributed throughout campus, targeting dorms, classrooms, and other student gathering places. The University cafeteria's electronic billboard, located in a high traffic area, was used to display an eye-catching ad. The event was mentioned in every library training session. A mass mailing of invitations was also delivered to all transfer and freshmen students one week before the event. It is imperative that all campus advertising outlets be exploited to their fullest potential, especially if the event is planned for the first or second week of a semester.

Advertising efforts were kicked into high gear one week prior to the event, which happened in early September. A Power Point display describing the event was showcased in the Library's lobby. Door prizes were stressed as the hook to spark interest. Departments were contacted and again asked to mention the Open House to their students. An article in the school newspaper was run and additional signs posted, including chalk ads on campus sidewalks. Open House bookmark advertisements were placed in all books that were checked out. An Open House banner was hung over the Library's entrance on the day prior to the event. Everything that could be done to get the word out was attempted and reinforced several times. Decorations throughout the building were used to heighten the feeling that something special was about to take place.

LOGISTICS

Staff and student volunteers, who had already gone through an event training session the week before, were in place thirty minutes before the Open House was set to start. The most important volunteers were the "greeters." Stationed at the entrance, they ensured everyone entering the Library was aware of the Open House and invited them to participate. Students who were willing to go through the tour were asked to fill out their name, address, and classification on the invitation. This information was important for event statistics as well as contacting door prize winners who were not present at the drawing. Once the invitations were filled out, students were given brief tour instructions and turned loose on a self-guided tour.

Six main Library locations were selected as the most important. These were reference, circulation, periodicals, the computer lab, the music library, and the main stacks. The committee decided on the four or five points that would be stressed at each stop. The points discussed at each location were what incoming students would find most beneficial. Reference stressed the fact that "if you don't know the answer, ask here," and added it was where students found reference books, indexes, electronic sources, and InfoTrac. The computer lab used e-mail access, Netscape, Microsoft Office products, and typewriters as its "need to know" facts. Signs and tour maps were available to assist students unfamiliar with the Library. Additionally, staff members were on hand throughout the building to direct stray students.

As students visited each tour location, the functions performed there were explained by a knowledgeable Library student assistant. Using students as tour guides helped reinforce the casual nature of the event. The committee hoped the impression would be given that if these students were comfortable in a library setting, why should others be anxious? A Library staff member was also on hand to assist the student guide with the more difficult questions or to help with stamping the student's tour invitations. Signs reiterated what the tour guide was describing. After each student went through the brief location overview, their invitation was stamped and they were given a small gift. For example, the music library handed out pens with the Library's name and web address printed on them and Circulation gave out fast food coupons. No student was to go away empty-handed. This was another incentive to take the tour. A demonstration of the computer lab services could be followed up by a bookmark printed with the Library's web address, so the student would have something to take away. The give-away item could be related to the department involved, such as copy cards at the photocopier demonstration, or just fun, like the candy distributed in reference. Most of all, it was of utmost importance that the student assistants and staff be friendly and approachable.

In addition to the tour locations, booth space in the Library's lobby was offered to other university departments. This would be a great way for other agencies to advertise services. The Open House must not just look inward at Library functions, but illustrate how the Library works in conjunction with other university services. After all, the campus is a community. For added impact, booths must be plainly visible in the main Open House activity area, either at check-in or near the food and door prizes. For additional emphasis, booths from other university departments could be included as part of the tour itself. It cannot be taken for granted that freshman are aware of every service on campus, even after attending intensive orientation sessions. Most students are overwhelmed their first semester, therefore reinforcement is crucial.

A Library booth was also included in the Open House centering in on the Library's instruction program by detailing training sessions and online research aids. The centerpiece was a Power Point display that reinforced the information given at the tour locations. Subject bibliographies (Pathfinders) were available as handouts to further emphasize the services offered in the Library.

As soon as the students had completed the Library tour, they were eligible for the food as well as participating in the door prize drawings. The staff at the food counters verified the students had a completed invitation before they were given access to the "snacks." It was stressed that the food offered were "snacks," meaning students could not expect to make a full meal out of the Open House refreshments. For example, bagels and cream cheese, assorted yogurts, and dessert items were the main offerings. These were complemented by salty snacks items, candy and soft drinks.

For maximum effect, the refreshments area needs to be combined with the door prize location. The drawings combined with the food contribute to the overall excitement. Students will become very interested in the progress of the door prizes and monitor the winnings. With food and prizes in one location, students will not have to rush through their munchies to ensure they get their names in the drawings. Additionally, containing the refreshment area is an imperative as the food donations might not always be "library friendly."

The Open House door prize drawings consisted of a staff member pulling the completed invitations out of a barrel and announcing the winner. For this, you need an energetic, outgoing person. This individual needs to drum up excitement in the prizes being drawn as well as effectively banter with the students. Depending on how many prizes you have, you can stagger the prize drawings throughout the event, saving the biggest prizes for last. Students should not have to be present to win; winners and their prizes were posted on bulletin boards for immediate viewing. Students who were present when they won were given a sheet of paper verifying which prize and its number. Prizes were handed out at a second, more secure, location. Students who were not present were called by staff members the next day or checked the winnings board in the Library's lobby. Remember, the door prizes are the event's hook and will be the major reason many students attend. Their marketing value must be played to the hilt.

POST-EVENT FOLLOW UP

Post-Open House activities are the last phase of the event life-cycle. Donors have already been thanked, but follow-up is important to continue the relationship. Some donors will want feedback about how their contributions were used while others may need pictures for their files. The library used the photographs taken at the Open House as a display in the Library's lobby. Photographs and the list of winners may also be displayed on the event's web page. The final post-Open House activity is to meet with all the staff volunteers to brainstorm on possible successes and failures. The input received will play an important part in planning for the following year. The process is now complete and steps are in place for future events.

One final point to consider is what to do with the remaining food, supplies, decorations? Consider donating decorations and candy to a children's advocacy and care center. Another source for non-perishable food items is a food pantry/night shelter for the homeless. It is important to re-use donations to both avoid wastefulness and spread the goodwill to organizations in greater need of support.

Looking back on the previous two Open House events, there may be a perceived imbalance between the organizational effort and the number of attendees. Out of a potential of 1,400 freshmen students, only 125 attended the first year whereas 173 attended the second year. These figures reflect the number of "official" library tour participants. While these low figures may seem discouraging, the positive press coverage in University publications, combined with encouraging feedback from students, staff, and faculty, indicate this event will build in numbers over the succeeding years. Potential library event organizers must realize that crowded university calendars, filled with competing events, may initially decrease attendance. To be effective, library public relations must be an ongoing outreach effort. It may take several iterations of an event to build a following and achieve your attendance goals.

CONCLUSION

In conclusion, the Open House is an effective and innovative way to publicize the library to new students who are both wary and unsure of their new environment. It will complement, not replace, the traditional library tours and bibliographic instruction sessions. The relaxed "party" atmosphere of the Open House begins the process of developing the valuable library skills students will use throughout their academic careers. An added benefit of the Open House is not only the strengthening of campus-wide and community bonds, but the opportunity for staff members to participate in a fun and "out of the box" approach to library outreach. Most of all, the Open House will show off your library in a new and innovative light to students, faculty, administration, and the community-at-large.

APPENDIX
Sample Letter

July 15, 1998

Jane Doe, Owner
Coffee and Tea House
2970 Park Hill at University
Ft. Worth, TX 76109

Dear Ms.Doe:

The Mary Couts Burnett Library at Texas Christian University will be hosting its *2nd annual Open House* for incoming freshmen on *September 1, 1998*. The slogan for this year's event is *"frog files: the truth is in here"* and the intent is to get new students familiar with the various services that the library can provide them during their tenure here.

APPENDIX (continued)

The entering freshman class will consist of approximately 1,300 students. This year's Open House is already a much anticipated event and we expect between 300-350 students in attendance.

We are requesting donations from businesses which are patronized by TCU community members. Please consider donating a gift certificate or other item which can be used as a door prize giveaway.

The Open House Committee is seeking to have a complete and confirmed list of donors by *August 15, 1998*.

Finally, I will be happy to display any marketing/promotional materials that you would like to provide. The library is also committed to advertising your donation on our web page which gets over 3,000 hits each day.

Thanks in advance for your consideration to this solicitation request. Please contact me with any questions you may have. I look forward to hearing from you.

Sincerely,

Alexia Strout-Dapaz
Reference/Business Librarian
Texas Christian University
P. O. Box 298400
Fort Worth, Texas 76129
257-5336 (Phone)–921-7447 (FAX)
a.stroutdapaz@tcu.edu

Outside the Exhibit Case:
An Undergraduate Library
Welcomes the Community

Eleanor Mitchell
Diane Zwemer

SUMMARY. In planning for a major traveling exhibit in UCLA's undergraduate library, outreach was a priority. Programming and publicity targeted segments of the campus and community both as participants and as attendees. This collaboration came to fruition in an exciting array of programs that brought many people into the library and demonstrated the strengths of collections, resources and services to new audiences.

UCLA's College Library, the undergraduate library that recently returned to its historic and award-winning Powell Library Building, was a site for the ALA-Smithsonian traveling exhibition, "A More Perfect Union: Japanese Americans and the United States Constitution." The Programs and Exhibits Committee of the Library surrounded the display of this material with several months' worth of diverse community and campus programming. Events involved staff, faculty, students, local K-12 teachers, members of the Los Angeles Japanese American Community, writers, film makers, even a movie star (this IS Los Angeles)! In addition to highlighting the strengths of UCLA's Library collections through traditional means, a variety of media and multimedia programs

Eleanor Mitchell is Head, College Library, UCLA. UCLA, Box 951450, Los Angeles, CA 90095-1450. Diane Zwemer is former Instructional Services Coordinator, College Library, UCLA.

[Haworth co-indexing entry note]: "Outside the Exhibit Case: An Undergraduate Library Welcomes the Community." Mitchell, Eleanor, and Diane Zwemer. Co-published simultaneously in *The Reference Librarian* (The Haworth Information Press, an imprint of The Haworth Press, Inc.) No. 67/68, 1999, pp. 187-201; and: *Library Outreach, Partnerships, and Distance Education: Reference Librarians at the Gateway* (ed: Wendi Arant, and Pixey Anne Mosley) The Haworth Press, Inc., 2000, pp. 187-201. Single or multiple copies of this article are available for a fee from The Haworth Document Delivery Service [1-800-342-9678, 9:00 a.m. - 5:00 p.m. (EST). E-mail address: getinfo@haworthpressinc.com].

187

and events supplemented the exhibit. *[Article copies available for a fee from The Haworth Document Delivery Service: 1-800-342-9678. E-mail address: getinfo@haworthpressinc.com <Website: http://www.haworthpressinc.com>]*

KEYWORDS. Community outreach, collaborative projects, traveling exhibits, Japanese Americans

INTRODUCTION

UCLA College Library staff focus on providing reference, instruction, and information resources for undergraduates, in support of the University's academic mission. Since the 1996 reopening of the historic Powell Library Building, after four years' of renovation and preservation efforts, that role has been expanded and redefined. Powell Library has become a center for undergraduates, housing library and computing facilities and offering a calendar of cultural and artistic programming from author lectures to musical performances to faculty presentations. Although the staff has become accustomed to the use of this facility for "extra-library" activities, the installation of a national touring exhibition in 1997 presented opportunities that challenged their notions of what was possible.

In 1995, UCLA's College Library was selected as one of twenty libraries in the nation to participate in the ALA-Smithsonian organized exhibition tour, "A More Perfect Union: Japanese Americans and the U.S. Constitution." The reasons behind the selection of this library as the site for this exhibit, the related strengths of local collections and the broad interest in the topic among community populations, were the same ones that led to a very ambitious calendar of enhanced and supportive programming and other activities. The exhibition proved to be the inspiration and the stepping stone for a host of events that brought together a diverse group of planners and participants from on and off campus, and attracted crowds of visitors to the library. The interest was so high, and the possibilities so boundless that the library staff members, as planners, were loath to leave any resource unmined, any potential audience uninvited. So, taking a broad view of the requirement that the host library provide both public programming and an opening reception, a committee of library staff and other interested faculty and students from the University began what amounted to a year's worth of planning and implementation.

Public library staffs are more accustomed to and often have as part of their mission, and their budgets, community outreach and public programming. Not so with this academic library. Staff had no experience with programming on this scale, nor background in the protocol of coordinating, not only across academic departments, but also with a range of players from city agencies to private organizations to local museums. There were no dedicated personnel to muster for the program, but a need to rely upon existing staff resources. Furthermore, the project started out with no budget other than basic funding provided by the UCLA Library to cover small expenses such the printing of flyers. Collaboration with more knowledgeable individuals and departments was an essential strategy.

PLANNING FOR OUTREACH

The process began with the College Library's five member standing committee, whose charge expanded from "exhibits" to "exhibits and programs." This redefinition continues to be a useful way to look at programming within the Library. The Committee's broader purview evolved from a static to a dynamic stance, from mere display to performance. The Committee was encouraged to think about creative ways to enhance programming by incorporating library resources and collections–through creation of bibliographies and reading lists, and displays of relevant library materials (both physically and on the Web)–into scheduled public events. The Exhibits and Programs Committee of the College Library served to coordinate, schedule, and communicate among planners and implementers in this decentralized program. These staff members also were responsible for resolving building use issues, and for those aspects of the programming that involved identifying expertise and resources from the library's existing staff and collections. They created balance and assured relevance among the programs; made certain that the Library's interests and goals were visible throughout the varied events; and coordinated a larger team of program planners, consisting of teaching faculty, departmental coordinators, and students with interest in particular aspects of the program.

Planning began with goal setting. With the initial aim being to provide a venue for public access to the traveling exhibition, the committee members developed three programmatic goals: (1) expand the exhibition theme to include interesting sub-topics, angles and related topics; (2) showcase the richness of library, campus, and community resources on the topic; and (3) reach as wide an audience as possible, beyond our primary users and Library colleagues. Key to tapping into the campus and community resources was the involvement of a mix of participants in the planning team.

This was, indeed, the first of the outreach efforts. The first task of the core committee was to identify the best persons and organizations to work with, in terms of the resources, expertise, and connections that they could bring to the planning table for the premier exhibit. With the advice of the UCLA Asian American Studies Center (AASC), the Library's primary exhibit partner, a larger committee was created, consisting of persons from various academic departments, student groups and community organizations that helped the Library gain entrance into a well-developed network of individuals and groups with established roles and existing programs. Through these mutually beneficial partnerships, the Library was able to relinquish responsibility for some events in their entirety, ceding control to groups and individuals with expertise or interest who could sponsor or co-sponsor events or programs and bring them to fruition.

THE CALENDAR

The availability of the traveling exhibition from the Smithsonian dictated the timeline for the programming. Once the application was accepted and the library selected as a site, two staff members attended an orientation meeting in September of 1995, in Washington, D.C.; participation for one member was funded by the institutional sponsors of the project, the American Library Association and the Smithsonian, while the Library supported the other staff member's attendance. At this point, they were made familiar with the exhibition materials that would be provided, were taught how to erect and dismantle the displays, and gained some sense of the content of the materials. With two years between this point and the scheduled arrival of the exhibition materials from the Smithsonian, there seemed a luxury of time. With a library move and building reopening taking place in the intervening time, and an equally ambitious roster of celebratory and instructional activities surrounding that event, the staff members on the Library's Exhibits and Programs Committee put planning on hold until spring of 1997.

The strategy was to develop a master calendar centered on the date of the installation, the only fixed moment that was beyond our control, and ending with its dismantling and shipping off to the next site. Events and programs were penciled in following that date, with the understanding that there be flexibility based on the availability of key participants. Venues and contact people were added as the additional information became available. Working back from the scheduled opening event, the committee used the calendar to identify decision points and deadlines, so that they could determine at any moment whether things were on track. In areas such as publicity, the calendar served to remind the committee members of publication deadlines for various news vehicles, and helped to fit the many meetings around the academic and other scheduled events that would affect availability of participants. The calendar supported one of the guiding principles, which was to build and layer events and activities whenever possible. A glance at the calendar identified open venues, unused blocks of time and places where one could fit in an additional screening, or another author event. It also guided the shaping of the programs. Considerations of timing, audience, conflict and sequence, were easy to work out with the overview so readily accessible.

EXTENDING THE REACH OF EXHIBITS

The venue was essential to planning. The placement of the core of materials provided as part of the ALA/Smithsonian traveling exhibit, consisting of five multi-fold freestanding panels, two banners, a laserdisk and kiosk, was a primary concern. The intention was to also use as many varied spaces as possible: the "quad," an open area in front of the Library building; the entrance foyer; display cases and performance space in the historic Rotunda; and the "cyberspace" of the World Wide Web. Additionally, events were planned that would be appropriate to and enhanced by their space.

The physical layout of the exhibit meant that anybody who stepped inside the Library doors experienced at least part of what was on display. At the entrance foyer to College Library, the laserdisk kiosk displaying interviews with former internees stood at the base of the stairs leading to the main library floor. Nearby a video player showed a continuous loop of clips depicting the Japanese American experience during the Second World War, compiled from the Hearst Metrotone Newsreels from the UCLA Film and Television Archives. Even visitors who entered the building intending to go to the computer lab, the study rooms or any of the other offices and departments located in Powell, would see and hear these displays.

Upstairs, the five multi-fold panels, each over six feet high, were centrally placed around the second floor Rotunda, permitting visitors easy access to the information on both sides. This is a heavily traversed area in one of the most popular spaces of the Library. Supplementing these panels were four exhibit cases in the College Library Rotunda that contained photographs and documents from the UCLA Library Special Collections, including the items from the Japanese American Resource Project (JARP), and University Archives departments. These items documented how the exhibit themes touched the lives of the UCLA community during the period of the internment. For example, included were reproductions of the student newspaper *The Daily Bruin*, with headlines such as "Edict Bans Japanese from Westwood," and "Army Rule Affects 175 Bruin Students." Also included were the final meeting minutes of Chi Alpha Delta, a Japanese American sorority that had to be disbanded due to the Executive Order, and letters from UC President Sproul, requesting transfers for Japanese students to colleges in states unaffected by the evacuation. These displays were particularly significant to UCLA's present day undergraduates, and to the alumni, some of whom were students at UCLA during that period.

The Japanese American National Museum, in Los Angeles, a primary partner in the planning of the events, identified interested community members and groups and provided the Library with access to some of their materials and collections. Security considerations prevented the display of several of the Museum's models of internment camps and guard towers. However, enlarged photographs of the camps from the Museum's collections, including some by Dorothea Lange from their exhibit, "Executive Order 9066," enhanced and enlivened the exhibition area. These large, somber, black and white photographs added a chilling, realistic effect.

A fifth exhibit case, located in the first floor book stacks, was filled with contemporary (1996-97) newspaper clippings from the *Los Angeles Times* and the *Daily Bruin* with articles relevant to race relations and redress issues for other ethnic groups, as well as for Japanese Americans.

Throughout the seven-week run of the exhibit, many people took the time to stop and read the panels and closely examine the materials in the exhibit cases. Some faculty from the Asian American Studies Center encouraged their students to see the exhibit. Often, the staff saw people taking notes on what they were reading. Occasionally, people would stop by the reference desk to talk more about the exhibit and how it affected them or their families' lives. Over 83,000 visitors viewed some or all of the materials on display from Oct. 30 through Dec. 18, 1997.

REACHING OUT
THROUGH DIVERSE PROGRAM PLANNING

One principle that guided the program planning was to build upon strengths. There was an effort to maximize and enhance a single event by expanding it through additional related or supporting activities. The Committee also planned to extend the experience of the exhibition through a range of media, including programming that encompassed live presentation, print, film, newsreel, music and movement, and the electronic formats. Additionally, there was an intention to branch out into areas with which the academic library staff had only marginal experience: developing bibliographies for K-12, planning programs for school teachers, hosting forums for experts from the legal to the literary worlds, screening films, and compiling newsreel footage.

One important factor that guided the Committee's approach was the recognition that no single event would have universal appeal. Though each program would be free and open, individual programs would have a specific angle and target audience. This would determine the composition of the program, its timing on the schedule, and where and how to advertise it. A typical busy undergraduate, for example, might want to attend the Grand Opening, and perhaps some of the screenings, but would probably only choose to attend programs when not attending classes on campus. On the other hand, members of the community at large, who might be drawn by programs such as the author visits, would rather not come to campus during the week, but would prefer weekends when traffic and parking are less likely to be a problem. Of necessity, the program targeted for public school teachers was a weekend event. Primarily, events for students, faculty and staff were held during the week while events targeting the community were held on weekends.

The Grand Opening serves as a perfect example of the blending of campus and community appeal. The variety of participants and activities on that day set the tone for future programs. At the stroke of noon, the festivities began with a bang, a resounding performance by UCLA's student drum and dance group, the Kyodo Taiko Drummers, on the steps outside the Powell Library Building. Although the program had been announced in both campus and community media, the sound and movement attracted passersby and drew others within earshot to the event. Following this, representatives from the Asian American Studies Center, the UCLA Library Administration, and the Nikkei Student Union, key players in the programs, shared a few words of welcome with the audience. The keynote speaker, actor George Takei of *Star Trek* fame and UCLA alumnus, spoke movingly about his family's internment experience in Arkansas. Then, the ceremony moved indoors to the main exhibit space in the Rotunda where visitors could view the panels and cases. The UCLA BookZone, the campus bookstore, was on hand to sell copies of Takei's autobiography, *To The Stars*. At a nearby table, Mr. Takei signed books for a long line of devoted fans.

This opening event demonstrates the careful orchestration that marked the entire months-long program, the attention to the diverse interests of the public and the maximizing of impact through building layers of events. An opening event for the general public was a requirement of the traveling exhibition; the College Library wanted to be sure to reach its own primary undergraduate clientele with the opening. To bring them in to the process and help make the exhibit more personal for them, the Nikkei Student Union was invited to become involved in the planning. One of their members, a UCLA undergraduate, spoke eloquently and personally to the gathered crowd about the exhibition themes. The Taiko Drummers appreciated the performance opportunity as much as the students enjoyed watching them. George Takei helped bridge the gap between current and former students. As a former internee at a camp, Mr. Takei also spoke to the interests of community visitors as he recounted his experiences. His Hollywood connection provided additional glamour. After all, TV camera crews rarely show up at libraries to interview librarians!

If the Grand Opening was the program of broadest interest and most popular appeal, other events were tightly wrapped about specific themes and topics that were more focused. The exhibit planning group, with their combined subject knowledge, networking skills and people connections, and insightful and personal suggestions for potential speakers, helped map out the entire programmatic schedule. They helped develop a full slate of programs that included those that had social relevance, were academically oriented, and had personal significance for both presenters and audience.

REACHING THOSE WITH SPECIAL INTERESTS

One member of the planning group was a faculty member from the Department of Social Welfare, whose area of specialization is the redress issue. Through a panel discussion titled "And Redress for All," he helped the Committee to broaden an exhibit theme from a narrow focus on redress for interned Japanese Americans to the ongoing debate concerning race in America. The panelists included representatives from organizations such as the Multicultural Collaborative, the Asian Pacific American Legal Center, the Los Angeles County Human Relations Commission, and a member of President Clinton's Initiative on Race. With additional publicity provided by the School of Public Policy, this program reached an audience broader than those only interested in Asian American issues. The university's newspaper, the *Daily Bruin*, also provided extensive coverage of the program, with a detailed article and analysis the following day that really caught the social debate issues.

Though the internment occurred more than 50 years ago, it is recent enough that a number of survivors and others affected by the Executive Order are still living in this Southern California community. Another panel discussion was called "Remembering the Internment: Japanese Americans Share Their Memories So That It Will Never Happen Again." This program was handled in its entirety by a Department of History faculty member at the suggestion of the AASC. It featured a panel of Japanese Americans, including UCLA alumni, who shared their personal experiences of being removed and incarcerated during World War II. This session was particularly well attended by community members, as was another program focusing on literature of the camps. This panel discussion, "Voices of Internment & Redress: Literature on the Internment Experience," was organized by the AASC and the English Department, and included a panel of five authors whose works touched upon the internment and redress issues. The BookZone again participated by having a table in the Library Rotunda to sell these and other related works.

One highlight of the program was a special screening of a new documentary film, "Beyond Barbed Wire" (a 1996 production of Mac & Ava Motion Picture Productions). This Seattle International Film Festival selection recounts the stories and memories of the Japanese American soldiers of the 100th/442nd/MIS military units of World War II, who fought in a segregated unit to prove their loyalty to this country. Arranging a venue, and finding funding for the costs associated with the screening seemed great obstacles to this program, particularly for a program committee already occupied with a number of complex details. A former UCLA student who had heard about the upcoming exhibit took charge and made arrangements with the film's producer for the UCLA Asian Pacific Coalition, the UCLA Campus Programs Committee and a local chapter of the Japanese American Citizens League to provide sponsorship for the screening. She also arranged a panel discussion to follow the screening, which featured the film's writer and co-producer, the director, a 442nd Regimental Combat Team veteran, a MIS (Military Intelligence Service) veteran, and the daughter of a 442nd veteran. This documentary screening was not the only motion picture event. In order to showcase other UCLA resources relevant to the exhibit and appeal to a broader community of potential visitors, a varied program of documentaries and other short films were selected from the UCLA Film & Television Archive and shown on Saturday afternoons in the Powell Library video-viewing lab.

The final program, sponsored by the UCLA Library, was targeted to library staff and others on campus interested in new digital technologies. Called "Documenting the Experience Digitally," it included presentations of three recent UCLA electronic projects relevant to the program topic. One was a new CD-ROM, *Executive Order 9066: The Incarceration of Japanese Americans During World War II* (published by Groliers in 1997) that details the internment experience through photographs, videos and text. Another panelist demonstrated UCLA Library's Ishigo Archive Digital Library Project, an electronically networked prototype for the storage, retrieval and delivery of primary source materials. The Ishigo Archive is part of the Japanese-American Research Project (JARP). The third presentation highlighted an interactive CD-ROM developed by the AASC, the *Asian American Experience,* that takes a broad look at the history of Asian immigration to the US and Asian American life. Beyond the presentations, these CD-ROMs were made available for users to access in a computer area adjacent to the exhibits in the Rotunda.

OUTREACH TO SCHOOLS, THROUGH TEACHERS

While the UCLA campus and the Library are open to the public, there are limited programmatic ways for an undergraduate library to reach out to the schools. The Committee felt that this exhibition would be particularly relevant to elementary, middle, and high school students, and sought ways to bring them to the Library. The AASC, through their contacts with local school board members, was able to bring about a program through schoolteachers that also reached school children. At the suggestion of the AASC and inspired by the planned exhibition and associated events, the Los Angeles Unified School District organized and conducted teacher in-service training sessions at UCLA about the internment. These sessions were timed to coincide with the program. The two-weekend professional development program explored how the internment could have happened in a democratic society, and the lessons that should be learned from it. The focus was on ways this material can be integrated into K-12 classroom instruction. The sessions included films, literary readings, and an array of presentations by scholars, writers and librarians, as well as individuals who were interned. The teachers' enthusiasm led to student visits, and brought many virtual visitors to the special bibliographies on the Library's web site for students.

VIRTUALLY EXTENDING YOUR REACH

One of the most exciting aspects of the programming was the development of an extensive web site for the exhibit. Not only does the web site include basic information about the exhibit and program schedule at UCLA, but it also points to many other sites relevant to Japanese American and Asian American history. It has sections appropriate for K-12 users and scholarly resources. The web site served as an organizing tool for planners as well as a communication vehicle for visitors. The web site is still available and can be found at: http://www.library. ucla.edu/libraries/college/JAexhibit/

REACHING OUT WITH A PUBLICITY CAMPAIGN

In seeking to attract the diverse audiences that were targeted for individual programs, it was clear that publicity needed to be specific and timely. The traditional methods and organs used to reach the UCLA student population, such as posters, flyers, the campus calendar and the student newspaper would be only a beginning. One Library staff member was assigned to oversee all the communications and publicity related to the programs and exhibits. Her key tasks were to identify appropriate outlets for publicity, and to provide information to them for inclusion in their publications and other forms of media.

On campus, both the student newspaper, *The Daily Bruin*, and the campus newspaper, *UCLA Today*, were contacted with information about scheduled programs and speakers. The academic departments involved with the programs also posted notices and distributed flyers to their students and faculty. The *UCLA Library News for the Faculty* carried a full-page article on the exhibit and related programs. Other programs were announced in the Library's staff newsletter. Campus electronic media were also important. In addition to the Library's web site devoted to the exhibit, the UCLA Library and the UCLA web pages included the programs in their listings of events. The UCLA BookZone's electronic announcements of upcoming book events provided another access point for potential visitors to discover this programming.

Beyond the campus, announcements of events were included in the newsletter of the Japanese American National Museum. Flyers were sent to the Museum and to a local Japanese American citizens' league for distribution. The connection of this series of events to the local Japanese American community was evident in the press coverage provided by their community publications such as *Kamai Forum* and *Rafu Shimpo*.

Two approaches were useful in providing publicity about the programs. It was important to distribute information about the program as a whole in the context of the overall schedule, which the Committee did through the use of a brochure. It was also necessary to publicize each individual event to the target population at a appropriate to the scheduled date.

GROWING AN EVENT INTO A PROGRAM: FOUR POINTS FOR SUCCESSFUL OUTREACH

1. Choose the Right Event

One key to the success of this program was the strength of both interest in the topic and resources in the area. The ALA-Smithsonian exhibition, around which the programs coalesced, was a big draw. In the wake of related programs held in recent years on campus, marking the fiftieth anniversary of the Japanese-American internment during the Second World War, there was a high level of interest already established. Individuals with expertise, involved in earlier programming, were identified. The Committee's research identified an existing network of local community organizations and resources that indicated strong likelihood of interest and support.

2. Build a Network of Human Resources

Another key to the success of this program was recognizing the need to broaden participation beyond the Library's own committee. The Library staff began by identifying a network of individuals who could bring different expertise, resources, perspectives, and constituents into the process. UCLA is rich in related resources, in campus libraries and special collections; films and videos in the Film and Television Archives; as well as nationally-known faculty and other experts in the Asian American Studies Center and other academic departments, with particular interests in areas such as literature, law, and public policy. In turn, their links to the broader community of interested people brought program participants and attendees. The Los Angeles area offers cultural resources and well-organized and identifiable community groups that enriched programming and boosted participation. The best way to ensure that the resources and expertise available locally became part of this program, and to overcome the departmental autonomy that can make partnering cumbersome, was to involve these key players in the planning. Whether they came with just strong personal interest, or professional or political clout, volunteer participation was critical to this effort.

3. Give Power to Volunteers

When the right people have been recruited, and the parameters of the program communicated, it makes good sense to let them run with their portion of the plan. Make them more than just volunteers. As appropriate give them the authority to make decisions and build their own events. Let them use their expertise and, in some cases, their financial resources, to extend the reach of your program. Though this involves relinquishing some centralized control, it is actually key to more meaningful community involvement and results in the development of some extraordinary programming far beyond the abilities of the core committee. Relationships like this help both sides achieve what each wants. For example, in promoting the linkage of this program with a teacher training event sponsored and planned by the Los Angeles Unified School District, the Library was able to help support their programmatic goals and to strengthen this community connection to UCLA and the Library, with minimal outlay of library staff time and effort. In another example, when a producer contacted the Committee with information on her own documentary film related to the exhibit theme, a volunteer from campus took on the complete responsibility for everything from finding funding to scheduling the event.

4. Understand and Build on Others' Agendas

In its collaborations, the Library recognized that its planning partners and co-sponsors also had goals for their involvement. It was mutually rewarding to support their objectives along with the Library's own. For example, the Asian American Studies Center provided critical guidance and support to the programming, but also benefited from increased visibility on campus. The Nikkei Student Union received exposure and encouraged new members. The campus book store actually sold books at author signings. The Film and Television Archives promoted their new CD-ROM. The local Japanese American Citizens league tailored a program to their members' interests. Finally, the UCLA Library was able to showcase the Powell Building, highlight the extensive JARP collection and hold a special event for potential donors. The thoughtful mix of approaches and content that surrounded this exhibit was precisely in keeping with the College Library's own interest in providing academic and intellectual programming for its primarily undergraduate constituency.

REWARDS OF OUTREACH

Outreach to the campus and community through this exhibit and the related programming served not only to meet the requirements and intent of the traveling exhibition, but also underscored the connection of the campus to the interests of the community. The programs and events reinforced the notion of the College Library as a center for cultural activity, and of the UCLA Library as a source of information and programming. They resulted in strengthened ties between the Library and campus departments and faculty, and provided learning opportunities for Library staff and primary clientele. The programs surrounding this exhibition demonstrated the strengths of the Library's collections, resources, and services to new audiences.

EXHIBIT AND PROGRAMMING ACKNOWLEDGMENTS

The following organizations received acknowledgment in all the Library's exhibit publicity:

- American Library Association
- Asian American Studies Center, UCLA (AASC)
- Dept. of Special Collections, UCLA
- Gila River Reunion Committee
- Japanese American Citizens League–Pacific Southwest Division
- Japanese American Historical Society of Southern California
- Japanese American National Museum
- Los Angeles Unified School District (LAUSD)
- Manzanar Committee
- National Coalition for Redress and Reparations
- National Museum of American History, Smithsonian Institution
- University Archives, UCLA Department of Special Collections
- UCLA Film & Television Archive
- UCLA Asian Pacific Coalition
- UCLA BookZone
- UCLA Nikkei Student Union

Developing a Liaison Program in a New Organizational Structure– A Work in Progress

Carla A. Hendrix

SUMMARY. This article describes the development of an expanded liaison outreach program in the context of a view of organizational structure that is characterized by a flattened organizational hierarchy, an emphasis on programmatic groups and a merger with college computing services. The goal of this liaison program is to provide consistent information to academic departments about library services, collection development and instruction, as well as information regarding computing services. The production of a liaison script to assist librarians in communicating information about rapidly changing services and technologies offered by a merged Division of Library and Information Services is outlined. The first years of the liaison program's development are evaluated in terms of the barriers to success and the benefits of such an expanded program. *[Article copies available for a fee from The Haworth Document Delivery Service: 1-800-342-9678. E-mail address: getinfo@haworthpressinc.com <Website: http://www.haworthpressinc.com>]*

KEYWORDS. Faculty liaison, librarian-faculty relations, university libraries, technology support, library instruction, combined library and computing services

Carla A. Hendrix is Associate Librarian, Collection Development/Acquisitions, Benjamin Feinberg Library, Plattsburgh State University of New York, Plattsburgh, NY 12901.

[Haworth co-indexing entry note]: "Developing a Liaison Program in a New Organizational Structure–A Work in Progress." Hendrix, Carla A. Co-published simultaneously in *The Reference Librarian* (The Haworth Information Press, an imprint of The Haworth Press, Inc.) No. 67/68, 1999, pp. 203-224; and: *Library Outreach, Partnerships, and Distance Education: Reference Librarians at the Gateway* (ed: Wendi Arant, and Pixey Anne Mosley) The Haworth Press, Inc., 2000, pp. 203-224. Single or multiple copies of this article are available for a fee from The Haworth Document Delivery Service [1-800-342-9678, 9:00 a.m. - 5:00 p.m. (EST). E-mail address: getinfo@haworthpressinc.com].

INTRODUCTION

The Feinberg Library at Plattsburgh State University of New York has had a formal outreach program through its liaison and instruction activities for many years. As in most college libraries, the last decade has seen enormous changes in the library in terms of organizational structure, the format and availability of information resources, methods of access to and delivery of those resources, as well as rapidly changing needs and expectations on the part of our constituencies, the faculty/staff and students of the college.

With these changes have come changes in outreach activities as the Library attempts to keep up with changes in technology, increased access to burgeoning sources of information, differing levels of technological expertise on the parts of librarians, students and classroom faculty, relatively static budgets combined with increased costs for resources and the technology to make these resources readily accessible to users whose expectations for immediate access to information grows exponentially.

This article describes a work-in-progress: the development of a liaison program that allows us to provide consistent information to our faculty/academic departments about library services, collection development and instruction, as well as information regarding computing services, from Web page development to hardware/software upgrades and campus networking priorities. This liaison program is conceived as a dialogue. While information about the topics above is expected to flow out to departments via the library liaisons, liaisons are equally responsible for bringing information back from departments. This information from the departments allows the Library and Computing Services to respond to concerns from academic departments and make changes and improvements in library collections, library and computing instruction and services, as faculty needs change or new academic programs are added.

In order to understand how the liaison program has developed, some background about our outreach programs, organizational structure and changes in access and delivery of information is necessary.

BACKGROUND

Outreach Activities

In the past, outreach at Feinberg took a fairly familiar shape. Since 1976, a liaison program has linked each librarian (both in public and technical services) with an academic department or departments. The focus of the liaison program was collection development. Librarian liaisons provided the point of communication for academic departments' requests for monographic purchases, recommendations for new periodical or serial subscriptions and information about new or changed academic programs. The budget for monographic allocations was divided among librarian liaisons based on a cost/use formula that divided funds by LC classification numbers. Reference materials were selected by the librarians in the Reference unit from a separate reference allocation. Reference librarians provided the majority of instruction to our students in a required "Introduction to Library Skills" course and via course-related instruction, usually a one-shot instructional session on tools and techniques specified by the instructor or jointly determined by instructor and librarian.

Network instruction was added to the mix seven years ago, when several librarians with particular expertise in online searching and the Internet were asked to join staff in Computing Support in offering workshops for faculty/staff about using electronic resources for their research activities. New or changed library services were promoted to the faculty through an irregularly published newsletter or by means of memos to all academic departments from the librarian supervising the service or from the Director of the Library.

In a world of card catalogs and print indexes where reliance on the materials owned by the library, supplemented by an active interlibrary loan service, was thought sufficient for undergraduate teaching needs, these outreach programs served well as vehicles for communication between library and academic department. If some liaisons and reference librarians were more active in their communication and their advocacy for their departments, it might have meant an additional periodical subscription or two for that academic department. By and large a faculty member's knowledge of a library's resources and how to use them, gained initially during their doctoral studies, was more than enough foundation to keep them abreast of the growth and change in information in their field. Furthermore, the roles of librarians, be it as reference librarians, catalogers, circulation or acquisitions librarians were relatively clearly understood by faculty, as were services such as interlibrary loan or reserves.

Organizational Structure

The organizational changes in the Library began in 1995. A survey of all library staff by the Director of Libraries identified the hierarchical structure as one barrier to effective communication, opportunities for creativity and experimentation and equity of workload, especially amongst librarians. The development of a flattened organizational structure based on a programmatic group concept is the subject of its own, as yet unwritten, article. Six programmatic groups emerged from this development: Instruction Services, Resource Access and Delivery, Information Services, Patron Services, Information Systems and Collection Development. Each group had at least five members, librarians, non-librarian professionals and senior support staff. Each group had a group leader chosen by the Director from librarians expressing interest in serving in that capacity. The Group leaders and the Director formed a seventh group, which served as a steering group, setting priorities and providing a bi-weekly forum for communication among groups. The Collection Development Group had as part of its responsibilities the development and maintenance of the liaison program.

As part of this re-organization of the Library's structure, the roles of librarians saw a significant shift. Four core responsibilities for librarians were identified: reference desk service (equalized for all librarians), classroom teaching (a one-credit required course, "Introduction to Information Research," course-related sessions and network instruction), liaison responsibilities and service on two programmatic groups. Liaison responsibilities had been focused on selection activities under the previous organizational structure. The selection of materials for the core collection would now be done by the four librarians on the Collection Development Group. Each librarian on the Collection Development Group selects basic materials by discipline (Humanities, Social Sciences, Sciences and General, which includes the interdisciplinary programs such as Latin American Studies, Canadian Studies, Minority Studies and Women's Studies). The role of the liaison now would focus on communication to the department(s) regarding all aspects of library services and from the department(s) back to the Library and to the appropriate programmatic group to address and resolve issues raised by faculty. The role of the liaison will be more extensively described under Development of the Current Liaison Program later in this article.

A year later, as all involved were just beginning to get their feet wet in this new organization, a second and more far-reaching structural change occurred. With the retirement of the Director of Computing Services, the Director of Libraries was asked to assume a new role as Dean of Library and Information Services. The Library was now part of a newly created division that included academic computing, administrative computing, systems management, network operations and instructional engineering. Many of these units, especially academic computing support and systems and networks, had responsibilities for areas of great technological change. As a result, there was a real need for the activities of these areas to be communicated and explicated to the faculty, who were suddenly finding themselves with new desktop computers with unfamiliar software, new Ethernet wiring and access to the Web. In response to this need, it was felt that the liaison role could be expanded to include the provision of information (if not direct support) to faculty regarding the myriad of technological changes that were now intimately linked with the resources and services provided by the Library.

Delivery of Information

The shape and format of information that a college library is able to provide to its community via ownership or access has seen rapid and radical transformation during this last decade. Nine years ago, librarians relied on a card catalog, print indexes, selected indexes on CD-ROM, the physical collection of materials and an ILL service seen as highly responsive with the addition of a fax machine! Now we count on an online catalog, Web-based indexes, including full text, access to all the resources of the Web and ILL delivery via the Internet to faculty desktops. The machines we had on our desktops, which brought us email and listservs, ftp and gophers, are the stuff of museums now. The powers of our present desktop machines could well seem obsolete in six months. Issues of interconnectivity (or lack thereof), seemingly constant needs for upgrades, monthly (and usually improving) changes to our interfaces have left librarians and classroom faculty with feelings of excitement and amazement at the vastness of the information resources (good, bad and indifferent). Perhaps more importantly for liaison/outreach activities, faculty now also experience feelings of inadequacy, frustration and a disturbing sensation that they may no longer possess the expertise to keep up with their disciplines, let alone stand before a classroom full of students as keepers of the keys to a store of information which they will open to their students as they guide them toward greater knowledge.

For librarians in their outreach roles, information on the infrastructure supporting the technology that makes access to information possible today is as important to their continued success as is knowledge of the contents and use of these access tools. It is not enough to be able to introduce a faculty member to the usefulness of the CARL REVEAL service. One should also provide information and guidance to that faculty member on whom to contact if the desktop machine crashes every time the faculty member attempts to add a title for email delivery of the table of contents. Outreach to students, especially distance learners, cannot be properly done without information on connectivity, compatible communications software and the realities of text vs. graphical Web interfaces.

Librarians at the Plattsburgh campus have taken a lead in incorporating instructional technology into courses and workshops. As mediated, computerized classrooms are set up on campus, other faculty look to us for information and expertise in becoming proficient in using the technology and also for collection support to assist in this incorporation of technology. This is not to say that librarians are expected to be experts in technical aspects of computing. Rather, librarians in their outreach functions should be able to keep the members of their liaison departments informed about technological changes that affect their teaching and research, as well as whom to contact on campus for more detailed information, about solutions to problems, or incorporating new software into their homework assignments.

DEVELOPMENT OF THE CURRENT LIAISON PROGRAM

As the Library moved into the new organizational group structure, the Collection Development Group was charged with defining the new role of liaisons, as well as devising a liaison program that would ensure that all academic departments received the same information from their library liaisons. At this time, the Library and Computing merger was still a year in the future. The charge to the Collection Development Group is quoted below from a handout developed by the Director of the Library in consultation with librarians who under the old structure had served on a library administrative group as department heads.

Creates for users a dynamic and integrated collection development program which balances traditional formats and electronic access while being responsive to the curriculum/program needs of faculty and staff. This group will serve as bibliographers for all collections in any given year; this group will also serve as the serials review committee.

Examples:	builds core collection	maintains conspectus
	monitors acquisitions formula	approval plans
	works with liaisons	serials review

During the first year of its existence, 1995-96, the Collection Development Group focussed on defining its role and the role of liaisons in the new group structure. The Group, meeting twice a month, developed the following document to define respectively the roles of the Collection Development Group and of the Liaison:

The Role of the Collection Development Group:

- Build, manage, and evaluate all collections by selecting basic materials in all formats, establishing policies, processes, and procedures for collection evaluation and by monitoring statistical information.
- Serve as a review group for budget monitoring and material acquisitions in overseeing all funds and providing liaisons with statistical/budgetary information.
- Design and maintain a liaison program.
- Annually identify the library goals, services and news to be communicated to the college community.

The Role of the Liaison:

- Serve as primary contact for Dept./Program, and participate in liaison program as developed by the Collection Development Group. Assist Collection Development Group in selection and evaluation.

This document, along with a draft of a liaison program, was brought to the Library Faculty for discussion and approval. The liaison program as initially defined after these discussions included four basic activities.

1. Maintain awareness of changes in scope and trends in the Dept./ Program and address these and other concerns with the Collection Development Group.
2. Promote awareness and use of library services and programs for faculty and students and provide updates on new developments in resources, both library-wide and subject-specific.
3. Communicate with other [programmatic] groups issues relevant to the Dept./Program.
4. Assist Collection Development Group in materials selection and collection evaluation.

The following year, 1996-97, saw the merger of the Library and Computing into the new division of Library and Information Services. Five more programmatic groups were created focussing on computing issues. Examples of these groups include the Computer Users Group and the Systems and Networks Group. At the same time, a multi-year program began to wire the campus for Ethernet connections and to survey faculty and administrative offices for planned upgrades or new desktop computer purchases. An educational technology initiative to integrate technology into classroom teaching was begun. The Library began offering telnet access to FirstSearch databases, the CARL/RE-VEAL service and a pilot full text database. Clearly there was much to communicate to the campus regarding all these changes!

Discussions at Group Leaders meetings raised the issue of how to best and most effectively communicate these plans and initiatives to the campus community. Initially, we discussed using staff from the computing side of the division to meet with academic departments to share information Ethernet connections and desktop computer upgrades. However, that required organizing another group of people from the Division to communicate the computing changes. It seemed most sensible that Library liaisons, all of who had established connections with academic departments, be considered the people responsible for the communication of information from all parts of the Division to their respective departments/programs. Additionally the Collection Development Group was asked to expand their concept of the liaison program to include "the promotion of services and updates on new developments" from all parts of the Division.

When the Dean proposed this new role for liaisons at a Library Faculty meeting, the responses of the liaisons to this expansion of their responsibilities was mixed. While all saw the logic of a single line of communication from the Division to the departments, many felt their knowledge of the more technical aspects of computing and networking were inadequate to the task. This was a legitimate concern, so it was agreed that the Collection Development Group would develop a "liaison script" outlining information to be shared with departments. Handouts, where appropriate, summarizing or expanding upon the "script" and names of contacts within the Division to whom faculty could address additional questions would be included in a liaison packet.

The Group Leader for the Collection Development Group called for suggestions from each divisional programmatic group for items to include in this "liaison script." The response was overwhelming. It was clear to the Group that it would be impossible to include all suggestions in a script designed for a liaison to present in roughly twenty minutes at an academic departmental meeting. Priorities needed to be set, so that the script did not become a laundry list of new developments and reminders about established services.

The Group spent the next few months identifying the items that could be included in the "liaison script." We determined that four to five major items were the maximum number that we could hope to communicate effectively. From a list of five broad categories–Computer Issues, Collection Development Issues, Grant Issues, Services (Instruction, Library, Information), and Miscellaneous–we settled upon three major categories–Collection Development, Information Services and Teaching and Technology as the three broad areas to be covered. Two documents for liaisons were prepared by the Collection Development Group: a handout for liaisons to distribute to members of their liaison departments and a four page narrative expanding on these categories, to be used either as background information for liaisons to read in preparation for their meetings or to use as a "script" to refer to when presenting the information to the academic departments (see Appendix). Handouts developed for particular services (CARL/RE-VEAL, ILL Copy Service) were provided. A schedule of the buildings covered in each phase of the Ethernet wiring project and the charge to the newly created Teaching, Learning, and Technology Advisory Group completed the packet. This packet of materials was distributed to each liaison with the understanding that they would communicate this information to members of academic departments during the last half of the spring semester of 1997.

How well did this first foray work into the development and distribution of a liaison "script" that combined information on both Library and Computing services? As there was no formal, quantitative assessment of the use of or response to the script provided to liaisons, results of the program's success are based on anecdotal evidence from conversations with and email from individual liaisons. Liaisons generally felt that the support of documentation and some structure to the information provided was most welcome in communicating with their liaison departments. Having information on whom to contact in Computing for technical questions made the provision of information about networking and computer upgrades easier than some had expected. When the questions became too technical, the liaison could provide the name, phone number or email address of someone who could respond in more detail to the question posed by the faculty member. Some liaisons reported back on the positive reception by the members of an academic department to both the information and the handouts.

There were as many models of distribution of this liaison program information as there are academic departments. While the Collection Development Group encouraged liaisons to meet with their departments, the Group did not prescribe any particular model. We believe that the liaisons are in the best position to know the most appropriate and effective means to distribute the information, as most liaisons have long-established working relationships with the faculty in their liaison departments. Also, the timing of completion of the "liaison script" and accompanying handouts in mid-spring semester made it difficult for liaisons to get on the agenda for a departmental meeting. Some liaisons did meet formally with their departments; some met with the department chair to review the information and materials; some met with the member of the department who served as the liaison to the library. Others summarized the information from the script in a memo to department members attaching relevant handouts. Some did not make use of the script at all, citing lack of time or insufficient interest on the part of their liaison departments.

In the second year of this program, 1997-98, the Collection Development Group was less successful in planning a cohesive, informative program of information for liaisons to communicate to their departments. While the Group did request input from all Divisional Group Leaders about new or changed programs and services for inclusion in a liaison script, response was much lower to the request in this second year. Possible reasons for this will be discussed under Barriers to Success later in this article. During the early part of the Fall semester, the Collection Development Group developed a list of topics to be developed into a script: Web access to CARL/REVEAL, new OPAC guide, public scanners, personal Web pages and serial holdings in the OPAC. However, the Group was unsuccessful in garnering the background information/handouts from Group Leaders necessary to draft a script of any substance. At the midpoint of the spring semester, plans were set aside for the year. The Group planned to develop the liaison script and presentation packet over the summer in conjunction with a new planning schedule implemented this year by the Dean. The initial stages of this third year of the program are briefly described in the next section.

BARRIERS TO SUCCESS

As the preceding section ends with a description of the failure of the Group to develop a second year program of outreach, an examination of the possible reasons for this lack of success seems the next logical topic for discussion. The Group (and most liaisons) are optimistic about the positive aspects of the program and fully expect to build on the modest success of the first year in developing a program for our third year. The barriers to success in the development of this program may be divided into three categories: Category 1, those barriers which historically have hampered library liaison and outreach activities and are well documented in the literature; Category 2, those barriers which have arisen as a result of recent changes and developments in technology and information resources, about which less has been written because such barriers have only recently emerged; and Category 3, those barriers which are particular to the Division of Library and Information Services at Plattsburgh, but are likely reflected on other college campuses and whose description may inform others seeking to develop or expand their liaison or outreach programs.

Identified Barriers

Category 1

- Variation in interest regarding library and technology services and programs on the part of members of academic departments.
- Variation in interpersonal skills and workload of both library liaison and department liaison to the library.
- Lack of balance between information flowing to departments and information flowing back to library and computing.
- Declining or static budgets for library materials.

Category 2

- Lack of base technology knowledge on part of library liaisons.
- Relative newness of relationship between library and computing.

Category 3

- Need for better communication between Collection Development Group and individual liaisons.
- Lack of time and value commitment to development of documentation of services and programs by individuals or programmatic groups.
- Lack of recognition on the part of systems and network staff of the importance to faculty of changes and new initiatives in their areas.
- Lack of clear, ongoing support for liaison program within the Divisional planning process.
- Lack of recognition on part of academic departments, specifically, and the college, generally, of the expanded role of library liaisons as emissaries of both the library and the computing services on campus.

The first four barriers listed have been referred to frequently over the years in the literature on bibliographic instruction (Radar 1992) and collection development (Latta 1992). The last of the four, declining or static budget, was cited recently in a useful article by Felix Chu on librarian-faculty relations regarding collection development (Chu 1997). Lack of base technology knowledge and the ambiguity of the respective roles of librarians and computing center staff are cited in Nancy Schiller's 1994 article describing an international survey she conducted on the instructional roles of academic librarians and computing center staff in Internet training (Schiller 1994). While the survey indicated emerging integration and cooperation, the emphasis must be on "emerging." These are new relationships, and as Schiller's survey results suggest, there is evidence of some competition, confusion and misunderstanding amongst and between staff in these two areas in higher education.

The last four barriers, while not unique to Plattsburgh, are not evident in the literature of librarianship. As the Collection Development Group has reviewed its progress over the last two years, and receives feedback from other programmatic groups and individual liaisons, it is clear that the Group needs to provide liaisons with more frequent reports on acquisitions and collection development activities. If the Group fails in its communication about the areas of library services for which it is primarily responsible, it is unlikely to be seen as a group through which information can flow about programs sponsored by other Divisional groups, whose programs and services need to be promoted and explained to faculty in academic departments.

The lack of commitment, both in terms of time and recognition of intrinsic value, to documentation of services and programs has made the task of promoting these activities briefly and clearly much more difficult for the Collection Development Group. If the model of a "liaison script" with accompanying handouts is to work successfully, documentation that clearly and succinctly informs the user of the value and uses of the service and gives how-to information for the novice user and tips for the more advanced user is critical. This is not to say that enormous amounts of staff time must be devoted to this documentation; indeed, much how-to documentation for electronic resources and services is available as help screens provided by a service or resource. In fact, the current philosophy of many of Plattsburgh's librarians and computing staff is that it is unnecessary to create any documentation beyond that provided on the help screens. My own experience is that the help screens are useless if you cannot give faculty a compelling explanation (however brief) of the value of the service to them and clear steps to accessing the service (at least on campus), so they can test its value for themselves. If faculty never access the service, it does not matter that the help screens are wonderfully clear and useful.

A fourth barrier, lack of recognition of the importance of systems and network changes to users of electronic resources and services is necessarily a process of education for all in higher education. While systems and networks staff have supported email and online catalogs for years, the exponential growth of electronic resources means more and more reliance on the campus units that are responsible for these systems and networks. Developing a sense of user service and an understanding of the consequences to user services of changes in systems and networks means a change of perspective for these computing staff. Plattsburgh is fortunate to have open-minded staff whose ability and willingness to change their perspective toward user service is fostered by being part of a larger division where service to users is a primary focus.

The planning process for the Division had acted against the timely development of an annual "liaison script" to use as a vehicle for communication and promotion of services offered by the Division. Until 1997-98, the planning retreat for Group Leaders and led by the Dean took place in the fall semester. As a traditional time of new beginnings in the academic life cycle, fall semester was seen as a good time to plan new projects and reflect on what had been done the previous year. In 1997-98, the planning retreat took place at the end of the spring semester. Not only does this coincide more with the fiscal year, but gives the Division members time to implement new initiatives over the summer for a fall semester start-up. This new planning cycle should allow the Collection Development Group sufficient time to determine which new initiatives or planned changes are of most interest or use to academic departments, develop the "script" and devise the supporting documents or have them developed by other members of the Division. In this planning cycle, library liaisons may take this information to their academic departments as early in the fall semester as possible, beginning the dialog at the start, rather than at the finish of the academic year. At the end of the fall semester of 1998-99, it is possible to report that this change in the planning cycle enabled the Collection Development Group to develop a liaison script for this third year. Focussing on the revision of collection development policies for each department in light of a new strategic plan and the identification of new academic program initiatives for the college, as well as providing updates on the progress of implementing a proxy server and a new email system, liaisons were able to contact their academic departments during the Fall semester to begin the dialogue. It is too early to evaluate the success of this year's liaison outreach program, but at least one barrier has been surmounted.

Lastly, it is a long-term process to acquaint the campus community with the changes that have occurred organizationally between the Library and Computing. Many of our faculty and administrators still view these two entities as entirely separate and have not yet learned to view librarians as liaisons not only from library but from computing services as well. Such simple things as lunching with faculty, serving on campus committees, attending campus events where in casual conversation the link between the two areas is mentioned is one of the best ways of educating others about the merger. No amount of memos, newsletters or homepages can match the effectiveness of a response by a library liaison to the mention of a faculty member's computer problem with the name of a contact, an explanation of the process for seeking help with a networking problem or for reserving a computer classroom. It is this sort of informal communication which will best educate the campus community to the role of the liaison and the organizational connection between library and computing.

BENEFITS OF THE LIAISON PROGRAM

While the program is still in the early stages of its development, there are already clear benefits that can be attributed to this liaison program. This list of benefits will presumably grow as the program matures. The following are benefits that may already be distinguished.

- Integrates information regarding developments, opportunities and changes in the technology infrastructure with information on traditional library services such as instruction and collection development; services which are increasingly dependent upon technology as electronic information resources grow.
- Allows communication to continue to flow to departments even in times of restricted budgets for traditional library materials. Liaisons can balance news about static monographic budgets or impending journal cancellations with information about exciting and new opportunities for faculty to access the Web, apply for grants to integrate technology into their classrooms or direct their students toward expanded offerings via full-text databases.

- Provides opportunities for liaisons to communicate about support for information literacy, for students and faculty, as network instruction activities are now a combined responsibility of library and computing staff.
- Enhances the image of library liaisons as knowledgeable about traditional library services, well informed about current trends in technology and organizationally connected to those most knowledgeable about new technologies on campus.
- Allows for uniform and consistent information to be provided to all academic departments regarding library and computing services–services which are increasingly intertwined and interdependent.

FUTURE DIRECTIONS

Given the rapid changes occurring in library services and information technology, it is difficult to project what the content of the liaison scripts will be in future years–or even next semester. With an understanding of some of the barriers to success that the Collection Development Group has faced, the first priority is to ensure that an annual script is developed that gives liaisons sufficient time to communicate the information effectively, combined with enough supporting information to assist them in promoting the use of our services and program to the faculty. The Group will need to continue to work to engage other programmatic groups in fostering this communication.

Neither students nor administrative staff figure currently in this outreach program, except by extension. Informed faculty will be better placed to encourage their students to take advantage of the services offered by the Division. Returning adult students and distance learners especially need the support of the library and computing services to most effectively take advantage of their academic programs.

Administrative offices will need to be information literate as more and more information useful to their work is online internally or via the Web. In fact, some discussion is underway in the Division of Library and Information Services about linking the programmers in Computing Systems with the administrative offices they have traditionally supported, thereby extending the liaison program into areas such as financial aid, registrar and career services. For the present our goal is to continue to develop our expanded liaison program to the point where we are genuinely satisfied with its effectiveness as an outreach model to academic departments.

Meanwhile, I take heart from a summary of a panel presentation wrap up speech, given by Evan Farber at the 19th National LOEX Library Instruction Conference in 1991. Evan Farber's concluding remarks were summarized thus, "He cautioned participants not to become impatient with implementing their own programs. Instead, concentrate on building relationships with teaching faculty and administrators, and continue to develop them." (LOEX 1992, 169) It is difficult to imagine wiser or more sustaining advice.

REFERENCES

Chu, F. T. 1997. Librarian-Faculty Relations in Collection Development. *Journal of Academic Librarianship* 23:15-20.

Latta, G. F. 1992. Liaison Services in Academic Libraries; An Annotated Bibliography. In *Liaison Services in ARL Libraries, SPEC; A Publication Series for Library Staff*, comp. G. F. Latta, no.189, 179-183. Washington: Association of Research Libraries.

LOEX Conference-Panel SUMMARY. In *Working With Faculty in the New Electronic Library*, ed. L. Shirato, 167-169. Ann Arbor: Pierian Press.

Rader, H. 1992. Library Orientation and Instruction–1990. In *Working With Faculty in the New Electronic Library*, ed. L. Shirato, 171-183. Ann Arbor: Pierian Press.

Schiller, N. 1994. Internet Training and Support: Academic Libraries and Computer Centers; Who's Doing What?. *Internet Research* 4:35-47.

APPENDIX

Library and Information Services
Update for Academic Departments

Collection Development:

- **Periodicals/Books: Working toward a reasonable balance in a time of rising periodical costs**
- Book recommendations are always welcome
- New Periodical titles requests are reviewed. Process takes time; funds are maintaining current titles
- Video requests over $100.00 require preview by requester before purchase. Contact Media Assistant, x2222, to schedule previews.

APPENDIX (continued)

Information Services:

- **Full-text database trial–Try it and let us know (on FLAIR menu, choose IAC Trail)**
- REVEAL/ILL Document Delivery for access to updating services and materials not owned by Feinberg
- FirstSearch: electronic access to wide range of databases and built-in ILL request form

Instruction Services:

- **LIB101: All subject specific sections in Fall '97. ADVISORS: encourage LIB101 enrollment early, especially for transfers**
- Course-related instruction: One time sessions geared to your course
- Training sessions: hour-long workshops on electronic resources, using software, Internet/Web

Technology and Teaching:

- **Ethernet connection schedule**
- **Faculty computer upgrade/replacement process**
- Educational Technology grants and Teaching and Technology grants support integration of technology into teaching
- Library and Information Services Web pages: If you have Ethernet access, take a look. There is a lot of information on teaching and technology and easy access to a variety of information resources for you and your students

Liaison Information for Visit to Departments

What follows fills out a summary of information that the Collection Development Group and Steering Group believe is important for liaisons to convey to their departments. Also attached is additional information on: Ethernet connection schedule, TLTAG's mission. The topics covered in a departmental visit this Spring should be able to be covered in 15-20 minutes. Questions from faculty on items not covered could be useful in deciding topics for a Fall visit, so please forward questions to Collection Development Group.

Collection Development, Information Services, Instruction Services, and Technology issues are the four broad categories to be covered.

Collection Development

Historically, our goal is to aim for a ratio in allocating monies for books/periodicals of 40/60. The chart attached is to give liaisons a sense of how we've steadily moved away from the ratio since the periodicals cut in 1989/90. *Why?* Periodical prices have risen steadily. This year's increase is 10%, or about $33,000, just to maintain our current subscriptions. We have not received comparable inflationary increases. Our current ratio of books/periodicals is 27/73. Encourage departments to look at subscriptions that are no longer used in their courses. (Looked at another way, our purchasing power for books is constantly eroded. We have moved from purchasing about 4,300 books per year to about 2,500 books per year.)

We are beginning the process of trying to find an appropriate balance between books, serials and electronic resources. The Collection Development Group is already reviewing Reference continuations. After an internal review, we can get a better sense of where we are. Departments can expect that we, as liaisons, will be back in the fall to discuss periodical costs more fully.

Implications of electronic full text access: Full-text databases and online versions of periodicals *may* mean cancellation of print versions. Vendors' pricing structures are too volatile to make any blanket statements about future impact on print subscriptions. Many "full-text" databases are selectively full-text.

What's in It for Me?

- There is money for books. We may see an additional infusion for Spring, so *encourage faculty book recommendations.*
- There is no money to acquire new periodical titles this year, but recommendations are being accepted for review and will be looked at case by case. In some instances, it **MAY** be possible to offer one-time money for books
- There is a small budget for videos, but at the moment outstanding requests exceed remaining monies

How to Make Recommendations?

- Books–we accept in any format: catalogs, an email message to liaison, book order cards and Web page electronic form
- Periodicals–Request form is necessary. Review process takes time and is usually done in the Fall. The form provides space for suggested cancellation of current subscription
- Videos–Requests in any form. Videos over $100 require preview and an evaluation form. The Media Assistant handles previews. *Previewing does work,* eliminating purchase of videos that sound good on paper

APPENDIX (continued)

Other sources of book funds (soft money)

- Coordinated Collection Development monies through regional library system in these areas: Canadian Studies, Environmental Studies (Lake Champlain Basin), International Business, Latin American Studies, Mass Media, Multicultural, Nursing, Women's Studies
- College Foundation funds for significant (read expensive) titles. Recommendations are reviewed and voted on by Library Faculty twice/year
- Student Club funds: Some student clubs (notably Art Resources Club) have raised money to purchase books students recommend. Encourage departments to work with student club. Money raised *may* be matched by the Library

Information Services

Below is a summary of services to highlight.

Full-Text Database Trial

- What it is
- Current IAC trial, feedback
- Implications

REVEAL/ILL Document Delivery

- What it is
- Information and help for setting up account. There is a handout describing how to access REVEAL, but it doesn't include the new book alert function or Web page access
- Ordering articles. See ILL Copy Service Form attached

FirstSearch

- What it is, coverage, ILL feature
- Web access coming

It is assumed that liaisons are familiar with these services; if not, check with someone more familiar with the service.

Instruction Services

- Subject sections of LIB101. Student advising (no waivers). If faculty don't understand, bring questions back to LIB101 Coordinator.

- Pre-planning course-related sessions. Requests need to be by 3rd week of classes; two-week lead time is needed. We're scheduling now for Fall'97. Contact Reference Assistant, x5191
- Variety of training sessions (databases, FirstSearch, Internet, etc.). Take schedule with you to department meeting
- Library homepage information about instructional services

Technology Issues

Wiring for Ethernet connections are being done on a phased basis following a survey done by Systems people. A list of buildings in each phase is below:

Phase I: This phase is essentially complete
Redcay
Myers
Hudson
Beaumont
133 Court

Phase II: This phase is in progress. CVH is near completion. Sibley will be next. Kehoe may be done by an outside firm
Ward
CVH
Sibley
Kehoe
Feinberg (completion of few connections)

Phase II also includes some other areas. Only faculty buildings are listed here. At the end of Phase II, about 85% of our full-time faculty/staff will be connected via Ethernet.

Phase III: (1997-1998)
Memorial
Yokum
Hawkins
Angell Center, etc.

There are Phases IV and V. There are plans for upgrades between 1998 and 2000!

Process for faculty computer upgrades/replacements

Surveys have been conducted by Computing Support to determine if computers had minimum requirements to run software for network connection.

APPENDIX (continued)

These surveys were distributed to department chairs by the Dean for prioritization. Efforts are being made to upgrade everyone, but, given funding, upgrades may need to be done by priorities listed by department chair. *Please refer any questions about the priority list to your liaison department's chair.*

Computing staff will make appointments with individuals to do necessary software installation.

If there is time/opportunity, please remind faculty that support for technology in their teaching is available through the Educational Technology and Teaching/Learning grants. Memos were sent out on each of these. The deadline for Ed Tech is mid-March and another request for Teaching/Learning proposals will come out next Fall.

For departments with access to the Web, mention the Division's Web pages and encourage faculty to use them.

Collaborative Learning:
University Archives
and Freshman Composition

Jeanine Mazak
Frank Manista

SUMMARY. The many concerns over the costs and benefits of higher education have created an often intense dialogue across university departmental borders. In response, many departments have moved to collaborative efforts to reinforce the necessity and usefulness of the Liberal Arts curriculum for students. Academic service departments, including archives, seek to have their resources more actively used by the student base. The authors collaborated on an assignment requiring student use of primary source materials held at the Michigan State University Archives and Historical Collections. The dialogue this assignment created and the projects it produced was of benefit to all involved: instructors, faculty, and students. *[Article copies available for a fee from The Haworth Document Delivery Service: 1-800-342-9678. E-mail address: getinfo@haworthpressinc.com <Website: http://www.haworthpressinc.com>]*

KEYWORDS. Library archives, library instruction, faculty liaison, library assignments

---

Jeanine Mazak is currently serving as Projects/Outreach Archivist, Michigan State University Archives and Historical Collections (MSUAHC), 101 Conrad Hall, East Lansing, MI 48824-1327. Frank Manista is a PhD Candidate in English at Michigan State University.

[Haworth co-indexing entry note]: "Collaborative Learning: University Archives and Freshman Composition." Mazak, Jeanine, and Frank Manista. Co-published simultaneously in *The Reference Librarian* (The Haworth Information Press, an imprint of The Haworth Press, Inc.) No. 67/68, 1999, pp. 225-242; and: *Library Outreach, Partnerships, and Distance Education: Reference Librarians at the Gateway* (ed: Wendi Arant, and Pixey Anne Mosley) The Haworth Press, Inc., 2000, pp. 225-242. Single or multiple copies of this article are available for a fee from The Haworth Document Delivery Service [1-800-342-9678, 9:00 a.m. - 5:00 p.m. (EST). E-mail address: getinfo@haworthpressinc.com].

The many and justifiable concerns over the costs and benefits of higher education have created an often intense dialogue across university departmental borders. In response to this, many departments have moved to collaborative efforts to reinforce the necessity and usefulness of the Liberal Arts curriculum for students in their remaining college careers and afterward in the "real world" experiences that will follow. Together, Jeanine Mazak and Frank Manista collaborated on an assignment requiring student use of the Michigan State University Archives and Historical Collections (MSUAHC) in a research project for the Department of American Thought and Language. The dialogue it created and the projects it produced benefited instructors, faculty and students, and posed some interesting ideas for the teaching of composition and the facilitation of student research. This article explores that collaboration. It is divided into sections, with each section alternating between the perspective of either Jeanine or Frank.

I.

In August 1995, the MSUAHC moved operations from the basement of the Main Library to a newly renovated facility across campus in Conrad Hall. In many ways the move was (and has been) advantageous for the unit. The trade-off, however, has come at the expense of the convenience of location, accessibility and exposure on campus, all of which affect student use of the facility.

The Main Library is situated at a more central location on campus, while Conrad Hall borders its East end, nestled between dormitories and the medical schools. Before the move, it was more convenient for instructors to include the MSUAHC on a general tour of the Main Library, scheduling both tours and orientation sessions during the same class period. With the move and the distance between buildings, instructors who desire to have an Archives' tour and orientation session must schedule a visit separately, and many instructors do not want to use two class periods for introductions to the separate research facilities. When having to make a choice between the two, the Archives is understandably often on the losing end, as most students will use a library more than an archives for general research purposes.

The lack of orientation sessions has not prevented instructors from using the Archives in assignments that gauge underclassmen's (mainly Freshmen) ability to use campus research facilities on campus. As in many university archives, the MSUAHC is flooded with a number of "ready reference," or vertical file, information requests, including those made by dormitory or student organization "ice-breaker" activities, with questions such as: "What is the tallest/oldest building on campus?"; and "When was your dorm built and who/what is it named after?" Much of the vertical file information has been developed as a result of these frequently asked questions.[1] These are handled quick and easily. However, the students sent in with a class assignment intended to "teach research techniques" are different. They too seek a short answer, but one requiring a little more detail than "ice breaker" questions: "Who was the University's first Dean of Women Students, when did she serve, and write a brief biography." Unlike a phone call, email or quick visit for a one or two word response, this student researcher must come in and undergo the typical researcher application process: sign the guest register, complete an application form, present identification card, and interview with the archivist on reference duty to assess his/her needs. Many times the instructor giving this type of assignment will contact the archives to notify the staff of the assignment and oftentimes forwarding a copy of it. However, there are times when an assignment is given without warning to the archives' staff. When a staff member calls to confirm and clarify the assignment, this person is more often than not informed that the assignment is not important enough to warrant a full class orientation, especially if the class has already been on a library tour.

Since many of these underclassmen researchers have not been through an orientation seminar or may never have been in an archive before, reactions to standard procedures range from confusion to hostility. In *Providing Reference Services for Archives and Manuscripts,* Mary Jo Pugh states that "If the research experience is not structured, students can be overwhelmed by research in the archives."[2] Perhaps the reactions of our student researchers are expressions of feeling overwhelmed. Oftentimes students, at this level, assume they will be directed to a book on the shelf that can be pulled down and opened to a page containing all the information they need. Even as an archivist quickly explains the procedures and the intent behind them, students often view it as unnecessary or a hassle. In casual conversations with students, they frequently express a sense of dread having to go to a research facility where they are required to speak with a staff person to request materials that are not allowed to circulate. Some students find intimidating the closed off rooms of an archives or special collections department and all the rules and regulations within. It is much easier to go to a terminal, enter a search query, and pick a book off of a shelf.

The issue of a general decline in archives' orientation sessions with increased use by instructors in course assignments was raised at a MSUAHC staff meeting a few weeks into the Fall 1997 semester. Discussed were ways to encourage the use of the archives by underclassmen in a structured manner that included an introductory orientation. There was also a need to expand and become more proactive in campus outreach programs to target faculty and student use. No longer were faculty and students able to "stumble into" the archives while wandering through the Main Library.[3] Fortunately, the MSUAHC has a history of working well with the University units and administrative offices served by our University Records Management Program. The MSUAHC also works well with "scholarly" researchers. Outreach initiatives over the course of the past year involved an aggressive expansion of the MSUAHC web site[4] and Internet access to collection research and University records management services that further strengthened connections to their respective constituents. But unlike University staff seeking records management services and advice and scholarly researchers seeking detailed information on a specific subject; the basic underclassman just learning the mechanics of the research process or faculty member seeking to enhance classroom learning is not always well served by a web site. There was a definite need to develop outreach programs to better serve this constituency.[5]

Discussion focused on defining the goals of our outreach initiative: increasing visibility on campus and use by faculty and staff, and how to reach this goal. The choice was made to reach out to instructors of underclass courses.[6] The MSUAHC staff selected the American Thought and Language (ATL) department to propose a program to work collaboratively with instructors to use archival resources in class projects. ATL was targeted because of the diverse nature of the program, not solely an English or history course, and because its students are primarily Freshmen. The Archives' director took the proposal to the chairperson of ATL, who in turn informed the ATL instructors. The Archives' staff received numerous calls concerning the MSUAHC proposal and spent time discussing holdings and how they may fit the tentative themes instructors were developing for their Spring 1998 semester courses. Despite the interest, it appeared as though there would be no takers. This was not a great surprise considering that our proposal was offered mid-term in the Fall–too late to incorporate into current class work and possibly too late for some instructors lining up themes for the Spring. However, one ATL instructor, Frank Manista, chose to collaborate with the Archives for the Spring semester.[7]

II.

For two years, Frank Manista has taught as an instructor in the ATL department. Devised in the early 1950s to be separate and notably distinct from the English Department, ATL emphasizes Freshman composition almost exclusively. ATL teaches basic composition from the standpoint of the distinct American landscape; therefore, as instructors, we assign authors that are noted as distinctly American and reasonably valued vis-à-vis the American ideology. In most mainstream first-year Freshman composition courses, if there is generally a literature component, the texts assigned usually come from several different time periods in order to give examples of exceptional writing and thinking across a broad spectrum and to offer a type of time-line where the students can begin to conceptualize how a country evolved politically and ideologically.

The pedagogical goals of any composition program are in part to assist students to become proficient in college writing, which includes composition, revision and editing; as well as preparation for college reading, thinking, and the writing process that are critical in the students' present and future courses. Over the course of the term, reading and writing assignments increase in complexity, as students improve in their abilities. Invention techniques, defining purpose and audience, critical writing, organization, integration of sources, style, mechanics and usage, collaborative learning and writing, and language awareness are included in the standard checklist of most first-year composition classes. The underlying agenda is always to teach the students to express themselves clearly and effectively through writing, as well as learning to read and think critically. Class time is generally and effectively spent reading and writing, practicing and developing those vital academic skills, building confidence and competence in the process. Throughout a given semester, students, on average, write four or five papers based on their reading of the class materials, in addition to library research.[8]

Despite the intent of the University, it has often been noted that Freshmen completing their first-year studies at MSU are still not proficient in the use of the University library system, often lacking in basic research skills necessary for later required courses. This, of course, places an undue burden onto the backs and syllabi of upper division instructors who must backtrack in order to teach some of those basic skills for their research-oriented courses.

The most common and unfortunate research tactic of students using the library seemed to be restricted to books that came up the quickest and easiest on the library computer card-catalog. Quite often, the texts the undergraduates find in their perusal of the library have little to do with their actual interests or projects; it seemed that part of the problem was the type of research assignment, as well as instructor expectations. Such typical search-and-destroy research methods are, more often that not, carelessly written and plagiarized collages that are of interest to neither the student nor to the teacher. Collaborating with the University archives seemed to be a possible means of generating student interest while simultaneously facilitating an assignment that would teach the students how to do research by themselves, rather than the typical mundane method of leading them by the hand to the card catalog machines and to the library stacks. The collaborative idea was to create an additional research project that the students would work on over the course of the entire semester that would use the university archives as the primary research facility. The project included a prospectus, an annotated bibliography, a research report, and a final oral presentation to be done at the end of the semester, in lieu of a final exam. Although an archives is often regarded as little more than a warehouse of old papers and scrapbooks from university football games, it is also an exceptional research facility that can be used to teach basic, fundamental research skills to any student at any level.

While developing the overall approach for the assignment, continuous communication between departments was crucial; from these dialogues, it was decided that the best assignment was one left open-ended, in fact vague, in order to force the students to put their own spin on it, rather than making the task initially a guessing game whereby they would spend considerable time trying to figure out what the instructor wants. Such an assignment gives the students, the staff of the archives, and the instructor space to move and work within a variety of interpretive stances. Frank Manista's full assignment appears at the end of this article (see Appendix), but this excerpt illustrates the simplicity of the project:

> You must go to the University Archives and Historical Collections located in Conrad Hall. From the materials the Archives has, you must research something that you find, not only personally interesting, but pertinent and relevant to Michigan State University and the development and evolution of American thought.

In class discussion, prior to the initial orientation visit to the archives, the class talked about some of the more famous collections housed there: the Wesley Fishel papers, the Vietnam Project collection, and some of the Civil War letters and diaries. As one may note, the project's outline simply states that the project itself must fit three criteria: it must interest the student, it must be relevant to the University, and it must participate in the development/evolution of American thought. Although some of the students expressed anxiety at the prospect of fulfilling these three criteria, they soon learned that the flexibility of the assignment and the storehouse of possibilities located at the archives made the demands reasonable. The projects and the project reports were well written, thoughtful and interesting.[9]

III.

The initial orientation session was very important for the archives' staff. It was the chance to put students at ease and prepare them for what is required of them as researchers, while explaining the unit's mission, holdings and services in a structured setting. The typical orientation session at the MSUAHC is as follows: Each student signs the guest registry, after which the student is given a packet of information which includes a researcher application, list of reading room rules, forms for photocopy and photo-reproduction services, and a photocopy of University-related manuscript material–usually a letter from a student during the turn of the century describing a social event or campus activity. Introductions are made of the archives' staff. At this point the archivist responsible for the orientation session stresses that part of the archivist's job is to assist the researcher, that the archivist is a "partner in research"[10] and will do everything possible, short of writing a researcher's paper and controlling the research process, to help. Then follows a discussion of the differences between an archives and a library including location and open hours, the researcher application process and security issues, accessibility via email, phone, and fax; procedures and precautions (again, security) and why they are in place and that they are evenly applied. It is noted that the same security requests made of a Freshman, looking up information on whom a residence hall may be named after, are required of all researchers that come through the door.

Emphasis is placed on the fact that as students of Michigan State University, the holdings of the archives are part of their history. An understanding of the history of this institution shows that the University is not just the athletic teams or a student's major or the dorm in which one resides. As a pioneer land-grant institution, Michigan State University has a history important not only to the institution, but also the history of the country and its system of higher education.

Examples of archival holdings are then brought out for the students to examine, including photographs of the early years of campus, student diary entries from the 1890s and 1920s describing social events on campus, manuscript materials from major collections, and secondary sources written with the aid of archival material. This part of the orientation, in many cases, is a student's first realization that the information found in books they use for reports and in class come from other sources. Putting on white cotton gloves and holding century-old diaries and early photographic images underscores the importance of preservation and security issues as they realize that they are holding a truly unique object, often the only one in existence.

After the lecture ends, time is spent fielding questions, initially directed by the instructor, but then dominated by students. Following this, any remaining time is devoted to informal research interviews with the archives' staff, perusing finding aids and old yearbooks. Then it is up to the students to return on their own. If the orientation session has been effective, the students will return knowing the staff is there to assist them, and may also have a new found respect for the materials and services provided.

Communication between instructor and archives staff is the key to any success with this type of project. Throughout the course of the semester, the instructor and project-coordinating archivist communicated regularly via email and had occasional meetings for coffee. The archives' staff made sure to listen to concerns and questions had by the students as they came in to work on their projects. Any questions or concerns the archives' staff had concerning the students were passed along to the instructor. Likewise, the students communicated their concerns with the archives to the instructor, who then passed these things along to the project-coordinating archivist.

The archives' staff did not plan on providing any extra or special services to the undergraduate students in terms of reference services that would not be applied to any other researcher. Still, working with a class of Freshmen students on a long-term research project was definitely challenging and time consuming. The archivists found that the students handled the materials with respect and care. The orientation to the facility had proved invaluable in these students' response to the process over those who had not had a structured orientation session.[11]

It is easy for an archivist to become accustomed to the "quick fix" questions usually posed by novice researchers; as well as to the "serious" scholar who only needs someone to pull materials and then stay out of the way. The coordinating archivist for this project found many of the generalizations concerning novice researchers accurate, such as when Pugh states "the enthusiasm and excitement that students bring to research can make working with them very rewarding."[12] The challenge came in staying focused on several different research projects at the same time, while also listening to student questions, concerns and comments.

Overall, the archives' staff adapted well to working with the student group, guiding them through collections, spending more time with them discussing their topics to see what their focus was, or if they even had one. It was difficult, on occasion, to fight the urge to direct their research. Doing so would have worked against the instructor's purpose for using the Archives collections in his course.

The archives' staff found that the novice researchers were not unlike those who have used the facility for years. One student mimicked a typical problem researcher–one who frequently uses the facilities but always finds something to complain about, such as hours and location. Had this student devoted all the time spent complaining in the facility to doing research, the time spent at the archives would have been halved. It was also interesting to observe and occasionally experience the dynamics of the students' teamwork, from the mini-celebrations of finding that key piece of information to the heated debates over the direction in which their project should move. A couple of times their excitement became disruptions, and the staff gently guided the students back to their project, a situation not commonly occurring at the MSUAHC.

IV.

As with any project assignment, problems can arise. The assignment was developed for partners, so that at any time when one partner could not do research, the other partner might be able to get some work done and share it. Excuses which lead to one partner doing the majority of the work or personality conflicts between partners occur as they would in any exercise where people are forced to work together. Keeping the lines of communication open between partners is obviously an essential component in the success of any project. The instructor should remain aware of the developments, but it is ultimately up to the students to solve any problems specific to their research and progress.

The success of the collaboration far outweighed these problems. One of the primary reasons for the project's success was the skills and efforts of the archives' staff. They aided the students by serving as guides through the collections. The students worked in pairs on a single project, not only to help facilitate their research, in terms of time and materials, but to reduce some of the workload thrust upon the archives. For this initial collaboration it also helped a great deal that there were only eight students in the class, allowing for even more flexibility in finding materials, as well as working with the staff. Each student had to write a separate prospectus, annotated bibliography, and final research report, but they collaborated on research and presented their findings together at the end of the semester. The archives was of great help in ensuring that the collections were always available for the students to come in and work on them at their convenience. The second, and perhaps most important reason, for the success of the assignment was that the projects created a sense of responsibility that regular research projects often fail to do. The majority of the materials at an archive are primary sources including manuscript materials, scrapbooks, departmental minutes, and notebooks. Because of the materials' often fragmented existences, these documents possess little or no secondary interpretation, which means that it is the job of the students researching to use and interpret the importance of the document. In this sense, more than a traditional research project, the students decide the direction of the project at the various stages noted above, which are read and commented on, but remain ungraded until the project is complete. In a similar method to portfolio grading, the students have numerous opportunities to change their project's direction, without penalty, as they go along, as long as they consult the instructor during routine progress reports. Thus they are continuously working collaboratively, with a partner, with the staff of the archives, and with their teacher.

Most research reports for Freshman composition seem to be poorly done rewordings of materials that most of the students either did not understand or did not care to put in the effort to understand. With the archive assignment, they could not simply reword another's scholarly research because of the character of the materials that they were looking through. Moreover, the collections are often more like doing a puzzle than research, since most of the materials are not in one place–they may be scattered throughout fifty cubic feet of papers and notes that the students then have to "assemble." The research may seem easy, in one sense, because one doesn't have to continue to consult a card catalog and run up to the stacks to see if the book or journal offers anything for one's argument. However, the task is intensely more demanding, since archival research is also the task of interpreting small amounts of information as one proceeds. Like football, archival research is a game of inches. The key lesson is, of course, that the students learn that all research is primarily an interpretive task, as opposed to the "book report" method that more traditional research assignments unfortunately generate.

In usual research assignments, students feel reluctant to throw out any book, since it took them the time to find it and hopefully read it. Furthermore, they think of books as more important than articles, mostly because books are bigger. With archival research, often there are very few books that are in a particular collection, and moreover the only thesis that may be surrounding a collection is that the materials therein are all part of an individual's scholarly interests, i.e., Wesley Fishel's numerous newspaper clippings before and after the Vietnam War.[13]

Working in an archives also meant that the students had to see their research and their methods as part of a web or matrix: what they discovered in one place or in one collection usually lead them to another collection or even to another facility. They could not work in isolation, because their own projects, chosen on their own, were based on collections that of course did not develop in isolation.

One group working on a project about the Clifton and Dolores Wharton Center for the Performing Arts found that they had to go to the Wharton Center to complete some of his research, not because the MSUAHC was ill-equipped, but because his research required that he had to go to the source facility itself. They contacted the Wharton Center prior to the visit, and the manager happily complied with a tour and access to records and photographs. This collection proved to be quite important, not only because of the Center's impact on the arts, but because the students, despite the prominence of the Wharton Center, had not realized that Clifton Wharton was MSU's first and only African-American president. The Wharton Center has helped to create and sustain many distinct cultures at MSU:

> [The Wharton Center] blends educational needs with unlimited opportunities for entertainment, and shows the audience and performers that Michigan State University can focus on other aspects of life [in addition to] agriculture . . . With education through [the] arts as its main focus, this center adds an elegant showcase of performances, and brings people into the community. (Student report)

The Center itself, which has been the site of U.S. presidential election debates, helps to present a different and culturally diverse face of the already well-known MSU community.

Two students working on the Vietnam Project collection, which chronicles MSU's involvement with the United States' initial contact in Vietnam, found that they had to do some additional research into the Wesley Fishel Papers, a separate but integral collection. Furthermore, they had to go to the Main Library for additional reading to contextualize hundreds of cubic feet of materials. As one group wrote in their report:

> [MSU] was called in to work with the people to [help] reconstruct their lives . . . after the Communist rebels began attacking

the government of South Vietnam . . . The relationship between MSU and Vietnam sparked a flame that eventually blew up into a war. (Student report)

A third group researched MSU's "Land Grant Status," which meant that they had to research the Morrill Act, legislation which helped to provide the beginnings of equal opportunity education for everyone, not just the elite and wealthy. This project lead the researchers to the Main Library as well to find additional materials regarding the Morrill Act and MSU's involvement in an effort that drastically changed the face of American education:

> [MSU] could never have evolved from a school [that primarily taught agriculture] to one that included majors such as psychology, business administration, and English . . . The Morrill Act has improved the quality and the quantity of our mass education and it has contributed to our nation's growth considerably. (Student report)

This project was also special because the two students put together a web page that not only had their research reports, their annotated bibliographies, and prospecti, but scans of some of their research, including a time line regarding Justin Morrill's efforts to get the Morrill Act passed.

V.

The experience also challenged the staff of the MSUAHC to examine our holdings and collections policy. In regards to the report on the Wharton Center and its impact on the University and neighboring communities, the staff was able to provide background information for the student including biographies on Mr. and Mrs. Wharton, the cost of the facility, the architects, and the campaign to build the center. Archival material was not, however, able to provide a chronology and/or programs of performances staged at the Wharton Center during its 15-year history. For this information the student was directed to the front office of the Wharton Center. Noting the missing subject materials, a review of the serials collection was made and it was realized that there had not been a regular collecting of programs and publications produced by the Center. Through this student's project the archives' staff was able to pinpoint a collection deficiency and build a partnership with the offices of the Wharton Center to receive back materials, as well as ensure the collection of future materials published through the Center.

Instead of conducting formal exit interviews with each student as the semester drew to a close, the project-coordinating archivist was able to attend the final class where the students presented the information gathered through their research. It was a greater testament to the efforts of all those involved, and a great deal more entertaining than an interview. The archivist was able to see the classroom application of the students' research project, and discovered the collaboration to be a success as each student group synthesized the information gathered from MSUAHC collections into very well done reports. It was apparent, not only from the visitor log at the MSUAHC, that these students worked very long and hard on their research papers.

VI.

The collaboration was incredibly successful, more so than could have been anticipated, because the students gained a great deal from the experience, both in terms of their writing and research skills, as well as from the knowledge garnered. In their final analyses of their work and their findings, they commented on their surprise at how important Michigan State University has been historically, which gave them pride in themselves and their University. The collaboration is something I plan to do again in my classes, since it helped to create interesting class discussions and certainly exceptional research papers and presentations.

Certainly having a small class size facilitated students' research and staff efforts; however, even larger classes can work effectively, provided that the instructor and staff talk regularly and prepare each other with the assignment, the class demands, and a schedule for the students to come in and work. The MSUAHC is indeed a valuable resource to the University and the surrounding community, both as a warehouse for important historical documents, and as an educational research facility.

VII.

Work in promoting student use of the MSUAHC, especially on the underclassman level, will be an ongoing issue for its staff, not only due to the remote campus location, but also in response to the constant change in student population. During the Summer of 1998 the MSUAHC staff redeveloped initial outreach goals, though the primary focus is still increased visibility and use. The small-scale success of the project with Mr. Manista's ATL 150 class is something that has been expanded and that the staff plans to continue. Recent revisions to the website include a new section for faculty and staff outlining orientation, tour and collaboration opportunities. Mounted during the summer, this information became available to instructors in enough time before the start of the new academic year. An MSUAHC archivist has been assigned the task of developing outreach activities. This person will conduct presentations before graduate teaching assistant seminars, residence life resource fairs, and the student oriented conference held on campus in late September and attended by faculty and staff from various colleges and universities. An updated brochure outlining services provided by the MSUAHC, as well as a bookmarker have been developed, and both of which have been distributed on various locations on campus.

For a Big Ten institution, the Michigan State University Archives and Historical Collections is a small unit. With a director, two full-time permanent archivists (including the University Records Manager) and one full-time temporary archivist, it is quite a task for the unit to provide for the research, records management and other archival needs of the community. Each professional takes on many tasks (such as reference desk duties) in addition to their primary job descriptions. If outreach work to underclassmen and the faculty educating them is well received the workload will become greater, but will be well worth the extra effort to support in every way the University's mission of teaching, research and public service.

REFERENCES

1. Maher, William J, *The Management of College and University Archives* (Metuchen, N.J.: The Society of American Archivists and The Scarecrow Press, Inc., 1992), 256. Maher notes that "The distinguishing features of most undergraduate use relate to their larger numbers, short inquiries, and repetitious cursory examination of a relatively narrow range of topics."

2. Pugh, Mary Jo, *Providing Reference Services for Archives and Manuscripts* (Chicago: Society of American Archivists, 1992), 19.

3. Dearstyne, Bruce W "Archival Reference and Outreach: Toward a New Paradigm," *Reference Services for Archives and Manuscripts* (The Haworth Press, Inc., 1997).

4. wwwmsu.edu/unit/msuarhc

5. Cross, James Edward, "Archival Reference: State of the Art," *Reference Services for Archives and Manuscripts* (The Haworth Press, Inc., 1997), 10.

6. Mayer, 261.

7. This would be the first time either Mr. Manista or Ms. Mazek would be involved in such a project. While working at MSUAHC in a variety of capacities since August 1996, it was not until Summer 1997 that she became responsible for class orientation, anchoring the reference desk and developing and maintaining the Archives' outreach projects.

8. One exception was a research project Mr. Maniste assigned based on the research methods from James L. Harner's *Literary Research Guide: A Guide to Reference Sources for the Study of Literatures in English and Related Topics.* MLA Publications, 1990. The students learned the use of the library facility within the scope of specific exercises that forced them to discover the available resources. They did not, however, have to write a formal research paper, and so their ability to synthesize the materials discovered was limited.

9. See *The Everyday Writer: A Brief Reference* ed. Andrea Lunsford and Robert Connors. New York: St. Martin's Press, 1997.

10. Pugh, 7.

11. One personal observation was that this group of students handled the materials, and the request for the materials, with more care and respect than this author has seen given by "serious scholars" working on long-term projects.

12. Pugh, 19.

13. Wesley R Fishel. Papers. UA 17.95, 83.45 cu. ft. 1921-1977 Wesley R. Fishel (1919-1977) joined the faculty of Michigan State University in 1951, teaching political science until his death in 1977. Regarded as an expert on Southeast Asia affairs, he served as close friend and consultant to Ngo Dinh Diem, President of South Vietnam in the 1950s. Fishel was best known for his role in the Michigan State University Vietnam Advisory Group (MSUG) technical assistance program (1951-1961), serving as its Chief Advisor from 1956-1958.

APPENDIX

Frank C. Manista, Instructor
ATL 150: Evolution of American Thought
Spring 1998
Research Project Assignment

You will conduct research with one partner, and you will also present together at the end of the semester; however, I am expecting you to write separately. You and your partner must write a separate prospectus, an adapted annotated bibliography, and research report. Furthermore, you and your partner cannot simply turn in the same writing, i.e., the same prospectus or the same report twice. Obviously, they will resemble each other and will be dependent on each other, but you must each do your own work, as well as work together.

The assignment is quite simple: you must go to the University Archives and Historical Collections located in Conrad Library. From the materials that the Archives has, you must find something that you find not only personally interesting, but pertinent and relevant to Michigan State University and the development and evolution of American thought, or, put differently, important to MSU and ATL 150. The majority of your research must come from the Archives, but you are not restricted to it. Obviously, research at the main university library will most likely be essential in the development of your project.

Specific Due Dates To Remember:
28 January: Visit to the University Archives and Historical Collections, Conrad Library.
17 March: Prospectus Due–2 pages, 300 words/page
This prospectus must be a detailed proposal of what you are going to research and why the material(s) interest you. Included in the prospectus, you must already discuss some relevant research that you have found at the Archives and how you plan to integrate additional materials that you have discovered. Think of the prospectus as the outline of the research report where you state the thesis and give your basic plan.
7 April: Annotated bibliography *DRAFT* Due
Although this is only a draft, it must still be typed. The final annotated bibliography must be no fewer than 10 sources; of those ten, try to use no more and no fewer than 3 book-length sources. The remaining seven must be scholarly articles in journals, magazines, and newspapers. For each annotation, you must include the title of the source with all relevant publication information *IN MLA FORMAT!!!* In addition to the publication information, you must include a brief analysis of each source explaining

APPENDIX (continued)

the basic content in the text, how it is useful to your project, and its value to the project as a whole. Each entry must be no fewer than 150-200 words. NB: With most archival research, you will be working with unpublished resources, so the book-length requirement may need specific adaptation for your project. See me regarding any questions.

8 May: 7:45-9:45am–Research Projects due

Including: Research Report, final Annotated Bib, and In-class Presentations.

Research Report: 5 pages, 300 words/page–the report is where you will explain what you found in detail in a fully developed essay explaining your topic's relevance to Michigan State University and to the "development and evolution of American thought . . . " In other words, you must explain not only what you found and its importance to Michigan State University, but why it is of import to this class: *ATL 150.*

Annotated Bibliography: See explanation above.

In-class, 10-15 minute Presentations: These are presentations to be done during the 2-hour, final exam period. They are to be based on the research report. You may either simply read from your report or you may read portions of your report and discuss what you found in a less formal method. It takes approximately 2 minutes to read a page, so reading your entire paper will take 10 minutes, leaving 5 minutes for questions and answers. I will time you, so plan accordingly. These presentations are part of your project, so if you use any visual aids or any other materials NOT in your research report, make sure you give them to me before the end of the period.

For those of you who are ambitious and computer literate, you may want to consider placing your report on the Net and putting together a web page for your project. If this is of interest to you, speak with me sometime BEFORE you actually attempt it: I can give you names of people who can help you set up your own web page, as well as other important information about keeping it and updating it. You would still have to do all the work as listed above, but you could place your prospectus, annotated bib, and report, as well as visuals and links, all on the net as your project progresses. You may also want to speak with Jeanine Mazak (mazak@pilot.msu.edu) at the Archives about the direction and methods you may want to take in putting together something like this.

Academic Library Outreach Through Faculty Partnerships and Web-Based Research Aids

Connie Jo Ury
Joyce A. Meldrem
Carolyn V. Johnson

SUMMARY. Electronic library services and myriad online resources are shifting the roles and workloads of academic reference librarians. Reallocation of staffing through a differentiated reference desk service model provides time to author curriculum-centered online research guides and tutorials, bibliographies, and webliographies. The expanding electronic information environment also opens new opportunities for teaching partnerships with university faculty. This article showcases a librarian's collaborative work with a history professor, noting student benefits/reactions and implications for future collaboration. *[Article copies available for a fee from The Haworth Document Delivery Service: 1-800-342-9678. E-mail address: getinfo@haworthpressinc.com <Website: http://www.haworthpressinc.com>]*

Connie Jo Ury is Library Outreach Coordinator, Owens Library, Northwest Missouri State University, 800 University Drive, Maryville, MO 64468 (E-mail: cjury@ mail.nwmissouri.edu). Joyce A. Meldrem is Head Librarian, Collection Management, Owens Library, Northwest Missouri State University, 800 University Drive, Maryville, MO 64468 (E-Mail: meldrem@mail.nwmissouri.edu). Carolyn V. Johnson is Information Librarian, Owens Library, Northwest Missouri State University, 800 University Drive, Maryville, MO 64468 (E-mail: carolyn@mail.nwmissouri. edu).

[Haworth co-indexing entry note]: "Academic Library Outreach Through Faculty Partnerships and Web-Based Research Aids." Ury, Connie Jo, Joyce A. Meldrem, and Carolyn V. Johnson. Co-published simultaneously in *The Reference Librarian* (The Haworth Information Press, an imprint of The Haworth Press, Inc.) No. 67/68, 1999, pp. 243-256; and: *Library Outreach, Partnerships, and Distance Education: Reference Librarians at the Gateway* (ed: Wendi Arant, and Pixey Anne Mosley) The Haworth Press, Inc., 2000, pp. 243-256. Single or multiple copies of this article are available for a fee from The Haworth Document Delivery Service [1-800-342-9678, 9:00 a.m. - 5:00 p.m. (EST). E-mail address: getinfo@haworthpressinc. com].

KEYWORDS. Librarian-faculty relations, library instruction, internet research aids, student consultations, assignment development

INTRODUCTION

The universe of reference and instructional academic library service is changing at an accelerating pace. According to Rapple (1997), "[m]any traditional conceptions of libraries and librarianship have little relevance today because of the proliferation of electronic technology" (p. 1). Considering the sheer amount of information available, coupled with expanding retrieval systems, the question becomes whether libraries can continue to provide traditional reference service and adapt to the demands generated by global electronic resources. Rapple (1997) states "[t]raditionally, reference services focused on helping faculty and students locate material within the four walls of the home library. With the advent of the electronic library, librarians must now teach not only these home resources, but also point to the existence of, and means to access, the vast aggregate of global material" (p. 2).

Libraries and librarians serve as bridges between patrons and their information needs. As bridges, librarians help faculty and students evaluate and choose credible print information and World Wide Web resources. In the (self-)publishing arena of personal and commercial Web pages, the need for assistance in evaluating the integrity of information is critical but familiar to librarians who have always assisted in evaluating resources. Bosseau and Martin (1997) compare traditional roles of librarians with current opportunities available to provide leadership in the selection of resources. They observe that "[q]uality control of information sources has always been encompassed within the processes of authority control and cataloging. Evaluation of Web sites for aspects of quality, reliability, and searchability is an activity which libraries are equally suited to undertake" (p. 2).

The role of librarians in the electronic age is also expanding in the area of instruction. Online tutorials and instructional course-specific library Web pages are becoming common. In addition, current librarian job advertisements stress the importance of Web-authoring skills and the ability to teach information literacy online to distance education students.

The emergence of electronic access to information will further redefine the instructional roles of librarians. According to Rapple (1997), "[n]ot only will librarians help faculty and students do research, they will also help faculty develop new pedagogical methods for the electronic age. Many will become much more active in curriculum design, in devising and evaluating assignments, in team teaching, and in teaching for-credit courses. They will become true partners and fellow educators with faculty" (p. 2). Haycock (1998) agrees with this assessment, stating that "[t]eacher-librarians who understand the [r]esearch search process, work with classroom colleagues to integrate the process in instruction and intervene early in student support, more effectively guarantee student success and academic achievement" (p. 1).

The role changes outlined above will also redefine the way in which reference service delivery occurs. In many libraries, the number of hours librarians spend staffing the Reference Desk has already significantly decreased. Engle (1995) describes changes in undergraduate reference service staffing at Cornell's Uris Library. Their Reference Desk is often staffed by paraprofessionals, and the hours when reference service is offered have been trimmed. Staffing and budget cuts, coupled with increased demands for instructional delivery, have necessitated these changes. Engle explains the rationale for these changes: "Along with the decrease in service hours and the general level of expertise and experience at the service desks, more librarians are working at multiple service points and teaching a larger variety of classes. Sharing skills working with specific user groups and the sharing of information about local resources is increasing. As a result, referrals are more informed. The reduction in desk hours for Uris librarians has allowed them to increase significantly their involvement in, and leadership of library-wide groups. They have also used the additional off-desk time to plan and develop services in the virtual library" (p. 13).

NEW SERVICE MODEL

Five trends leading to specific, state-of-the-art responses in Reference Desk and instructional services offered by Owens Library at Northwest Missouri State University include:

- increasing requests for instruction to student and faculty groups;
- dwindling numbers of reference questions at the Reference Desk;
- growing numbers of hits on resources on the Owens Library Web page;

- decreasing print material circulation and declining door count numbers;
- reducing the number of librarian positions.

Owens' librarians are increasingly in demand to instruct student and faculty groups in the use of electronic services and resources. Instructional requests increased by 46.3% between the academic years 1992-1993 and 1997-1998. Conversely, the need for a Reference Desk service point is waning. The number of questions at Owens' Reference Desk has declined 33.9% from 1992-1993 to 1997-1998.

Owens Library's Web site was launched in the summer of 1996. Statistics regarding the usage of this page have been recorded since June 1997. In that time period, the number of pages has grown from 63 to 225, an increase of 257.1%. Along with the growth of the Web site, the use of these resources has grown phenomenally from 132,425 hits in the fall of 1997 to 182,122 hits in the spring of 1998, an increase of 37.5%. During this limited time period, the number of pages increased from 120 to 225, an increase of 87.5%.

The door count and circulation of print materials have declined as students access electronic resources from their residence halls. The 1997-1998 academic year was a pivotal year because a personal computer was provided in each residence hall room at Northwest Missouri State University. In addition, the fully networked campus supplied each faculty member with a notebook computer. For the first time since the 1992-1993 academic year, the door count showed a decrease for 1997-1998. The total number of patrons entering the library fell by 9.9%. With the networked environment and campus-wide access to personal computers, students' access to virtual resources has broadly expanded while the circulation of print materials has declined by 24.7% between 1992-1993 and 1997-1998. In response to this trend, Owens Library has mounted bibliographies of in-house print sources on the library's home page to market traditional research materials.

Since 1992, shifts in staffing patterns and allocation of salary funds have resulted in a reduction of librarians with reference expertise. In addition, professionals from other departments formerly able to provide reference are no longer comfortable with the evolving online reference environment.

The five trends described above have significantly impacted the way in which Owens Library faculty deliver reference service. The new paradigm supports a differentiated Reference Desk model where graduate and undergraduate students provide peer-to-peer information services for "frontline" general questions. Questions of a more in-depth, complex nature are immediately referred to scheduled information professionals, including librarians and paraprofessionals. This peer-to-peer model enables information professionals to produce and update online instructional materials and content-rich Web resources. We emphasize proactive information services that include class presentations, hands-on workshops, faculty office calls, and student research consultations by appointment.

PARTNERSHIPS

One new information service involves information professionals partnering with departmental faculty in a variety of subject areas. An example of Owens Library's proactive approach to partnerships is the teaching dyad formed by Library Outreach Coordinator Connie Ury with History, Humanities and Philosophy Assistant Professor Janice Brandon-Falcone. During the Spring of 1998, Ms. Ury worked with Dr. Brandon-Falcone to deliver instruction in an upper level history class entitled *Advanced Topics: American Religious History.* As part of the requirements of a graduate level independent seminar, Ury attended the undergraduate class each day and developed a peer-to-peer relationship with the students. She also completed many of the same research assignments as those of the students, thus establishing her credibility. In addition, Ury created a class Web site entitled *Advanced Topics: American Religious History.* This site included the class syllabus, links to online reading assignments, links to student midterm projects and final papers, and a link to an online peer evaluation form for the students' midterm projects. The URLs for all Web page titles (hereafter italicized) are included in Appendix A, along with an annotation describing each resource.

Ury met with each student early in the semester for one-on-one *Student Research Consultations* to help him/her focus a research topic and initiate a research strategy. During this meeting she:

- modeled a research strategy;
- helped each student identify areas of possible focus within a chosen topic; and

- mentored the students as they developed and employed search strategies.

World Wide Web resources developed by Owens' librarians set the agenda for these one-on-one appointments. Ury also created a research page, *History of Religion in America*, that outlined the five-step search strategy particularly applicable to this class:

1. Use print resources listed in the *Selected Religion Sources in Owens Library* and *Selected History Sources in Owens Library* to locate background information about a subject available in Owens Library.
2. Employ search strategies listed in the *Religious Research Guide* and the *Historical Research Guide* to retrieve information from the *Owens Library Catalog* and periodical indexes listed in *Find the Subject Database You Need*.
3. Use *Newspaper Sources* to locate newspaper literature providing primary information available in Owens Library about a topic.
4. Access resources available on the *American Religion WWW Resources,* the *Religious Studies WWW Resources,* and *the Online Searchable Newspapers* webliographies.
5. If you want personalized assistance with your research, make a *Student Research Consultations* appointment at the Information Desk in Owens Library or contact a member of the *Information Services Team*.

Each student was required to write a midterm project about a general area of American religious history. The constraints of the midterm projects were outlined in the class syllabus (Brandon-Falcone, 1998) as follows:

1. From the research topic that you select for your research paper, you will engage in some broad-based, background research initially.
2. By Mid-Term, you will have researched and annotated [i.e., briefly reviewed the contents and its utility] five book sources and 3-5 web sites that are useful sources of information on the topic. You will also prepare a short essay introducing your topic. If there are any questions that your topic poses for you in your research, the short essay might be the best place to begin to for-

mulate questions about the material. For those of you who are computer literate, you may create your own HTML document on a separate disc for Ms. Ury to FTP to the class web site. However, you are not penalized for being illiterate in HTML. Simply type up your essay, your annotated book sources (using standard Turabian style), and your annotated web sites (with address) and bring it to class or Ms. Ury. Your peers will be required to view your project and to respond with a peer evaluation form. By midterm, the background research to your paper topic should be completed (as well as most of your paper Bibliography). We will spend a day or so in class allowing for the presentation of Web contribution. (p. 2)

Ury assisted the students in converting their projects to HTML format. She also posted their projects to the World Wide Web. Access to the projects was provided by the previously mentioned course Web site *Advanced Topics: American Religious History.* Ury wrote a midterm project herself, thus increasing her credibility with the students as a fellow researcher.

To establish her credibility as a faculty member, Ury taught the class three times as listed below:

- American Judaism was the title of the first presentation. She used Microsoft PowerPoint to enhance the lecture and highlight important topics. The research completed for this presentation formed the basic premises behind her midterm project.
- The second presentation was entitled *Country Music: The White Soul of the United States Working Class.* She created this presentation in HTML format and displayed Web pages as she interacted with the class.
- Ury also spent time in class helping students learn appropriate skills for evaluating World Wide Web resources. She used a Web page entitled *Evaluating World Wide Web Resources* to model appropriate selection of credible and reliable material.

After students created their midterm projects, they evaluated one another's work using a *Peer Review* form. Each student was offered the opportunity to work with Ury to incorporate peer suggestions before Brandon-Falcone graded the assignment.

The final projects were focused on a narrow aspect of the students' midterm projects. Building upon the knowledge gained through one-on-one *Student Research Consultations,* students focused their research on a specific idea, group or persons from the field of American religion. Once again Ury helped the students to convert their papers to HTML format and posted the papers to the World Wide Web.

STUDENT BENEFITS

While working with the students to create the midterm projects and the final papers, Ury was able to highlight correct citation of print and online sources in Turabian format. In addition, she worked with students to develop a personal research heuristic through the use of online research guides. Students also gained experience in judiciously selecting print sources and online resources. They learned to evaluate the credibility and reliability of both material formats and to single out scholarly resources for their research.

STUDENT REACTIONS

Students were surveyed via e-mail about their reactions to this unique partnership. Six of eleven students responded to the survey for a return rate of 54.5%. The following descriptive data was gleaned from this small sample. The authors recognize the limitations inherent in generalizing from such a small sample. We have also incorporated anecdotal data based upon interaction with the students throughout the semester. Student presentations at a campus-wide quality symposium further supported the data presented below. When asked what was most and least valuable about the library instruction provided for this class, students identified two strengths of the experience: learning how to create annotated bibliographies and discovering the value of Owens Library's online bibliographies and webliographies.

When queried about the benefits and liabilities of placing their midterm projects and research papers on the World Wide Web, students identified the value of the online documents as additional resource material when preparing for tests. Another benefit was the initial evaluation of the document by peers in addition to the instructor. Students felt this process enhanced their work because they partnered with one another to create quality research projects. Students also took pride in the quality of their work because they knew it was available to a wide audience on the Web. The primary liability cited by students was the time consuming aspect of converting documents for display on the Web.

IMPLICATIONS FOR FUTURE PARTNERSHIPS

Although this small sample of students was highly satisfied with the experience, the Owens Library Information Services Team has determined that delivering instruction in this manner is extremely labor intensive. Three aspects were particularly time-consuming: creating Web pages that taught research skills and recommended sources (approximately 70 hours total); attending class (three hours per week); and converting student assignments to HTML format (approximately 60 hours total). Web page use statistics validate the time spent creating the online resources over the other two aspects because the online resources have a wider audience.

In light of this information, Owens Library has chosen to create and maintain research guides, bibliographies, and webliographies to respond to student information needs. Concentration is placed upon academic departmental subject areas requiring students to conduct extensive research. A total listing of Owens Library's research guides, bibliographies and webliographies is available on the Owens Library *Course/Subject Resources* Web page. As these resources were recently reorganized on the Web page reproduced in Appendix B, the magnitude of this task became apparent. The need for these subject specific resources is demonstrated by the high use rate of the Owens Library *Course/Subjects Resources* page during the 1997-1998 academic year. It ranks fourth in usage among the 225 pages available on the Owens Library site. Additional data regarding the use of our resources includes the following:

1. Pages resident on this site were accessed 328,042 times during the academic year.
2. The *Owens Library* front page was accessed 103,955 times for 32.08% of the total hits.
3. The *Owens Library Catalog* page was accessed 64,429 times for 19.89% of the total hits.

4. The *Search for Articles* page, which allows users to connect to online periodical indexes, was accessed 60,529 times for 18.68% of the total hits.
5. The *Owens Library Course/Subjects Resources* page was accessed 31,997 times for 9.97% of the total hits.

Reference personnel have decided this high level of usage from a student body of 6,000 warrants the efforts required to fill in the gaps apparent in high use subject areas. Our new role of creating and updating online bibliographies, webliographies, research tutorials, and evaluation guides supports classroom instruction, as well as individual research projects. The differentiated Reference Desk service model described earlier reallocates staff time for further collaborative Web resource development. It also offers us opportunities to partner with departments when developing new web resources without labor intensive time spent in the classroom.

REFERENCES

Bosseau, Don L. and Susan K. Martin. 1997. Responsibility and opportunity: moving the library to the forefront. *Journal of Academic Librarianship* [Online] 23 (4):313-15. Available: EBSCOhost/MasterFILE FullTEXT1000/9710062328 [accessed 24 August 1998].

Brandon-Falcone, Janice. 1998. Advanced Topics American Religious History Syllabus. [Online]. Available HTTP:http://www.nwmissouri.edu/~0500627/history/syllabus.html

Engle, Michael O. 1995. Forty-five years after Lamont: the university undergraduate library in the 1990s. *Library Trends* [Online] 44 (2):368-87. Available: SearchBank/Expanded Academic ASAP/A17726346 [accessed 24 August 1998].

Haycock, Ken. 1998. Early interventions in student research. *Emergency Librarian* [Online] 25 (4):29. Available: EBSCOhost/MasterFILE FullTEXT1000/437478 [accessed 24 August 1998].

Rapple, Brendan A. 1997. The librarian as teacher in the networked environment. *College Teaching* [Online] 45 (3): 114-17. Available: SearchBank/Expanded Academic ASAP/A20108532 [accessed 24 August 1998].

APPENDIX A

Advanced Topics: American Religious History
http://www.nwmissouri.edu/nwcourses/history155/religion/
This page is the Web site for the course taught by Dr. Janice Brandon-Falcone.

Advanced Topics American Religious History Syllabus
http://www.nwmissouri.edu/~0500627/history/syllabus.html
This page is the online syllabus for the course taught by Dr. Janice Brandon-Falcone.

American Judaism
http://www.nwmissouri.edu/nwcourses/history155/religion/midtermprojects/connieury/index.html
American Judaism is the midterm project authored by Connie Ury for the American Religious History course.

American Religion WWW Resources
http://www.nwmissouri.edu/library/religion/americanreligion.html
This page is an annotated webliography providing hyperlinks to sites related to American religious history.

Can American Judaism Be Described? Or Has the Assimilation of American Jews Altered the Uniqueness of Judaism?
http://www.nwmissouri.edu/nwcourses/history155/religion/papers/CONNIEURY/
This page is a paper authored by Connie Ury for the American Religious History course.

Country Music: The White Soul of the United States Working Class
http://www.nwmissouri.edu/nwcourses/history155/religion/country/
This page features an online presentation created by Connie Ury for the American Religious History course.

Country Western Music: The White Soul of the United States Working Class
http://www.nwmissouri.edu/nwcourses/history155/religion/papers/connieury2/
This page is a paper authored by Connie Ury for the American Religious History course.

Course/Subject Resources
http://www.nwmissouri.edu/library/courses/courses.htm
This page, reproduced in Appendix B, is the page that provides links to

APPENDIX A (continued)

research guides, bibliographies, and webliographies authored by Owens Library staff.

Evaluating WWW Resources
http://www.nwmissouri.edu/library/search/evaluate.htm
This page is a teaching tool designed to demonstrate assets and liabilities of using resources on the World Wide Web. It contains hyperlinks to credible and questionable resources.

Find the Subject Database You Need
http://www.nwmissouri.edu/library/articles/databases.htm
This directory recommends Owens Library electronic and print periodical article indexes for specific subjects. It provides hyperlinks to indexes available to Northwest Missouri State University students on the World Wide Web.

Historical Research Guide
http://www.nwmissouri.edu/library/history/research.html
This guide leads Northwest students through a heuristic for historical research. It includes hyperlinks to resources that will facilitate the research process.

History of Religion in America
http://www.nwmissouri.edu/library/religion/researchamericanreligion.html
This research guide leads the students in the History of Religion class through a research process specifically addressing their assignment.

Information Services Team
http://www.nwmissouri.edu/library/teams/infoteam.htm
This resource is the home page for the Information Services Team that is responsible for reference and instructional services in Owens Library.

Newspaper Sources
http://www.nwmissouri.edu/library/newspapers/newspapers.html
This page lists newspapers available in Owens Library. It specifically appeals to those interested in historical newspapers.

Online Searchable Newspapers
http://www.nwmissouri.edu/library/newspapers/newssites.htm
This page provides selected hyperlinks to online newspapers.

Owens Library Catalog
http://www.nwmissouri.edu/library/catalog/owens.htm
This page is the Web based interface to the Owens Library Catalog.

Owens Library Home Page
http://www.nwmissouri.edu/library/index.html
This is the front page of the Owens Library's Web presence.

Peer Review
http://www.nwmissouri.edu/nwcourses/history155/religion/peereval.html
This is an online peer review form for the American Religious History class.
It includes a feature allowing students to submit their evaluation of a page to
the course instructor.

Religious Research Guide
http://www.nwmissouri.edu/library/religion/research.html
This guide leads Northwest students through a heuristic for religious research. It includes hyperlinks to resources that will facilitate the research
process.

Religious Studies WWW Resources
http://www.nwmissouri.edu/library/religion/
This page is an annotated webliography providing hyperlinks to sites related
to world religious history.

Search for Articles
http://www.nwmissouri.edu/library/articles/webindex.htm
This page provides hyperlinks to Web-based periodical article indexes available to Northwest Missouri State University students on the World Wide Web.

Selected History Sources in Owens Library
http://www.nwmissouri.edu/library/courses/history.htm
This page is an annotated bibliography of historical reference sources available in Owens Library.

Selected Religion Sources in Owens Library
http://www.nwmissouri.edu/library/religion/bibliography.html
This page is an annotated bibliography of religious reference sources available in Owens Library.

Student Research Consultations
http://www.nwmissouri.edu/nwcourses/library/services/paper.htm
This page describes a one-on-one research consultation service offered by
Owens Library Information Services personnel.

APPENDIX B

NORTHWEST MISSOURI STATE UNIVERSITY

OWENS LIBRARY ⌐

Course/Subject Resources

These research, print and Web resources have been compiled by Owens Library information professionals. Access to items marked with a green paw print (🐾) is limited to users on campus.

Press Control/F and enter keywords describing a subject OR select a letter below:

[A] [B] [C] [D] [E] [F] [G] [H] [I] [L] [M] [N] [P] [R] [S] [T] [U] [W]

Subjects (A to Z)	Research Guides, Presentations, and Tutorials	Print Sources in Owens Library	WWW Resources
Agriculture			WWW Resources
Biography	Research Guide	Library Sources	WWW Resources
Business	Research Guide	Library Sources	WWW Resources
Company Research	Research Guide	Library Sources	WWW Resources
International		Library Sources	WWW Resources
Management Information Systems	Finding Articles About MIS Topics		MIS Tools WWW Resources
Online Searchable Newspapers			WWW Resources
Statistics		Library Sources	WWW Resources
Tax Accounting			WWW Resources
Careers		Library Sources	WWW Resources
College Choice		Library Sources	WWW Resources
Computer Science/ Information Systems	Research Guide		
Computers & Society	Research Guide		WWW Resources
Copyright	Copyright Resources		
Drama	Research Guide	Library Sources	WWW Resources
Education	Research Guide	Library Sources	WWW Resources
Children's Literature		Library Sources	WWW Resources
Distance Education			WWW Resources
Elementary Math			WWW Resources
Learning Disabilities			WWW Resources
Multicultural Education	Research Guide		WWW Resources
Secondary Lesson Plans			WWW Resources
Secondary Math			WWW Resources
Teachers			WWW Resources

IV. OUTREACH IN AN ACADEMIC LIBRARY: OVERVIEW, ISSUES, AND BACKGROUND

Improving ADA Access: Critical Planning

Margaret McCasland
Michael Golden

SUMMARY. *The Americans with Disabilities Act of 1990* (ADA) motivated libraries all over the United States to evaluate their accommodations and services to patrons with disabilities. This article presents a case study of the Texas Tech University Libraries project to meet the needs of their patrons in relation to ADA. The study focuses on including adaptive technologies in the library environment to aid blind, hearing, visually and physically-impaired patrons and increasing library staff awareness

Margaret McCasland is User Instruction Librarian, Texas Tech University Libraries, Lubbock, TX 79409-0002. Michael Golden, is Science Librarian, University of Missouri-Kansas City, 102 Miller Nichols Library, 5100 Rockhill Road, Kansas City, MO 64110-2499.

[Haworth co-indexing entry note]: "Improving ADA Access: Critical Planning." McCasland, Margaret, and Michael Golden. Co-published simultaneously in *The Reference Librarian* (The Haworth Information Press, an imprint of The Haworth Press, Inc.) No. 67/68, 1999, pp. 257-271; and: *Library Outreach, Partnerships, and Distance Education: Reference Librarians at the Gateway* (ed: Wendi Arant, and Pixey Anne Mosley) The Haworth Press, Inc., 2000, pp. 257-271. Single or multiple copies of this article are available for a fee from The Haworth Document Delivery Service [1-800-342-9678, 9:00 a.m. - 5:00 p.m. (EST). E-mail address: getinfo@haworthpressinc.com].

of the needs of patrons with disabilities. Findings from the study will also benefit school, public, and special libraries that are evaluating their access for patrons with disabilities. *[Article copies available for a fee from The Haworth Document Delivery Service: 1-800-342-9678. E-mail address: getinfo@haworthpressinc.com <Website: http://www.haworthpressinc. com>]*

KEYWORDS. ADA, Texas Tech University Libraries, JAWS, zoom text, CCTV, disabilities, adaptive equipment, library access

INTRODUCTION

A student was recently using the online catalog for the Texas Tech University Libraries. He sat down, adjusted his earphones, and started investigating the catalog. He selected the catalog from the libraries' Web page. Using the catalog, he performed a Boolean subject and author search and located several titles that interested him. He printed off the bibliographic information and presented it to the libraries' book retrieval service. While waiting for his books to be delivered, he investigated the World Wide Web for the first time. Within the next hour, he had his books in hand, checked out, and he was ready to go home to read them. Does this sound like a rather normal library occurrence? Maybe not, since the student in this case was totally blind. Previously, he had never used the library catalog on his own or used the Internet. He always had to have someone help him locate what he needed. What made this empowering discovery possible? First was his willingness to try new technologies. Second was an online catalog that did not incorporate a lot of graphics or frames. Finally, a computer program that would read the screen contents to the patron and a library staff with the knowledge of how to use the equipment and how to teach a patron to use it. All of these did not happen overnight and definitely not by some fortunate accident. A conscious plan had to be created and put into place in order for our patron to be able to find what he needed. That plan is what we will present in this paper.

THE LAW

While there are many federal and local laws affecting public institutions in general, there are three that affect libraries directly when considering access for disabled patrons. These are Title VII of the Civil Rights Act of 1964, Section 504 of the 1973 Vocational Rehabilitation Act, and the Americans with Disabilities Act of 1990 (ADA). The Rehabilitation Act of 1973, as amended in 1992, protects persons with disabilities from discrimination in services, programs and opportunities supported by federal funding. Section 504 insures that all public facilities are to remove all architectural structures that prove to be barriers to disabled patrons. Public entities receiving federal funds are responsible for barrier removal. On July 26, 1990, President George Bush signed the ADA into public law 101-336 and it took effect January 26, 1992. This law directs public and private libraries to provide services to people with disabilities that are equal to services provided to citizens without disabilities. This law, ADA, is divided into four parts: Title I; Title II; Title III, and Title IV. Title I removes barriers that have prevented qualified individuals with disabilities from having the same employment opportunities that are available to people without disabilities. For example, since July 26, 1992, all libraries receiving federal assistance must have formulated a plan for wheelchair accessibility.[3] Title II states that "no qualified individual with a disability shall, . . . be excluded from participation in . . . the services, programs, or activities of a public entity . . . "[1] A "qualified individual with a disability" is defined as any person with a disability "who, with or without reasonable modifications to rules, policies, or practices . . . meets the essential eligibility requirements for the receipt of services . . . provided by a public entity."[2] Title III prohibits discrimination on the basis of disabilities by private entities in places of public accommodation. Title IV covers the providing of communication services and auxiliary aids to the public. The ADA differs from Section 504 in that it specifies how patrons with disabilities will have access to library information, programs, and resources. Libraries that do not provide equal access to these services will be subject to Title VII of the Civil Rights Act of 1964, which states that individuals can bring private lawsuits to stop discrimination. It is the goal of Texas Tech University Libraries to help patrons achieve equal access to library materials regardless of their disabilities or other special needs.

THE LIBRARY

Texas Tech University is in the city of Lubbock, one of the largest cities in the Texas Panhandle. The University has a sprawling campus with more than 24,000 enrolled students. The Texas Tech University Libraries include the University Library, the Government Documents Depository, the International Cultural Center Library, the Architecture Library, and the Southwest Collection/Special Collections Library. The Libraries' Web-based information system includes the catalog, electronic citation indexes, full-text databases, catalogs of other libraries, and links to other campus and reference information sources.

The only libraries comparable in size to the Texas Tech University Libraries are located more than 320 miles away in either Dallas to the East or Albuquerque to the West, making the Libraries an oasis of information in the Southern Plains. The Library maintains borrowing agreements with small colleges and universities in the Texas Panhandle and Eastern New Mexico to provide access to resources that would otherwise be unavailable to users unaffiliated with Texas Tech University. Patrons from the community are welcome to use any of the resources available in the public areas of the Library. Because it is a major information resource in the area for both the academic and public sectors, the Library also serves a large number of patrons from the business community and from area public schools. ADA access problems encountered in the Texas Tech University Libraries are the same ones found in many school and public libraries so the solutions derived from this study would apply to any institution trying to improve services for handicapped patrons.

Access to the University Libraries is extremely important to patrons with disabilities. The most important issue is that there are no alternative libraries in the South Plains where they can find comparable resources. Physical access to the building is another critical issue since the campus Center for the Visually Impaired is located in the University Library building and many visually impaired students using the center are moving through the Library even when they are not using library services. Ease of use is another major consideration. Most of our students are trained in public schools in the use of adaptive equipment by the Texas Commission for the Blind, but some students may not have experience with any adaptive technology because they lost their sight later in life or moved to Texas without prior training. With technology increasing their opportunities in education and in the job market, more and more patrons with disabilities are enrolling for classes and using our services.

THE PROJECT

A project was formulated to evaluate access to the library collection for students with special needs such as those who are permanently or temporarily visually impaired, have low mobility, learning disabilities, or hearing impairments. Consultations were held with people who had expertise in many different areas. Librarians met with the Director of the Center for the Visually Impaired, the Adaptive Technology Specialist for the Texas Commission for the Blind, the Assistant Dean of Students with Disabilities, and occupational therapists from the Texas Tech University Health Sciences Center. A blind student worker at a public library was consulted about improving access for handicapped patrons. University students and staff were consulted about difficulties in the library and what they needed to effectively access the collection and work on assignments.

From these consultations, several areas of concern were found. Although we had provided adequate wheelchair access, directional signs pointing out adapted locations were not visible to students in a wheelchair. No text enlargement or voice access was available for computers or print materials in the library so that visually impaired students had to depend on a librarian to facilitate their research. No reader-scanner was available for the students to use to read library materials independently. The electric door into the library was hidden behind a post with low visibility signs indicating its location. Library Express, a paging service available to all students, provided access to stack materials but few students with disabilities were aware of it.

The study also brought out several other facts. First, configuring workstations with equipment for handicapped students does not reduce the number of workstations available for general use. Second, placing adaptive equipment in public areas and making it accessible to all patrons enhances access to extremely small print materials, including many Government Documents Depository items. Third, visually handicapped students have better access if the Library uses the same adaptive equipment and software as used by the Center for the Visually Impaired. Staff time is more effectively used if students are already familiar with the equipment and software and can use it with a minimum of point-of-use instruction.

It was determined that the principal focus of the project would be to address the problems of signage and adaptive equipment for the visually impaired. Students with learning disabilities and hearing impairments would be adequately served by programs already in place in the Library such as the Library Express paging and copy service, research consultations, and reserved study carrels. Information would be distributed to those students and they would be encouraged to take advantage of those programs. Access for these students should be continually evaluated to insure that the services and equipment were working and that changes in the library did not negatively impact their ability to use the resources.

THE IMPLEMENTATION

The first phase of the project was the selection and installation of adaptive equipment, improving access routes, and visible signage. The staff agreed that the equipment needed to be first put in place so that problems could be addressed and all changes made before any training was attempted.

Navigation within the library was made easier by installing an Information Desk near the entrance to the library, which is staffed during library hours. Desk personnel offer assistance in answering basic questions about the library as well as giving directions to patrons. Handicapped students needing assistance are greeted at the Information Desk as they enter the Library. They are conducted by student assistants from the desk to the proper service area and are given assistance in elevators when appropriate. Maps of our multilevel library are also available at the desk.

Physical access was improved with new signage mounted on a vertical surface visible from a seated position at the entry to the Reference Area. Directional signs visible from a seated position were installed on the outside of the library so that students could easily find the wheelchair ramp and electric door. Workstations in the Reference Area were moved so that they were visible from the entry and extra space was provided around the adaptive workstations to facilitate wheelchair access. An oversized trackball was installed on the workstation for low-mobility students. Visually impaired students indicated that their needs would be met by a Closed Circuit Television (CCTV) unit to enlarge print materials, a reader-scanner to read print, and a workstation with an enlarged display and a screen reader. The capability of saving materials to a disk so that they could use it at home was a high priority.

The Closed Circuit Television (CCTV) unit chosen is a Telesensory Chroma Plus with color select. This stand-alone unit displays printed material in a variety of enlarged print sizes and colors and can reverse colors so that visually impaired or color-blind persons can select the display that is most visible to them. The students requested a large monitor so that more text was visible on the screen at one time and reduced their need to scan. This equipment has been reliable and trouble-free. The students have found it easy to use and have required no training in order to use it effectively.

The Arkenstone and Hewlett Packard reader-scanners were considered but not purchased. Although the scanners were lower in price, both had to be used in conjunction with a computer and we felt that more students could use the equipment at one time if the person using the scanner did not tie up the computer as well. The reader-scanner selected was a Xerox Reading Edge, a stand-alone, transportable, optical scanner that will read most typeset and typewritten material using a Dectalk speech synthesizer. This unit can translate a wide variety of printed materials including books, magazines, photocopies and documents with multiple columns into spoken words. Earphones may be attached for privacy and the text can be saved to disk to be used at a later time. This scanner reads a page no matter how it is oriented on the scanning table so that visually impaired patrons do not need to actually see the text or to position the page carefully on the scanner. It can be interfaced with other computer devices allowing the user to read, write and store information and is connected to a Blazie Drive to allow data storage on 3.5″ disks. It does work slowly and we found that a stand-alone unit was not as important as it seemed in the beginning. In retrospect, we would select a faster scanner with a high rate of accuracy such as the Arkenstone or HP.

The workstation with JAWS for Windows and ZoomText has been the most heavily used piece of equipment in the project. JAWS (Job Access With Speech) for Windows is adaptive software designed to operate with a Dectalk Speech Synthesizer to read the display on the computer screen. This allows visually impaired patrons access to the Library catalog, citation databases, and the Internet. While designed with the priorities of the blind user in mind, JAWS offers both audible and visual output for the sighted user. There are many screen reading software packages on the market including Vocal-Eyes and Window-Eyes from GW Micro Inc.; Slimware by Syntha-voice; and ASAP and ASAW by MicroTalk. We selected JAWS because the Texas Commission for the Blind routinely uses JAWS in its technology program for visually impaired clients. Since the Texas Commission for the Blind trains most of our visually impaired patrons in its use, we felt that we could limit the point-of-use training by selecting the same software. Although JAWS has worked well for some applications, it will not accurately read Web tables and frames. Since the Texas Tech University Libraries' catalog is Web-based, voice access to the collection is limited. The current version of JAWS should be able to handle Web materials more accurately.

The workstation also included ZoomText, an adaptive software package that allows the visually impaired user to magnify the screen display. Most of our visually impaired students are low vision rather than blind, so it has given most of the students successful access to the Library catalog, citation databases, and the Internet. It is economical, easy to use, has several magnification settings, and requires no special hardware to work. It has been so popular with the students that we have added a second workstation to take care of the demand. The new station uses ZoomText Xtra that includes a voice synthesizer as part of the package.

Even programs like JAWS and ZoomText Xtra are not helpful to our patrons if the graphic interface of our WebPages and online catalog is difficult to read. Much thought was put into the design and presentation of our online catalog and Library Web site. A text version of the catalog is linked at the top of the page so the link is one of the first items to be read. This makes it easier for the user scanning with a reader that reads from the top of the page, such as JAWS. Frames have not been used in constructing the various pages and graphics have been kept at a minimum. Screen reader programs that do not recognize frames will read the top line from one frame, the top line of the next, back to the second line of the first frame, second line of the next until the text is completely scrambled. By eliminating these features, our patrons who have screen-reading devices at home are able to access our catalog and databases online. Once the needed bibliographic information is obtained, online document retrieval forms can be used to request items, which can be sent to the patron, or be picked up at the circulation desk. These simple changes to the Web page have allowed access to our collection and other library services well beyond our physical library buildings.

THE TRAINING

The next and probably most important step was to train the staff and the patrons in the use of the equipment. The staff needed to have a good working knowledge of the adaptive equipment available in the Library in order to direct patrons to the appropriate area. Also, if the staff were not adequately trained in the use of the equipment, they would not know how to provide initial guidance to the patron or to solve problems as they arise. An essential goal of the project was to have the equipment available to the public whenever the library was open so most of staff would be able to assist patrons with the equipment.

The librarians involved initiated the project because they saw the need for services and were committed to providing access to handicapped patrons and they received unqualified support from the Texas Tech University Libraries administration. We found that two people who work effectively together and who have backgrounds in handicapped access issues accomplish much more than a single person. The project began with one project coordinator, the User Instruction Librarian, Margaret McCasland. For the training phase of the project, Michael Golden joined the team to serve as second coordinator for handicapped access and a second person allowed the training program to move forward with much greater speed. As with many such library projects, this was a volunteer duty for librarians involved and each had core responsibilities in other areas.

Not all libraries are fortunate enough to have staff with prior experience in working with handicapped users and librarians must find ways to become familiar with handicapped access issues. The first and best way is to get acquainted with the handicapped users and ask them what they need. Many of the problems pointed out by patrons are embarrassingly obvious. Real life examples are wheelchair access signage visible to a standing person but invisible from a wheelchair, Braille door numbers that are placed over the top of the door, and restroom doors that are wide enough for wheelchair access, but too heavy for a wheelchair patron to open.

Another way to become familiar with disabled patron needs is to research the literature on disabilities. Much has been written about disabilities since the ADA took effect in 1992, but the following books are of special relevance to ADA issues and to library patrons with disabilities in general. The first, by Donald Foos and Nancy Pack, is titled *How Libraries Must Comply with the Americans with Disabilities Act (ADA)*. The second is *Library Patrons with Disabilities* by Ray Turner. A third is *Preparing Staff to Serve Patrons with Disabilities* by Courtney Deines-Jones and Connie Van Fleet. Another useful source is *Libraries and the Empowerment of Persons with Disabilities,* a Special Issue of *Library Hi Tech,* Volume 14, Number 1, 1996. If a library is concerned about compliance with ADA or just with serving all its patrons more effectively, then these publications should be required reading.

For initial staff orientation and training in handicapped services, we contacted a group that specialized in vocational rehabilitation training. We felt that they would be aware of the issues involved in teaching visually impaired students to use equipment. Unfortunately, this group did not have expertise in the type of adaptive technology installed on our workstations. After much time was spent trying to pull together a training program for the staff, we accepted our error and reluctantly found another trainer. We contacted a local visually impaired technology specialist who had worked with the University and with the Library before. Since he was a former visually impaired student and a heavy library user, he had great insight to what was needed to aid our patrons.

The final training plan was the result of joint discussions about what the Library wanted and what the technology specialist felt was needed in order to prepare staff to help patrons. After a plan was set up to introduce our staff to the JAWS program, we decided to divide our staff of approximately twenty persons into groups of not more than six. We then surveyed our staff to determine which times were best for training. We decided upon morning sessions to fit in with our trainer's schedule and when the Library was not busy. Sessions were limited to one hour to accommodate the staff's busy schedule.

Each session began with an introduction by the trainer and the staff. For some staff members, this might have been their first encounter with a visually impaired individual and was a planned part of the training. Getting acquainted with a person with a disability allows staff members to overcome some of their discomfort and allows them to get to know the individual as a person, rather than just as a disability. The trainer had a dynamic personality and humorous approach, but made people recognize that a little thought had to be invested when helping a visually impaired patron. The need for clear verbal communication became much more apparent. For example, we learned not to simply shake our heads to answer a yes-or-no question. The sessions were hands-on with a staff member volunteering to sit at the keyboard and gradually search the Library's Web pages and online catalog using only the JAWS commands and the keyboard. Use of the mouse was not allowed so staff would learn to use the program as a visually impaired patron would. This allowed our staff members to gain experience using the equipment and allowed time for problems to appear while the trainer was available to answer questions. Small group sessions allowed everyone to see the screen on the handicapped accessible computer and allowed staff to freely ask questions instead of being inhibited by a larger group. Handouts of commonly used commands were given to each staff member and several Braille copies were permanently placed at the reference desk.

Many of the Texas Tech University library staff volunteered to learn how to use the adaptive equipment and many developed an interest in services for disabled students. This willingness has been greatly appreciated by patrons needing this assistance. Staff began to greet disabled students on campus and offer to help when they came in the library. Meetings were held with the disabled student counselors in the Dean of Students' Office and in the Texas Commission for the Blind campus office to publicize the new services. Students who were reluctant to come to the Library because of past frustration are now regular users and some have joined the student staff. We are pleased with the opportunity to get to know our patrons with disabilities and better serve their needs.

Although we have JAWS for Windows installed on one handicapped access workstation and ZoomText and ZoomText Xtra installed on two units, our work is far from over. Staff and patrons alike continually face many challenges in using the software. Library workstations offer a choice of either Internet Explorer or Netscape for the patrons to use as an Internet browser. JAWS requires slightly different keyboard commands depending upon which browser is used. Patrons tend to use their favorite browser and staff needs to be aware of the differences in the command structure. Also, each upgrade of the software has a new set of commands and new problems to challenge even the most dedicated staff.

Another ongoing problem is that, as in many libraries, our staff has a wide range of technical skills. Some staff members have low technical skills, and some are able to program and troubleshoot on their own. Learning one set of commands for JAWS is a major task, but learning two very similar sets of commands for different browsers creates an additional burden. The multitude of commands is also confusing for the visually impaired patrons even though they use these programs every time they use a computer. There is no solution for this problem as long as software programmers do not use a common command language for adaptive programs. Also, staff found that some scanners come with keypads that feel similar but have different configurations which patrons find confusing. It creates barriers to using the scanner if a patron owns a scanner with a different configuration. In these cases, direct intervention of a reference librarian is needed for the patron to learn the appropriate keys for the equipment available in the library. Our librarians are now more able to help patrons find what they need because they have gained a basic knowledge of the systems and are aware that problems at the terminal may result from incorrect commands.

The project has been an outstanding success, but problems still exist and new ones will appear because it is an ongoing project involving people and changing technologies. The knowledge and experience our staff gained through this project allows them to be able to help patrons with handicaps have barrier-free access to library collections and Internet information. They have benefited from learning to cope with the problems encountered by users of these technologies and gained respect, understanding, and compassion for students and other patrons in our library who have special needs.

THE FUTURE

As we look to the future, we see that there is a lot to be done towards the training of our patrons, staff and ourselves in facilitating access to the Library and Southwest Collections. The work that has been accomplished has dramatically improved access to the library but an ongoing concern in our program is that we not become complacent about our achievements. Technologies and techniques change many times faster than we can keep current with equipment and training. As we offer more access, more handicapped students use our services. It is a prime concern of most librarians that we accept the growing task of continuing to provide access to our collections. In the future, we have plans to seek a grant to support training for both staff and patrons and to upgrade our adaptive equipment. We want to establish an ongoing orientation program for our handicapped students and new Library staff members. Continuing evaluation of the program will be a critical part of the future and will give us the ability to respond to new challenges and to take advantage of new technologies in meeting our goal of equal access to information for students with disabilities.

REFERENCES

1. Public Law 101-336, 101st Cong. 2nd Session. (26 July 1990), *The Americans With Disabilities Act of 1990*, Section 202.

2. Michael G. Gunde, "Libraries and the Americans with Disabilities Act," Chap. 1 in *How Libraries Must Comply with the Americans with Disabilities Act (ADA)* (Phoenix, AZ: Oryx, 1992).

3. Ray Turner, *Library Patrons with Disabilities*, (San Antonio, TX: White Buffalo Press, 1995).

4. Texas Commission for the Blind, *Strategic Plan for the 1995-1999 Period*, 1994.

APPENDIX

Product Listing

JAWS for Windows
Henter-Joyce, Inc.
11800 31st Court North
St. Petersburg, Florida 33716-1805
Phone: (813) 803-8000
Toll Free: (800) 336-5658
Fax: (813) 528-8901
E-mail: reseller@hj.com
Internet: www.hj.com

ZoomText and ZoomText Xtra
Ai Squared
P.O. Box 669
Manchester Center, VT 05255-0669
Phone: (802) 362-3612
Fax: (802) 362-1670
E-mail: zoomtext@aisquared.com
Internet: www.aisquared.com

Kurzweil Reading Edge Scanner
Xerox Imaging Systems, Inc.
Telesensory OCR Products Division
9 Centennial Drive
Peabody, MA 01960
Phone: (800) 248-6550
Fax (Sales): (508) 977-2148
Fax (Support): (508) 977-2434
E-mail (Sales): readingedge_sales@xis.xeroc.com
E-mail(Support): readingedge_support@xis.xerox.com

Blazie Drive
Blazie Engineering, Inc.
105 E. Jarrettsville Road
Forest Hill, MD 21050
Phone: (410) 893-9333
Fax: (410) 836-5040
E-Mail: info@blazie.com
Internet: www.blazie.com

Telesensory Chroma Plus
Telesensory Corporation
520 Almanor Avenue
Sunnyvale, CA 94086
Toll-Free: 1-800-804-8004
Direct: (408) 616-8700
Fax: (408) 616-8753
E-mail: info@telesensory.com
Internet: www.telesensory.com

Instruction and Outreach
at Colorado State University Libraries

Teresa Y. Neely
Naomi Lederer
Awilda Reyes
Polly Thistlethwaite
Lindsey Wess
Jean Winkler

SUMMARY. The Colorado State University Libraries' instructional outreach services have undergone significant changes since the reorganization of Reference Services in January of 1998. The new organizational structure created a separate group for instruction, outreach and staff training, which includes the extended university programs position (distance learning), and a new position, the undergraduate instruction librarian. This new group gives the Libraries an avenue in which to provide focused instruction to the Colorado State University community and limited outreach to campus affiliates and the Fort Collins community. This article discusses outreach activities before and after the reorganization including services to specific populations such as African Americans, Hispanics, distance learning populations and extension ser-

Teresa Y. Neely is Interim Personnel Librarian and Staff Development/Training Coordinator, Naomi Lederer is Undergraduate Instruction Specialist, Awilda Reyes is Reference and Business Librarian, Polly Thistlethwaite is Coordinator of Reference Services–Instruction, Outreach and Staff Training, Lindsey Wess is Library Technician III, Reference Services, and Jean Winkler is Catalog Librarian, all at the Colorado State University, Fort Collins, CO 80523-1019.

[Haworth co-indexing entry note]: "Instruction and Outreach at Colorado State University Libraries." Neely et al. Co-published simultaneously in *The Reference Librarian* (The Haworth Information Press, an imprint of The Haworth Press, Inc.) No. 67/68, 1999, pp. 273-287; and: *Library Outreach, Partnerships, and Distance Education: Reference Librarians at the Gateway* (ed: Wendi Arant, and Pixey Anne Mosley) The Haworth Press, Inc., 2000, pp. 273-287. Single or multiple copies of this article are available for a fee from The Haworth Document Delivery Service [1-800-342-9678, 9:00 a.m. - 5:00 p.m. (EST). E-mail address: getinfo@haworthpressinc.com].

273

vices, undergraduates, and disabled students. *[Article copies available for a fee from The Haworth Document Delivery Service: 1-800-342-9678. E-mail address: getinfo@haworthpressinc.com <Website: http://www.haworthpressinc.com>]*

KEYWORDS. Library instruction, multicultural outreach, minority user groups, liaison relationships

INTRODUCTION

For many years outreach activities at Colorado State University Libraries (CSUL) have stemmed primarily from the Public Services division, which encompasses Reference Services, Access Services (loan and reserve), and Interlibrary Loan (ILL). Until recently, instructional outreach services to the Colorado State University (CSU) and Fort Collins communities have been comprised of general and subject specific invited instruction, general library orientation, and services for extended university programs and extension services.

In January 1998, the CSUL reference services department reorganized itself from divisions of duties and responsibilities by subject to division by function, creating a separate group for instruction, outreach and staff training. This article will focus on the outreach and instructional activities both before and after the reorganization, including outreach to African Americans and Hispanics and the disabled. Before reorganization, outreach was limited to subject specialists working in conjunction with the extended university programs librarian (distance learning), and cultivating the liaison relationships with academic subject disciplines. The new organizational structure provides a focused effort on outreach activities that was not previously present.

BACKGROUND

Colorado State University is a land grant institution founded in 1870 as Colorado Agricultural College. It is a Carnegie I class research institution and has more than 22,000 students enrolled in undergraduate, graduate and professional degree programs. Currently, the University has approximately 1,400 faculty in eight colleges and 55 academic departments. The CSU University Libraries consists of the main library, Morgan Library, and three branches–the veterinary teaching hospital branch, the atmospheric sciences branch, and the engineering branch–and provides instruction, outreach and access to information resources and training for the entire CSU campus including branch and satellite campuses, extension services, and distance learning programs.

INSTRUCTION AND OUTREACH AT COLORADO STATE UNIVERSITY LIBRARIES

In general, instructional services for the Libraries has consisted of a University group or academic department contacting the Libraries administration or specific librarians and requesting assistance for general orientation and/or specialized instruction. CSUL continues to provide this type of support to University constituencies; however, it is now a more centralized operation, with resources, faculty and staff devoted to instruction and outreach. The position description of the instruction, outreach and staff training group (instruction group) coordinator includes a cornucopia of instruction and outreach-related duties, including coordinating and developing educational programs for users on and off campus; promoting instruction across campus and beyond; providing support for subject specialists in their teaching; organizing the evaluation of publications, guides, and web-based instructional tools; monitoring and recommending upgrades for electronic information teaching lab equipment; and planning and evaluating reference staff training programs. To that end, the selection of professional library staff for the group make-up was relatively easy; however, it was also limiting. In addition to the coordinator, this new group includes two new professional librarian positions, the undergraduate instruction specialist and the web librarian. Also included are the extended university programs librarian position, three reference librarian positions and two support staff positions.

Since the group was formed it has been busy attempting to find its place within the overall structure of Reference Services and the University Libraries system. There was an immediate need to address a large population of faculty, staff and graduate students in the wake of the disaster and a journal substitution project. Primary patrons were basically uninformed about how the Libraries could attend their needs with a greatly depleted collection. The instruction group developed and advertised, via a campus-wide electronic listserv, instruction sessions having "CSU EVENT–Fast, Free, Easy Library Research From Your Home or Office" in the subject line. Email on this listserv has the potential to reach each faculty and staff member and most graduate students at the University. These 90-minute sessions feature finding on-line full-text articles on topics of the participant's choice; setting up personal interlibrary loan (ILL) delivery profiles to make use of the Libraries' Fast Interlibrary Loan service for speeded delivery of flood damaged journals; minimal instruction in the use of *SAGE*, the Libraries' online catalog; and the most difficult part of each session, outfitting each participant with *Uncover Reveal* profiles for e-mail notification of current journal contents. A packet of public service flyers (handouts) which contain information about the databases and resources presented is distributed to each participant during the sessions.[1] The sessions are billed as "Library Research Through the Internet: The Basics" and are taught by instruction group staff as either general sessions in the Libraries' state-of-the art electronic information labs, or as subject-specific sessions in various campus college or department facilities. An informal survey to collect data on the status of campus-wide computer and technology facilities was completed by a member of the instruction group and based on the available facilities and other factors; the first subject-specific sessions were held at the College of Business. The business librarian, had she not already been a member of the instruction group, would still have been invited along for her liaison relationship as well as to instruct the subject-specific full-text part of the session. One of the dilemmas the instruction group faced was how to fulfill its goals and objectives, while at the same time not duplicate or take away from the liaison relationships already in place between reference librarians and academic departments. This problem was solved by including the appropriate subject librarian when planning instruction sessions for a particular subject. The email advertising these sessions also includes a reminder to participants to contact the appropriate library subject specialists for subject-specific sessions.

The response to the general sessions has been nothing short of phenomenal. The instruction group could not have anticipated the number of interested individuals who would RSVP, attend, and complete evaluation forms. A recent advertised session, limiting the class size to 30, received more than twice the anticipated numbers within two hours of email notification, prompting the scheduling of an additional session to be taught at the same time. The promising response rate calls for careful planning and timing of future sessions which are currently being scheduled on a more regular basis. Additional sessions have been scheduled for each month of the fall 1998 semester.[2] Evaluative feedback has been positive and encouraging and based on numerous requests, current sessions are now extended to two hours.

Since the dormitories on campus have been hardwired, the instruction group plans to take these popular instruction sessions directly to undergraduates, and are also in the process of developing a University Libraries newspaper flyer for the fall semester, highlighting the Libraries' services and resources, and changes that have recently taken place. Other outreach from the instruction group has come from the individual efforts of the undergraduate instruction specialist, the extended university programs librarian, subject specialists, and liaison relationships with ethnic advocacy offices and groups on campus. With the appointment of the new Colorado State University Libraries' dean, Camila Alire, there is a renewed focus on outreach and the Libraries will offer for the first time in the fall of 1998, honors internships to students enrolled in the CSU Honors Program. Collaborative efforts between the Libraries, the Honors Program, and the ethnic advocacy offices have been focused on securing honors students in general, and minority students, in particular, who are also enrolled in the honors program.[3]

UNDERGRADUATE INSTRUCTION OUTREACH AT CSU

Prior to the creation of the undergraduate instruction specialist position, there was not a concerted effort on the part of the Libraries to contribute to the overall undergraduate experience at CSU. The education subject selector developed and maintained the Libraries' curriculum collection and was also the liaison to the first year composition program. CSUL also offers a one-credit course, *Library Research Skills* (LI 301), which in the past has been taught by any of the professional librarians on staff. In addition, most subject librarians serve as liaisons to the academic departments and provide individual and specialized instruction and support to faculty, staff and students. The undergraduate instruction specialist position provides for a more

focused effort on the undergraduate population. This position currently has no collection development responsibilities; however, it has
enormous potential for instructional outreach at the academic research
library level based on liaison relationships with departments such as
the CSU Online Writing Center, and partnership development with the
K-12 community.

Naomi Lederer was appointed as the undergraduate instruction
librarian in 1996. The position, a new one, wished for in the early
1990s and created in 1996, acts as the liaison to the First Year Composition program, and provides support and tailored instruction for
special populations such as K-12, various University offices and targeted user groups. There are more than eighty sections of the Composition course taught each academic year, so providing instruction
sessions for individual sections is not possible. Instead, the undergraduate instruction specialist coordinates with the director of the composition program, designs web pages specifically for the program,
meets with new Graduate Teaching Assistants (GTAs) each fall semester, and teaches library instruction sessions for related Composition courses. In addition, this librarian teaches library instruction sessions to sections of the course when requested.

The web pages developed by the undergraduate instruction librarian are the main focus for instruction to the Composition course and
other undergraduate and related outreach. The philosophy behind
these pages is to enable students to learn research skills in or out of
the classroom. GTAs are encouraged to use the pages in their classes
and subsequent feedback from this group has been positive. The
undergraduate instruction librarian has also met with librarians and
media specialists from the local secondary school district to discuss
the web pages designed to teach students how to do library research.
Using the web pages as a beginning point, these sessions focus on the
types of skills that are critical for high school students to know–
whether they are planning to attend college or not. Community college outreach has also been an important, although a rare part of this
position. Other outreach opportunities include invitations to present
at the Fort Collins Internet Festival and "Tech Talks" in the Fort
Collins Public Libraries. These sessions have promoted the Libraries' collections and services, and, have further cemented the
relationship between Colorado State University and the Fort Collins
community.

Other outreach includes participating in special campus initiatives, such as Preview CSU, a two-day orientation to the University for new freshmen and their parents, where the librarian has the potential to reach 3,000 students and 2,000 parents each summer; providing instruction sessions for several junior and senior high schools, and other students in the Fort Collins community; and providing instruction sessions to groups not covered by collection development specialists. For example, there is instruction outreach to advanced composition courses, the Bridge program–a summer program for incoming freshmen, the International English Program, technical journalism courses, and new athletes.

Although other professional librarians still have the opportunity to teach *Library Research Skills* (LI 301), the Libraries' one-credit eight-week course, the undergraduate instruction specialist is the primary contact. This course provides another form of outreach in that it has the potential to reach a wide variety of students and provides a broad spectrum of information skills throughout the University. The course is required for Consumer Science majors and results in approximately 20 students per year enrolled in addition to voluntary registrants.

SERVING THE HISPANIC AND LATIN AMERICAN COMMUNITY AT COLORADO STATE UNIVERSITY

As the business librarian at Colorado State University Libraries, Awilda Reyes is responsible for developing collections as well as cultivating liaison relationships with the faculty, staff and students who make up the five departments in the College of Business (accounting, computer information systems, finance and real estate, management, and marketing). As a Hispanic member of the Colorado State University community, she has the opportunity to work directly with two student organizations that support the largest minority student population on campus.[4] The Latin American Student Organization deals with foreign students who come from Spanish-speaking countries. Awilda serves both as counselor for cultural activities, and as liaison between the library and the students. Like most students from ethnically diverse populations, these students feel more confident and more comfortable dealing with a Spanish-speaking person and a friend when they are doing research. The second student organization is El Centro Student Services, an organization serving Chicanos, Cubans, Hispanics, Latinos, Mexican-Americans, Puerto Ricans, Spanish-Americans and members of the University and local communities.[5] This office offers assistance with students and their transitions to the Colorado State University community; academic, personal and social counseling; and provides community outreach programming in and around Fort Collins. In her position as liaison and in her capacity as a librarian, Awilda assisted the office in the reorganization of a small library of books, periodicals, and films dealing with issues of concern to Chicano/Hispanics/Latinos. She also regularly attends cultural and social activities and forges personal relations with these students, which has opened the doors of the library in a different way. As liaison, Awilda takes advantage of opportunities with both of these organizations to promote library services by informing students of the various Hispanic-related resources available and accessible in the Libraries.

Each summer top Latino high school students from across the nation come to Colorado State University to participate in the Lorenzo de Zavala Youth Legislative Session. This intensive, three-day program is part of the National Hispanic Institute. By using a youth legislature and supreme court as forums to debate ideas and propose solutions by researching political, legal, and social issues, the Lorenzo de Zavala Youth Legislative Session focuses on planning the future of the Latino community. The subject areas to be researched by the students changes each of the three days of the Session. Instructional sessions at Morgan Library for these students include lessons on the use of *SAGE*, the Libraries' online catalog, and various print and online resources which provide information on the Hispanic population. In addition, students are introduced to and instructed in the use of print and online legal resources to assist them in their research.

SERVING THE AFRICAN AMERICAN COMMUNITY AT COLORADO STATE UNIVERSITY

According to fall 1997 data, the total student minority population at Colorado State University is 10.5 percent, or 2,335 of the total student population (22,344). The most recent statistics show that minority student enrollment has steadily increased from 9.6 percent (2,020) in

1993 to the current status. Totals for resident and nonresident African American undergraduate and graduate students are 318 or 1.4 percent of the total University population.[6] With numbers this small, it is imperative that some sort of focused outreach is done.

The CSU Office of Admissions sponsors many recruitment and retention efforts throughout the academic year. Each summer for the past 6 years, the Black Issues Forum (BIF) has been held on the CSU campus. This program was initially developed as a recruitment tool focused on high school students of African descent in the state of Colorado. Since its inception, the program has steadily grown and now includes many students from out of state each time it is held. The University Libraries, through its Black diversity liaison, Teresa Neely, plays an integral part in the success of BIF by providing access to staff, resources and collections for extended periods of time during the three-day program. Students conduct intensive research and the results are presented in a public forum on the last day of the program. Each year the format changes from either debates, town hall sessions, or general group presentations. Students also learn how to evaluate, use and present the results of their research, prepare annotated bibliographies, and work collaboratively in groups.

Black Student Services, like El Centro, is a part of the Student Affairs Division at CSU. Each semester this office teaches a class for at-risk students titled *The African-American Success Project*, which is designed to increase retention and graduation rates of students of African descent. As the liaison to Black Student Services at CSU, Teresa works collaboratively with this group to encourage the academic, professional, cultural, and personal development of all students of African descent enrolled at the University. Liaison activity with the African American Studies department in CSU's Center for Applied Studies in American Ethnicity includes materials selection, library instruction, and direct library support for students, faculty and staff. As a liaison, students are often referred to the library for one-on-one consultation to complete course requirements.

As a member of the African American community on campus, Teresa also serves as a direct contact for community and University members who require African and/or African American-related information.

DISTANCE LEARNING
AT CSU/EXTENDED UNIVERSITY PROGRAMS

The extended university programs librarian (EUP) provides library support for distance learning populations and services at Colorado State University. This position is jointly supported by the Division of Educational Outreach (Division) and the University Libraries. The Division administers the majority of the credit and non-credit off campus programs. These programs cover a variety of disciplines and are delivered internationally in a variety of ways. As a member of a land grant institution, the University Libraries support numerous extension stations and agents state-wide, as well as a video-based distance learning program. Formerly the SURGE program, it is now called the Colorado Distance Degree Program. This program offers master's degrees in business, computer science, engineering, statistics, and vocational education; and also a second BS in computer science, and doctorate degrees are available in some engineering fields. The University also offers correspondence study and telecourses, and operates the Denver Center for Continuing Education, which "represents an extension of University resources to the people and businesses of metropolitan Denver."

Prior to 1995, in order to provide adequate services to all students at a distance, the extended university programs librarian worked closely with subject specialists to provide specialized services to this population. In 1994, the business librarian and the extended university programs librarian conducted a survey of the then SURGE professors, and interviewed representatives from Continuing Education and the Office of Instructional Services, which distributes the video tapes, to determine the best method to deliver specialized instruction to the distance learning populations. It was then determined that the best method would be to produce a video.[7]

The primary focus for the extended university programs (EUP) librarian is to improve network-based access to library resources for distance users. Students, faculty, and staff working off campus want instant solutions to their problems and needs–just like students on campus. But unlike students on campus, remote users often find (or imagine) themselves stranded without library support for their course work. Surpassing remote users' modest expectations is easy and makes them particularly gratifying to work with. They are effusive in their thanks for even basic service.

News about remote access to library resources is maintained and regularly refreshed on CSU's Distance Users web pages.[8] The pages contain detailed information about obtaining remote access to library databases via the web and telnet, and also include web links to IAC databases and other databases available in test mode through the Triple I Web Access Management software. The distance user pages also feature automated forms for requesting material available in the library, plus the ILL request module for unmediated home mail or fax delivery to distance users.

Flyers and updates in CSU's distance education catalogs provide information on important print-based resources distributed to every distance education student. A 10-minute library instruction video, funded by the Division of Educational Outreach for distribution to all students taking distance courses by videotape, is currently in the works to update the videos produced in 1995.[9]

CSU's MBA program for distance learners uses EMBANET–a pavilion of web-based services to support distance learning including e-mail, chat rooms, and discussion groups. The EUP librarian maintains an e-mail presence there, providing information and answering research and access questions for groups and individuals.

One-on-one training and classroom instruction are essential to CSU's service for remote constituencies. Funded by a grant from the USWest corporation obtained by the University Libraries' in conjunction with CSU's Cooperative Extension program, during the 1998 spring semester, the EUP librarian traveled to several Cooperative Extension offices around the state providing on-site staff training on library resources available through new grant-funded workstations. Cooperative Extension agents have also flocked to library training workshops offered at annual on campus meetings. Off campus users (particularly those based nearby) have also attended the "Fast, Free, Easy" workshops offered on campus in order to get hands-on experience with library resources.

Serving a different off campus constituency, the EUP librarian has established regular hours at CSU's Denver Center where MBA, occupational therapy, and human resources classes take place. The EUP librarian conducts in-class training sessions in the Denver Center learning lab and holds office hours nearly weekly in that off campus location.

Personal training sessions, either in-person or on the phone, in conjunction with successful hands-on student experience provide the best introduction to library resources and open doors for subsequent phone and e-mail contact. By expanding remote access to electronic subject indexes and full-text resources through both training and technology, the EUP librarian actually creates a demand for material delivery and student-initiated research assistance.

OUTREACH TO THE DISABLED AT CSU LIBRARIES

Individuals with visual or hearing impairments, movement or strength limitations, cognitive limitations, repetitive motion injuries, or learning disabilities can all benefit from the availability of assistive technology. Within a library setting, assistive technology provides users with disabilities with decisive means to access information. For more than a decade librarians and staff from the Colorado State University Morgan Library have actively embraced assistive technology issues by offering users with special needs state of the art equipment as well as reference and retrieval service.

From the beginning, trained library staff were available to assist disabled users. In an effort to provide effective service to users with disabilities, several staff assistance scenarios have been attempted through the years. At one point the library tried initiating a program where users could walk-in unannounced and trained staff would be on call for immediate, one-on-one assistance. Another scenario involved assigning a pager to specific staff throughout the day. Staff from various public service points throughout the library could page a specific number and reach a member of the assistive technology team whenever needed. Both "on call" scenarios proved to be problematic because an assistive technology team member sometimes could not be located when needed. Trying to mesh pager assignment and staff schedules also became convoluted, often leaving portions of the workday with no staff coverage at all. The current policy now requires that prospective users contact the coordinator for assistive technology and make an appointment for assistance and training.

Keeping library staff abreast of the current state of affairs in the assistive technology room is accomplished in a number of ways including an assistive technology equipment and related services public service flyer, which details all of the services available at Morgan Library to assist disabled users as well as describes the equipment and resources that are available for use in the assistive technology room. Regular staff training and refresher courses are given to library staff who volunteer for the special appointment assistive technology team.

Beyond the library, outreach efforts have been ongoing with several campus departments to coordinate efforts and best meet the needs of university students with disabilities. The Colorado State University Office of Resources for Disabled Students (ORDS) recently recognized Morgan Library with the Outstanding Effort Award for the department on campus best meeting the needs of Colorado State students who have disabilities. The campus Assistive Technology Resource Center (ATRC) coordinators have been instrumental in recommending to the library new technologies in the field of assistive technology. In an effort to direct students to the library both ORDS and ATRC staff meet regularly with the Morgan Library assistive technology coordinator and her team. The Committee for Disabled Student Accessibility (CDSA) comprises a third campus group that is essential for ensuring that assistive technology efforts on campus remain current and effective. Much of the continued funding for the equipment and software for the assistive technology room derives from the CDSA and its generous support, including gifts of a new Macintosh-based assistive technology workstation, and two large screen monitors. CDSA students also meet with the library Assistive Technology team on an annual basis to review current needs and make recommendations for enhancements and additions to the library resources. The current array of equipment includes an Arkenstone Reading System, a Juliet Brailler, an Internet workstation with JAWS for Windows, and a word processing workstation with Dragon Naturally Speaking and Aurora.

Future plans for the assistive technology effort at Morgan Library include seeking ways to fund a full time coordinator position.[10] The person in this position would review, evaluate and make recommendations for new equipment, including upgrades and replacement; act as liaison with other campus departments; work more closely with disabled students; and keep abreast of Americans with Disability Act guidelines for the library at large.

FUTURE

The future for outreach and instruction at Colorado State University Libraries is promising and the instruction, outreach and staff training

group are leading the Libraries as it develops programs and dissemi-
nates information about resources and services to the University community at large. Opportunities for local and community outreach are
also a possibility and the Libraries continue to be dedicated to providing a full range of services to each member of the University community, both on campus and off, as well as limited services to affiliates
and constituents.

REFERENCES

1. After the disaster in the summer of 1997, the University Libraries' made
agreements with libraries, regionally and nationally, to deliver flooded journal articles within 3 business days; *Uncover Reveal* is an ASCII-based service of The Uncover Company. The service is respectable, however the user interface is awkward
and not user friendly. Frustrated by the long convoluted telnet access to the database,
Polly Thistlethwaite developed a public service flyer for the "Fast, Free" sessions,
titled "17 Easy Steps to Uncover."

2. See CSU Libraries Calendar of Events <http://mantalibrary.colostate.edu/
calendar.html>.

3. See CSU Libraries' Honors Student Intern Program <http://mantalibrary.
colostate.edu/pers/honors.html>.

4. The total minority student population in fall 1997 was 10.5% or 2,335 of the
total 22,344 students enrolled. Hispanic students made up 5.02% (1,123) of the total
population; Asian American students–630 (2.82%); Black students–318 (1.42%);
and Native American students–264 (1.18%). *University Facts at a Glance 1996-
1997.* Colorado State University, Office of Budgets and Institutional Analysis, 1998.
See Office of Budgets & Institutional Analysis, CSU <http://www.colostate.edu/Depts/
OBIA/obiapub0.html>.

5. Colorado State University's Student Affairs Division includes advocacy offices which represent the federally protected classes These are El Centro Student Services, Asian/Pacific American Student Services, Black Student Services, Native
American Student Services and Women's Programs and Studies.

6. From *Enrollment Data, Fall 1997* Office of Budgets and Institutional Analysis, CSU <http://www.colostate.edu/Depts/OBIA/obia.html>.

7. Two videos, one general and one for business students, were developed, pro-
duced and distributed to SURGE students See *Colorado State University Libraries–
Your Vital Connection,* assoc. prod., Teresa Y. Neely, Susan Schwellenbach and Joseph Schwind, 10:55 min., Colorado State University Libraries' and Colorado State
University Office of Instructional Services, 1995, videocassette; *Colorado State University Libraries–Your Vital Connection–Business Information,* assoc. prod., Teresa
Y. Neely, Susan Schwellenbach and Joseph Schwind, 13:50 min., Colorado State
University Libraries' and Colorado State University Office of Instructional Services,
1995, videocassette; and Teresa Y. Neely and Susan Schwellenbach, "Library support to distance learning students in the business disciplines," in Abbass F. Alkhafaji,

ed., *Business Research Yearbook–Global Business Perspectives* v. I (Lanham, MD: University Press of America, 1994), pp. 955-960.

8. See <http://mantalibrary.colostate.edu/distance>.

9. See end note # 7.

10. Jean Winkler, catalog librarian, is the current coordinator for disabled students, devoting less than 1/4 time to the position.

Outreach
at a Public, Academic, Regional Library–
Texas A&M University-Corpus Christi

Denise Landry-Hyde

SUMMARY. Bell Library at Texas A&M University-Corpus Christi has reached beyond its walls to utilize as well as to enrich the diverse community resources in our midst. In terms of distance education library support, the purpose is to compensate libraries that support A&M-Corpus Christi students living in their locales. In terms of consortium arrangements, we have played an integral part in the creation of the Coastal Bend Health Information Network, which is a unique blend of local college/university libraries and local hospitals. We have implemented the rather novel idea of having a specialized library, specifically a hospital library, outsource its library operations to our university library. When the local Art Institute of South Texas was brought under the university's organizational umbrella, Bell Library's contribution was to provide acquisition, processing, and cataloging support for Art Institute library holdings. We have entered into a Memorandum of Understanding with a "sister library" in Mexico. In summary, Bell Library strives to know and cultivate community interests that parallel our own. *[Article copies available for a fee from The Haworth Document Delivery Service: 1-800-342-9678. E-mail address: getinfo@haworthpressinc.com <Website: http://www.haworthpressinc.com>]*

KEYWORDS. Library outreach; public, academic, regional library; distance education; distance learning; consortia; special libraries; medical libraries; art libraries; outsourcing; special collections; archives

---

Denise Landry-Hyde is Information Literacy/Reference Librarian, Bell Library, Texas A&M University-Corpus Christi, 6300 Ocean Dr., Corpus Christi, TX 78412.

[Haworth co-indexing entry note]: "Outreach at a Public, Academic, Regional Library–Texas A&M University-Corpus Christi." Landry-Hyde, Denise. Co-published simultaneously in *The Reference Librarian* (The Haworth Information Press, an imprint of The Haworth Press, Inc.) No. 67/68, 1999, pp. 289-298; and: *Library Outreach, Partnerships, and Distance Education: Reference Librarians at the Gateway* (ed: Wendi Arant, and Pixey Anne Mosley) The Haworth Press, Inc., 2000, pp. 289-298. Single or multiple copies of this article are available for a fee from The Haworth Document Delivery Service [1-800-342-9678, 9:00 a.m. - 5:00 p.m. (EST). E-mail address: getinfo@haworthpressinc.com].

289

In 1989, Corpus Christi State University became a part of the Texas A&M University System. In Fall 1994, the name of the institution changed to Texas A&M University-Corpus Christi. With that name change came a change in status for the university. It grew from a two-year, upper-level institution into a four-year university with freshmen and sophomores in addition to upper-level undergraduates and graduate students. Practically overnight, the library's user group changed dramatically. Younger students populated the campus, and the number of students living on campus increased. Since 1993, a year before the change in status, enrollment has jumped by 1,500 students–a 33% increase (Strahan 1998). The university library, Bell Library, like most other academic libraries, has had to serve a broader range of students–varying in age, diversity, mobility, and level of expectations–"great expectations."

DISTANCE EDUCATION

As is true for most other university libraries, distance learning has become extremely important. Distance students increasingly expect to fulfill university coursework without setting foot on campus. A&M-CC students are no exception. Certain university programs hold classes in several other cities. The Nursing Program, for example, holds distance education classes in Laredo, Victoria, Temple, and Weslaco. The College of Education's Occupational Training and Development Program teaches classes in Laredo, Weslaco, Beeville, and El Paso. The students in all of these areas need curriculum support with regard to library research. The local libraries do not always have sufficient materials to meet the needs of distance education students. The nursing students probably have the greatest need for library support. The medical literature is very specialized and is typically fairly expensive. Libraries at the distance education points usually do not have the necessary medical literature. Bell Library's former director, Ben Wakashige, had been working out an arrangement whereby A&M-CC would pay to the institutions our students use locally a certain dollar amount to help cover the cost of services. Services would include interlibrary loan, circulation, reserve, reference, and use of periodicals. A&M-CC would pay those institutions $2 per student credit hour for undergraduates and tentatively up to $9 per graduate student credit hour. A&M-CC students pay a Library Use Fee of $2 per student credit hour each semester, but distance students are not receiving full library service for this fee. While this plan has not yet been put into effect, a sample, written agreement has been drawn up to be signed by both parties. The letter would be addressed to the library directors at each institution our students use, and money would be sent to those institutions (Wakashige 1998).

This is a novel approach to providing formal library collection support at distance locations. But as the number of students, traditional and non-traditional, taking distance education classes continues to grow, this kind of agreement becomes increasingly necessary. Oftentimes, proper library support is the *last thing* considered in distance education, yet it is so *critical* in terms of students' ability to fulfill course requirements. The average public library, for example, would be incapable of in-house support of very specialized nursing classes.

The instruction librarian advised both the Education and Nursing Faculties that she would be willing to teach library classes at the distance locations. Fortunately for Bell Library, the geographic distances are not so great as to prohibit this solution. In areas where distances are too great to travel, the library instructor would have to use teleconferencing, the Web, or some other distance education technology to deliver class content. What sometimes happens is that the library instruction staff at the distance library will teach classes for other schools' students. We have done this on occasion here at Bell Library. The class load has never been overwhelming. This is, at least, another option for meeting students' library instruction needs.

CONSORTIUM AGREEMENTS

Consortium agreements are another way libraries have reached out to one another and shared needed resources. A recent outreach development in which Bell Library has been a founding member is the formation of a consortium known as the Coastal Bend Health Information Network. The consortium is made up of college/university libraries and hospitals in the Coastal Bend area, a multi-county area. The goal of CBHIN, which has been funded by the South Texas Health Initiative (a state-supported initiative aimed at improving the caliber of health care in South Texas, a traditionally underserved area of the state), is to provide ready access to health information by students and professionals associated with health care in the Coastal Bend.

The valuable store of information in area hospital libraries has been opened up for university faculty/student use. On the other hand, college/university libraries are sharing their resources with those hospitals. A full-time Project Librarian and two FTE classified employees staff the project and make more direct access to health-related information possible. In its first year, FY 96, participants in the consortium included four institutions of higher education in the Coastal Bend which provide health-related programs and four Corpus Christi hospitals. As of September 1998, one additional college and several other area hospitals will have joined the consortium, so membership has increased. Each institution will pay a membership fee of $200 per year. This should help participants "own" the program. The project will also allocate $5,000 per institution to go towards the purchase of databases. The various institutions will have to make up any price difference (Gibson 1998).

CBHIN provides access to several health-related databases, including Medline, CINAHL, and the Health Reference Center, the latter of which is aimed towards consumer needs. The databases are accessible through the World Wide Web using Windows and Netscape software.

Rapid document delivery is another aspect of this program. In the medical world, the speed with which health information is disseminated is critically important. Therefore, the program ensured that each participating institution would have ARIEL, which utilizes the Internet and FAX capability to speed document delivery. Not every participating institution had ARIEL prior to the formation of the consortium, so the CBHIN has brought technological advances to members who had previously lacked that capability. A Union List of Serials of health-related periodicals located in the participating institutions has been compiled as part of the project. This helps considerably in locating institutions that have needed journals. An agreement among participating institutions helps to ensure that requested periodical articles will be faxed within *two working days*, if they are located at a participating institution. If the article is not available locally, the interlibrary loan request will be forwarded to a commercial document delivery vendor selected by the program or to another library. Oversight of the expenditure of South Texas Health Initiative funds is provided by

Briscoe Library of The University of Texas Health Science Center at San Antonio.

The CBHIN Project Librarian trains health care professionals, library, and hospital staff in the use of electronic information resources, including Internet sources. The program also provides training for library and hospital staff on effective document delivery procedures and techniques, so the institutions without trained staff will be able to conduct their own document delivery activities.

Another novel development in which Bell Library has played a crucial role is the outsourcing of library operations at Driscoll Children's Hospital in Corpus Christi to the university library. Driscoll Hospital pays the university approximately $100,000 per year to run its library operations, which includes hiring of a librarian and a paraprofessional, and purchasing and processing all items for Driscoll Hospital. Bell Library has in place the expertise and computer resources, such as OCLC membership, to provide these services. And the arrangement is a *revenue producer* for the university. These days, university administrators are increasingly looking for ways their institutions can make money (Wakashige 1998). The outsourcing arrangement also makes hospital library holdings available to students and faculty. Bell Library's Catalog Staff did retrospective conversion of 598 hospital library holdings, and these items show up in the university's online catalog. So anyone searching the online catalog is able to access these materials. As of FY 97/98 Bell Library began purchasing and processing all items for Driscoll Hospital (Shupala 1998).

Bell Library's director and university administrators spent voluminous hours putting this arrangement with Driscoll into effect. By all indications, both the university and the hospital are extremely pleased with the outcome. Prior to this arrangement, the Driscoll Hospital Library did not have the desired staffing level nor optimal technological capability. These needs have now been addressed (Wakashige 1998). The hospital is also a member of the Coastal Bend Health Information Network and therefore is able to get rapid document delivery of needed medical journal articles.

PARTNERING WITH THE ARTS

Texas A&M University-Corpus Christi has found a way to bring a local art museum under the organizational umbrella of the university.

In September 1995, the Art Museum of South Texas in Corpus Christi affiliated with A&M-CC after more than a year of discussions and efforts of university and museum officials. The museum actually operates as a department of A&M-CC. "'The partnership will provide many additional opportunities to expand art education programs for our students, faculty, and this entire region,'" said University President Robert Fergason (*Island University News* 1995).

Bell Library's role in this partnership has been the addition by its Catalog Unit, with help from a couple of other university librarians and staff, of 1,133 items to the library's online catalog. There are an estimated 500 items left to catalog. As of FY 98/99, Bell Library is responsible for the purchase and processing of all new items for the Art Institute (Shupala 1998). So once again, the arrangement seems to be mutually beneficial to both groups. "'The partnership provides an opportunity for two recognized educational institutions to join forces, which furthers arts programming across the region,'" said Bill Otton, Executive Director of the museum (*Island University News* 1995). And another specialized collection has been made available to a wider group of users by the addition of its holdings records to the university's online catalog.

A unique art project which opened to the public in March 1996 is housed in Bell Library. Jim Edwards, Visiting Professor of Art, working with faculty and administrators, opened the Texas Art Archives. The focus of the archives is on modern contemporary art and artists of Texas from the mid-'60s to the present. No one else in the state is concentrating on this, according to Jim Edwards. Art and information on Texas artists can be viewed on slides which make up a part of the archives collection. Video tapes are also available, one series being "Artists and Art" in which Texas artists have been interviewed in their studios. Flyers, catalogs, and publications round out the collection. Information and records in the archives are being cataloged and indexed for easy access by visitors. Students have helped and will continue to help develop the archives. This participation is good training in archival work for these students. The Texas Art Archives was three years in development and is a "dream come true," says Jim Edwards (*Island University News* 1996). Bell Library provided the space for this project to become a reality.

REACHING OUT TO THE PUBLIC LIBRARIES

Outreach has also been accomplished between local academic and public libraries. Bell Library's collection has been weak in current bestseller kinds of reading material. The library has had to spend its acquisitions money on works that directly support the curricula of instruction and research at the university. Some years, as is true for all public academic libraries, funding has been lean. So there have been few purchases of popular fiction titles. To address this situation, our Associate Director for Public Services, Nancy Cunningham, approached the director of our local public library to see if we could become a kind of small branch library of the public library and periodically receive books of a popular nature for users. The public library has been very supportive of this effort. This will not be a very large selection but will simply make it easier for members of the university community to obtain popular titles. This academic and public library joint venture will result in better service for these library users (Cunningham 1998).

COMMUNITY RELATIONSHIPS

Community outreach by Bell Library has taken many forms. One example involves the local chapter of the American Association of University Women which was interested in finding a home for its archives. The chapter recently celebrated its 70th anniversary, so the records of this group are rich in detail on the social/cultural life of Corpus Christi. The president of the local chapter approached the Information Literacy Librarian who is both an A&M-CC librarian as well as an AAUW member. A meeting was then arranged between AAUW representatives and the Head of Special Collections and Archives at the university. It was agreed that both parties had a mutual interest in preserving the archival records of this group. Since the university now has a Women's Center for Education and Service as well as an academic minor offered in Gender Studies, the interests of AAUW paralleled those of the university. Working together, each could enrich the other's programs. For example, during the annual celebration of Women's History Month, members of AAUW attend any number of university-sponsored programs and events held in honor of women's achievements and contributions to our society. The local chapter also provides a scholarship each year to some deserving female student to attend A&M-CC. Another noteworthy development is the effort to establish a student chapter of AAUW on campus. The Information Literacy Librarian recruited a library staff member to set into motion the steps that would lead to the creation of this chapter. This staff member is extremely active in community efforts and was excited by the prospect that a student chapter could be formed. With input from other university personnel, two faculty members willing to serve as mentors to the student group were recruited. The local AAUW chapter has a real desire for our students to continue their memberships well after their college days are over. With the imminent establishment of the student chapter, exposure of another generation of women to the work of this national group has been accomplished.

INTERNATIONAL RELATIONS

Outreach by Bell Library not only extends to local and area communities, however. It has an international dimension, as well. It extends across the state's border. In March 1996 the library signed a "Memorandum of Understanding" with the library of the Instituto Technologico y de Estudios Superiores de Monterrey in which our libraries would act as "sister libraries." Under this agreement, both universities said they would provide access to each other's online catalogs, engage in interlibrary book loans agreeing to deliver books to one another within a 48-hour period, seek ways including workshops and staff visitations in which library staffs could share and exchange ideas and expertise, and establish an automated document delivery program between the two libraries.

Beginning in Spring 1998, the libraries actually began a *staff exchange* in which a library staff member from one institution visits the other library for about one week, minimum. The program includes paraprofessionals as well as professionals. During this time, the visitor learns about how the other library operates. Ideas and suggestions are exchanged on both sides. The length of the visit makes it possible for the visiting staffer to truly immerse himself/herself in that library's operations. A one-day visit would hardly be worthwhile, particularly considering the distance between Corpus Christi and Monterrey. The staff exchange has been a major success story. Four staff exchanges have occurred as of this date, and another is planned for Spring 1999. Employees on both sides are ecstatic about the program, and the possibilities are practically limitless. The exchange has also been a morale booster. Plans are to continue the exchange, having as many library staff as possible making the visits. One of the exchanged staff members, Jose Gonzalez, who played a large role in getting this program up and running, participated this year in the International Book Fair held in Monterrey annually (Gonzalez 1998). The Memorandum of Understanding has widened our perspectives and involved both staffs in positive co-operative experiences.

A final stellar example of library/community outreach and cooperation is the recovery of the "lost" manuscripts of Jovita Gonzalez de Mireles, a South Texas Mexican-American writer. Urged by scholars to locate the papers of Gonzalez de Mireles, Dr. Tom Kreneck of Special Collections and Archives alerted local community people of the Library's interest in both Jovita and her educator husband, E. E. Mireles. Corpus Christi lay historian Ray J. Garcia serendipitously led Kreneck to the papers, which had come into the possession of another Corpus Christi resident, Isabel Cruz. Ms. Cruz generously donated the Mireles Papers to Special Collections and Archives. Dr. Jose E. Limon of the University of Texas at Austin visited the department and conclusively identified two missing historical novels entitled *Caballero* and *Dew on the Thorn* within the Mireles Papers. Both manuscripts have now been published and constitute important additions to South Texas Mexican-American literature. These works would have been lost to scholars and members of the general public alike had a number of community people and organizations, including the library, not come together to discover and care for these treasures. This story is a positive example of "a cooperative endeavor in which the library played a central role" (Kreneck 1998). Dr. Kreneck, in his article on the discovery of the manuscripts, quotes J. Frank Dobie, the well-known Texas folklorist, as saying that libraries are "'a community's most civilized achievement'" (Kreneck 1998).

In conclusion, in terms of distance education library support, particularly the idea of compensating libraries that support our students living in their locales; consortia agreements, including the unique blend of local college/university libraries with local hospitals; the novel idea of a specialized library, specifically a hospital library, outsourcing its library operations to a university library; bringing an art institute under the university's organizational umbrella and an art archives under the library's roof; exchanging staffs and ideas with a "sister library" in Mexico; and knowing and cultivating community interests that parallel our own, Bell Library has demonstrated its willingness to reach beyond its walls to utilize as well as to enrich the diverse community resources in its midst.

REFERENCES

Cunningham, Nancy. 1998. Interview by author. Corpus Christi, Texas, June.

Gibson, Sally. 1998. Interview by author. Corpus Christi, Texas, July.

Gonzalez, Jose. 1998. Interview by author. Corpus Christi, Texas, 17 August.

Island University News. 1995. TAMU-CC, Art Museum of South Texas Celebrate New Partnership, 29 September.

————. 1996. Mary and Jeff Bell Library is home to Texas Art Archives, 10 April.

Kreneck, Thomas H. 1998. Recovering the "Lost" Manuscripts of Jovita Gonzalez, the Production of South Texas Mexican-American Literature. *Texas Library Journal* 74(2): 76-79.

Shupala, Christine (ADULB042). (1998, 27 July). *Art Museum and Driscoll.* E-mail to author (ADULB025).

Sloan, Bernie. (1998). *Library Support for Distance Learning* [Online]. Available: http://www.lis.uiuc.edu/~sloan/libdist.htm [1998, 4 June].

Strahan, Amy. 1998. More Students Are Choosing Area's Four-year Universities. Corpus Chrisi Caller-Times, 20 July.

Wakashige, Ben. 1998. Interview by author. Corpus Christi, Texas, June.

Outreach to Distance Learners:
When the Distance Education Instructor Sends Students to the Library, Where Do They Go?

Jean S. Caspers

SUMMARY. It is the responsibility of any institution offering distance education programs to provide library resources and services for its students. In contrast to traditional students who can find the library on a campus map and go there, distance learners need orientation in order to "find their way" to their library. Librarians must be proactive in their efforts to make the library visible and accessible to these students. Library resources and services must be made available in ways compatible with the needs of students in these programs. The processes of designing, marketing, providing and evaluating appropriate library services demand continuous outreach to the distance education community. *[Article copies available for a fee from The Haworth Document Delivery Service: 1-800-342-9678. E-mail address: getinfo@haworthpressinc.com <Website: http://www.haworthpressinc.com>]*

KEYWORDS. Distance education, library instruction electronic reference, outreach, university libraries

INTRODUCTION

Responsibility for the provision of library support for distance learners rests with the institution offering courses or programs. The

---

Jean S. Caspers is Distance Education Librarian, The Valley Library, Oregon State University, Corvallis, OR 97331-4501.

[Haworth co-indexing entry note]: "Outreach to Distance Learners: When the Distance Education Instructor Sends Students to the Library, Where Do They Go?" Caspers, Jean S. Co-published simultaneously in *The Reference Librarian* (The Haworth Information Press, an imprint of The Haworth Press, Inc.) No. 67/68, 1999, pp. 299-311; and: *Library Outreach, Partnerships, and Distance Education: Reference Librarians at the Gateway* (ed: Wendi Arant, and Pixey Anne Mosley) The Haworth Press, Inc., 2000, pp. 299-311. Single or multiple copies of this article are available for a fee from The Haworth Document Delivery Service [1-800-342-9678, 9:00 a.m. - 5:00 p.m. (EST). E-mail address: getinfo@haworthpressinc.com].

1998 revision of the *ACRL Guidelines for Distance Learning Library Services* states:

> Library resources and services in institutions of higher education must meet the needs of all their faculty, students, and academic support staff, wherever these individuals are located, whether on a main campus, off campus, in distance education or extended campus programs, or in the absence of a campus at all . . . Students and faculty involved in distance learning programs are entitled to library services and resources equivalent to those provided for students and faculty in traditional campus settings. (ACRL, 1998)

These statements serve as the guiding principles for the provision of library services to distance learners.

Within the text of the ACRL guidelines, the need for outreach to the learning community is suggested thus: "Because students and faculty in distance learning programs frequently do not have direct access to a full range of library services and materials, equitable distance learning library services are more personalized than might be expected on campus" (ACRL, 1998). This is true because the situations of distance learners differ from those of on campus students. Indeed, in many cases, the situations of different students within the same distance education program may vary widely.

When distance education services are initiated, the full range of library services available for on campus students in the same discipline must be identified and used as the baseline for planning. Appropriate services can be offered only if the unique needs of the students in distance education programs is known; and the students for whom these services have been designed will be able to utilize them only if they are effectively informed. The continued value of the library's services will depend on a continuous process of evaluation and improvement in response to the assessment of these services over time.

A great deal of outreach is required to achieve these results. Outreach efforts will involve contacts with administrators, faculty, librarians on campus and at other libraries, and students enrolled in distance education courses.

DEFINING THE DISTANCE LEARNER USER GROUP

The terms distance learning or distance education are employed to describe either independent study or classroom learning that takes place away from the main campus of the home institution. Although face to face teaching involving faculty who travel to meet with student groups is well established and often takes place at great distances from the home institution's campus(es), some definitions, such as this put forth in a glossary of distance education terminology on the Web, limit the definition to courses where ". . . students and instructors are separated by physical distance and technology, often in tandem with face to face communication, is used to bridge the gap" (College of Engineering, UI, 1995). Courses supported by technologies which can support distance learners increasingly include a mix of students, including both distance learners and students located on the home campus. Therefore, "distance education" as a term is seen by some as giving way to "distributed education" (Dede, 1996; Ruhig-DuMont, Barton, and Rhimes, 1995).

A student who needs unique distance education library services can be defined as one whose residence is too far away for him/her to reasonably be expected to regularly travel to the home campus library to study, and who also does not come to campus for class. It is important that each institution determine the characteristics of the set of students who will be eligible for any special services, such as subsidized materials delivery to their homes or to a site in their community. Once these have been determined, it is the responsibility of the librarians at the home institution determine ways to identify and reach out to these students.

BECOMING PART
OF THE DISTANCE EDUCATION COMMUNITY

Writing about services for ethnic populations and immigrant groups, Keller states: "To accomplish their mission and guarantee their future role as an information center, libraries and librarians need to enhance two things: their relationship to the communities they serve, and their approach to marketing library programs and services to their communities" (Keller, 1996). In a similar way, it is crucial for the distance education librarian to actively become part of the distance education community, especially as related to programs emanating from the home campus.

One of the first tasks of a distance education librarian is to identify and meet the people involved with distance education offerings emanating from the institution. During this process, questions such as the following must be answered. What courses of study are offered? Who, if anyone, gathers and catalogs this information centrally? How can the library get advance notice of distance education offerings? Who is the main point of contact in the central (or in the various dispersed) offices overseeing distance education programs? Are there web courses? Are they identified as part of the centralized (if any) distance education efforts, or are departments offering them independently? Are all continuing education and/or distance degree students enrolling through the registrar's office? Are there distributed education courses which include students both on campus and those who should qualify for distance learner library services? Where do the students reside and/or attend class? What local libraries might they have in their communities? Although some of these questions can be answered by campus publications, web sites, or catalogs, personal networking with program administrators is critical.

Outreach efforts to students via the teaching faculty are often effective because faculty have a direct line to the students. If faculty encourage students to utilize the resources of the home library, they will be likely to pay attention to that recommendation. Librarians should seek collaborative relationships with faculty, identifying the research needs of students in their classes, and working out the details of the most appropriate ways to meet these needs.

Traditionally, the library has been a place where people come to work with materials and librarians. As educators are designing virtual classes and working with students who cannot be expected to travel to the home institution's library, the traditional view of what librarians can do to serve students remotely must be made explicit. Instructors' expectations of what librarians can and will do for distance learners often need to be expanded. From the point of view of an educator, Elizabeth Burge emphasizes the need for proactive outreach by librarians thus:

> I am always confronted with the problem of how to move learners sensitively and consistently out of their "teach me" passive,

receptive attitudes, and develop the skills and desire to take responsibility for their learning . . . It is a tricky problem to solve
and often requires rapid judgements around feasibility and timing
of interventions designed to prompt and support learners . . .
There is a real limit to the energy and time I am prepared to spend
on checking out how responsive and connected the library staff
want to be. If my initial expectations of them are low, then I have
to decide how I will deal with that result; some days I am even
too weary to think about the problem, so . . . I take the path of
easiest action and don't call the librarian. (Burge, 1991, 15)

In order to avoid exclusion from the education process, the distance
education librarian must take steps to raise expectations of the teaching faculty concerning the ability of the library to provide research
support leading to student success in distance education courses. If
training workshops for distance education faculty are offered, the
distance education librarian should be a presenter at this training. As
distance offerings are listed each term the distance education librarian
should make contact, informing faculty of the types of services available and opening discussions about the students' library needs for
success in the course. These discussions may result in new ideas for
library services or new approaches to them, or simply to a new awareness on the part of the faculty member of how existing library services
are workable for their students' needs. Collaborative planning involving librarians and faculty as partners with a common goal of fulfilling
the course goals is the ideal situation.

Whether or not collaboration with all faculty members is accomplished, materials providing orientation for the students should be
available. These may include newsletters, brochures, handbooks, videos, and web pages. Contact information for the distance education
librarian and the reference desk, along with the URL for the library's
web page, should be included in the distance education department's
course catalog. On program and individual class web sites, links to the
library's services should be provided.

A great deal of outreach is involved in arranging for the placement
and delivery of orientation information: contact with the course catalog
editor; with the program directors (to gain the professors' names and
contact information early enough to make contact); with the subject
librarians who contact the professors; with web page editors managing

sections of the university and the library's web, which would be good places for a link to the distance education library services web page. Examples of such pages are widely available on the web (Sloan, 1998).

Library research instruction may be delivered to each class by means of face to face teaching at a class site, via interactive television, as a collaborative faculty participant on a class e-mail list or electronic conference, or by other direct means utilized by the course instructor. If the librarian is not invited to present library instruction directly, delivering packaged instruction or making it available are other options. Some libraries uses a web tutorial or online course for this purpose. Indeed, even if the librarian is invited, having the web tutorial in place for follow up is an asset. Many examples of online instruction can be found on the web (LOEX, 1998; Scholz-Crane, 1997).

One on one instruction which grows from a reference call or email query is another way instruction is delivered by librarians at the home library, and, similar to reference transactions in the library building, this is often the manner in which much teaching about the library research process occurs. A toll free number, or the librarian's offer to return a student's call at the library's expense, facilitates this type of teaching. E-mail transactions, particularly as follow ups to a telephone conversation, are often appropriate for the delivery of personalized, detailed one on one instruction.

Burge makes the observation that opportunities to interact with distance learners can enhance the student's feeling of being supported by the home institution. "You are relatively neutral territory for learners who are caught in a power differential with their teacher or tutor and there is scope for you to use that special status to support learners affectively as well as cognitively and logistically" (Burge, 1991, 14).

The role of the distance education librarians is often to serve as a generalist reference librarian, answering many questions, but referring specialized questions to subject librarians as appropriate. In a library where distance education service is integrated into the library's existing structure, outreach to subject librarians internally is critical. If subject librarians are well informed about distance education developments in the departments to which they are assigned they will be better able to integrate service to distance learners into their work load. This communication works two ways. Often it is the subject librarian, not the distance education librarian, who is first to learn about new distance education programs which are being planned by an academic department.

Getting materials to the student is a primary responsibility of the home institution. Unless the home institution is maintaining a branch library or devoting sufficient funds to maintain collections to support their programs at a host library, there is no reason to expect libraries in the student's location to have the materials needed for a course. The home institution must be ready to deliver materials expediently to the student.

Replicating the functions of the interlibrary loan transaction is a core method used by many libraries (Fritts, 1993; Grudzien and Jones, 1995). Electronic delivery, and electronic repositories of articles, such as those offered by subscriptions to full text services, can be an excellent way to assure that the distance learner with Internet access has direct and fast access to information provided by the home institution. A librarian working collaboratively with a faculty member packaging a course may find a new role as co-developer of the resources to be read by the students, collecting an "electronic bookcase" delivered within the course materials on CD-ROM or via the web course (Burge, 1991, 16). Of course, copyright issues must be carefully considered in these processes (Gregory, 1997).

The distance education community surrounding the institution's off campus course offerings is likely to include many people and groups which are not visible on campus. These people may include some teaching faculty, who may not maintain an office on the home campus. They may include administrators at each partnering host institution, such as a community college in another town.

WORKING WITH THE COMMUNITY BEYOND THE HOME INSTITUTION

Partnerships between university and community college libraries are becoming routine. Programs which build on the two-year programs offered at community colleges which allow students to complete a baccalaureate degree without relocating generally involve such partnerships. Community colleges are also frequently partners with universities offering graduate level degrees. Generally the degree-granting institution, where the student is enrolled, is referred to as the "home" institution. The community college, where the student may physically attend upper division or graduate level classes and receive other student services, is known as the "host" institution. There should be an agreement between the home and host institutions delineating the extent to which library services will be provided by the host library. The home institution librarian should initiate this process. The librarians at the host institution must have the means to conveniently assist students to connect to the home library's resources and services. At the least, this means access to the student library orientation materials in print and/or electronic form, and an ongoing relationship between the home and host library staff. When there is an ongoing concentration of students at a particular host institution, resources in the form of core library materials or funding may be provided to the host institution's library by the home institution. The details of these arrangements will vary greatly depending on variables such as the nature of the programs offered as compared to the existing community college library collections, the ability of the home institution to deliver appropriate research resources to the students in a timely manner, and the policies and mission of the community college.

Even when the home library offers excellent services, students will use local libraries to a great extent. In a survey of students enrolled in an off-campus doctoral program at Oregon State University, 20 students who resided in various communities from 40 to 1,200 miles from campus reported using 28 unique libraries instead of or in addition to the OSU libraries. Of these, ten were academic libraries at four-year institutions, thirteen were community college libraries, four were public libraries, and one was a special library (Caspers, 1997). Similarly, in a study of Deakin University graduate off-campus students, Macauley found that over 86% of 190 respondents reported using "libraries other than their home institution library for their thesis research" (Macauley, 1997).

Although they will be welcomed as primary clientele in their public library, unless that library has a mission which includes collecting and providing access to materials appropriate for the student's research, the information search process at the local library can become quite frustrating. If the student is not seen as a primary client at a library, such as at a private academic institution where he or she is not enrolled or employed, there may be further frustration at the circulation desk. The student may be denied circulation privileges or charged a fee for a library card. This may result in ill will on the part of the student towards both the local library and the home library if no reciprocal agreements have been arranged. It also creates antipathy on the part of the local librarians towards the degree-granting institution. Dugan coined the phrase "victim library" to describe the role of the local library in this scenario (Dugan, 1997). Outreach to local librarians to establish reciprocal agreements and/or to ensure that the librarians have information for efficiently refering students to the home library is important. If the referrals result in successful outcomes for their patrons, these librarians will be likely to gain confidence in future referrals, thus becoming partners in a satisfying process which fulfills the missions of both libraries involved.

When student populations are not concentrated but dispersed over multiple locations it is inefficient to forge formal agreements with each library a student might use. Courses delivered via the World Wide Web are a contributor to the geographic dispersal of students. Of course, the use of the web is one potential solution to offering library services to students independently of other libraries. This is certainly a powerful tool for reaching students who have access to the web.

If the home library provides services via the web, however, it cannot be assumed that all distance learners have the same level of access to these services that on-campus students may enjoy. Simply substituting a Library Home Page for the types of outreach described above is not sufficient. Students who are not taking their courses via the web may or may not have made arrangements for web access. They may or may not be able to spend sufficient time at public terminals in unaffiliated libraries. There may or may not be computer labs accessible by arrangement at host institutions, and even when there are, without orientation by librarians, students may not think about doing library research (as opposed to web surfing) from a computer lab. The student in any of these situations may need technical assistance in order to gain access to library services provided via telnet, password information for access to bibliographic databases which require passwords, or information and help in establishing access via a proxy server if the home institution provides one. Therefore it remains crucial that students receive orientation information in print format via their professors and/or directly from the home library. The print material should make it clear that they will be able to have personalized assistance to obtain the research support they need from the home library whether or not they have access to the web.

The distance education library community also extends to those who do similar work. There are many distance education librarians in the world who are available for connections, and many opportunities for professional development in this arena. Joining the Distance Learning Section of the Association of College and Research Libraries Division of ALA is a good way to get connected with other librarians doing this work (DLS, 1998).

Keller recommends several key points for establishing community connections (Keller, 1996, 42-3). Using them as a model, a similar list can be utilized for establishing connections with the distance education community:

Determine the community's demographic profile.

- Survey your students.
- Meet with your administrators.
- Collaborate with your teaching faculty.

Encourage library staff to learn about distance education programs.

- Present a brown bag.
- Encourage them to collaborate with teaching faculty.
- Provide them with partnership support when they do.

Serve on campus committees related to distance education.

- Use your personal connections with library and/or distance education department senior administrators to get appointed.
- If a relevant committee does not exist on campus, initiate it!

Serve on professional committees at the state, regional and/or national level related to:

- distance education librarianship.
- distance education in general.

Meet with users and involve them in determining how the library can provide better service to meet their needs.

- talk with teaching faculty.
- meet with administrators.
- interview, survey and hold focus groups with students.

Take advantage of opportunities to speak at conferences.

- in the library community.
- in the distance education community.
- in the broader higher education community.

Develop your marketing skills and expertise.

- take classes in community relations and marketing.
- meet with your institution's public relations experts and ask their advice.
- take a distance education course as a student.

EVALUATION OF DISTANCE LIBRARY SERVICES

Evaluation is a necessary component of distance delivery services. Information about the numbers of students enrolled in distance education programs, their locations, and the courses of study in which they are engaged should be updated each term. Data indicating the numbers of reference contacts, materials requests received, items delivered, and turn around time should be compiled regularly. An excellent tool for considering what data to track has been designed by the Statistics Committee of the Distance Learning Services (DLS) section of ACRL (Statistics Committee, DLS, 1998). Qualitative information gathering indicating student satisfaction with the library's services and collections (and access to collections) should also be gathered.

Obviously every contact with a distance learner or faculty member delivering distance classes affords the opportunity to ask for feedback about the effectiveness of the library's support, and this informal method is important. However, more formal assessment should also be pursued. Focus groups of known heavy library users (for instance, graduate students) can be conducted, as can surveys distributed with cooperation from a faculty member directed to a class as it concludes its term.

If the distance education office surveys students regularly, it is useful to work with their survey team to insert library related questions into their survey. A question regarding whether the students were aware of the home library's services is particularly helpful in both assessing the effectiveness of marketing, and in increasing the faculty and/or distance education office's understanding of the need to market library services. This vehicle for surveys is also more likely to include students who are not receiving services: a sample which will be left out by surveys distributed directly to known library users such as students in classes with whom the librarians have worked.

The purpose of assessment is, of course, to improve service design, marketing efforts, and the delivery of services. Improvement efforts should be continuous, with changes being considered in response to input from users, and implemented as appropriate.

Outreach to other libraries via networking and benchmarking research is also critical for distance education library services. The opportunities for creative solutions to new situations about in this field of service, and keeping abreast with developments and ideas implemented by other libraries is another avenue for effective service improvement.

CONCLUSION

Outreach is integral to the success of distance education library services. From the initial stages of the design of services through their marketing, delivery, evaluation and improvement, broad and continuous communication efforts on the part of librarians engaged with distance education is crucial.

Without outreach efforts to determine student needs, services may create barriers rather than access. Without aggressive marketing efforts, students may believe their only option is to burden their local library with their research needs. Without the cooperation of teaching faculty, students may not have the opportunity to learn how perform research using the most appropriate resources. Without regular evaluation, needed improvements to the service may not be identified. Without networking with other distance education librarians, opportunities to enhance services in new ways may not be considered. Without library services conducive to student success, the home institution may lose students to schools with better programs.

REFERENCES

Association of College and Research Libraries (ACRL). 1998. "Guidelines for Distance Learning Library Services." *C&RL News 59:689-694.*
Burge, Elizabeth J. (1991). "Relationships and Responsibilities: Librarians and Distance Educators Working Together." In *The Off-Campus Library Services Confer-*

ence, Albuquerque, New Mexico, October 30-November 1, 1991. ERIC ED339383.

Caspers, Jean. (1997). Unpublished report. Oregon State University, Corvallis, OR.

College of Engineering, University of Idaho. (1995). Glossary of Distance Education Terminology. [Online]. Available HTTP: http://www.uidaho.edu/evo/dist14.html

Dede, Chris. (1996). "The Transformation of Distance Education to Distributed Learning." *Western Cooperative for Educational Telecommunications News.* [Online] Available HTTP: http://www.wiche.edu/telecom/news/newsdede.htm

Distance Learning Section (DLS) of the Association of College and Research Libraries Web Site (1998). [Online] Available HTTP: http://ecuvax.cis.ecu. edu/~lbshouse/home.htm

Dugan, Robert E. (1997). "Distance Education: Provider and Victim Libraries." *Journal of Academic Librarianship 23*: 315-318.

Fritts, Jack. (1993). "Sharing the Load: A Model for Interlibrary Loan/Circulation Cooperation." *Journal of Interlibrary Loan, Document Delivery & Information Supply 4*: 55-66.

Gregory, Vicki L. (1996). "Delivery of Information Via the World Wide Web: A Look at Copyright and Intellectual Property Issues." IN *The Association of College and Research Libraries Conference: Nashville, TN.* [Online] Available HTTP: http://www.ala.org/acrl/paperhtm/e40.html

Grudzien, Pamela and Maryhelen Jones. (1995). "Internal Partnerships for External Sourcing: Interlibrary Loan as Supplier-Provider for Off-Campus Students." In *The Seventh Off-Campus Library Services Proceedings. San Diego, CA, October 25-27, 1995.*

Keller, Shelley G. (1996). "The Secret Power of Community Connections." *The Reference Librarian 54*: 29-44.

Library Instruction Round Table (LIRT). (1997). *Library Instruction Tutorials.* [Online]. Available HTTP: http://Diogenes.Baylor.edu/Library/LIRT/lirtproj.html

LOEX. (1998). *LOEX Clearinghouse for Library Instruction (Online Tutorials section).* [Online] Available HTTP: http://www.emich.edu/~lshirato/loex.html

Macauley, Peter. (1997). "Distance Education Research Students and Their Library Use." *Australian Academic and Research Libraries: AARL 28*: 188-197.

Ruhig DuMont, Rosemary, Lyle Barton, and Ilec Rhimes. (1995). Distributed Academic Technologies: Changing the Face of Teaching, Learning and Research. In *Realizing the Potential of Information Resources: Information, Technology & Services: The Cause Annual Conference, New Orleans, LA. Nov. 28-Dec. 1, 1995.*

Scholz-Crane, Ann. (1997). *Web-Based Instruction Center.* [Online] Available HTTP: http://crab.rutgers.edu/~scholzcr/cil/

Sloan, Bernie. (1998). "Individual Library Web Sites for Distance Learning Support." [Online] Available HTTP: http://www.lis.uiuc.edu/~sloan/libdist.htm

Statistics Committee, Distance Learning Section (DLS). (1998). *Uniform Statistics Data Collection Form.* [Online] Available HTTP: http://ecuvax.cis.ecu/~lbschouse/explain.htm

Index

Academic libraries. *See also* specific
libraries
handicap-accessible Web pages of,
5-28
Bobby 3.0 online evaluation of,
13-20
browser compatibility errors on,
18-19
frequency of accessibility errors
on, 16
recommendations for
improvement of, 7,11-12,
16-18,20,23-24
relationship to Association of
Research Libraries rank, 10,
13-14,19-20,25-28
relationship to Carnegie
Classification, 10,13,19-20,
25-28
relationship to Yahoo!'s
"America's 100 Most Wired
Colleges" rank, 10-11,19-20,
25-28
*Academic Libraries and Outreach
Services* (Jesudason), 152,158
ACRL. *See* Association of College and
Research Libraries
Advertising. *See* Publicity campaigns
African-American community, library
instructional outreach for,
278-281
African American Cultural Center, 152
Alire, Camila, 277
American Association of University
Women (AAUW), 295-296
American Library Association (ALA)
as "A More Perfect Union:
Japanese Americans and the
U.S. Constitution" exhibit
sponsor, 187,190

Annual Conference, 42
Distance Learning Section, 308
Americans with Disabilities Act
(ADA)
Internet access and, 6-7
libraries' compliance with, 259. *See
also* Assistive technology;
Computer workstations,
handicap-accessible; Web
home pages, handicap-
accessibility of
guides for, 266
Titles, 6-7,259
America Online, 33
*America's Children: Key National
Indicators of Well-Being*
(Federal Interagency Forum
on Child and Family
Statistics), 86-87
Apple Computer, 9
Application sharing, 38
Archival outreach
faculty-librarian relationship in,
232-233
for undergraduates, 225-242
Archives
Bloom Southwest Jewish Archives,
60-61,67
improvement of accessibility of,
58,64-66
Michigan State University Archives
and Historical Collections,
225-242
ARIEL, 292
Arizona Agricultural Networked
Information Consortium, 58
Arizona Board of Regents, 148
Arizona Historical Society, 61
Arizona (ship), Pearl Harbor, 59,61,67
Arkenstone Reading System, 285